ACTIVE BRAVE CONVERSATIONS

Classroom voices
that support and advocate for
belonging and inclusion

Andrew B. Campbell

Pembroke Publishers Limited

© 2025 Pembroke Publishers
538 Hood Road
Markham, Ontario, Canada L3R 3K9
www.pembrokepublishers.com

All rights reserved.

No part of this publication may be reproduced in any form or by any means electronic or mechanical, including photocopy, scanning, recording, or any information, storage or retrieval system, without permission in writing from the publisher. Excerpts from this publication may be reproduced under licence from Access Copyright, or with the express written permission of Pembroke Publishers Limited, or as permitted by law.

Every effort has been made to contact copyright holders for permission to reproduce borrowed material. The publishers apologize for any such omissions and will be pleased to rectify them in subsequent reprints of the book.

Library and Archives Canada Cataloguing in Publication

Title: Active brave conversations : classroom voices that support and advocate for belonging and inclusion / Andrew B. Campbell (Dr. ABC).

Names: Campbell, Andrew B., author.

Description: Includes bibliographical references and index.

Identifiers: Canadiana (print) 20250246465 | Canadiana (ebook) 2025024652X | ISBN 9781551383781 (softcover) | ISBN 9781551389745 (PDF)

Subjects: LCSH: Multicultural education. | LCSH: Culturally relevant pedagogy. | LCSH: Teachers—Training of. | LCSH: Anti-racism—Study and teaching. | LCSH: Race—Study and teaching.

Classification: LCC LC1099 .C36 2025 | DDC 370.117—dc23

Editor: Kat Mototsune
Cover Design: John Zehethofer
Typesetting: Jay Tee Graphics Ltd.

Printed and bound in Canada
9 8 7 6 5 4 3 2 1

Contents

Introduction   *5*

Chapter 1:
Becoming a Champion for EDIA and Anti-Oppressive Practices
by Andrew B. Campbell (DR.ABC) and Saffiyyah Waithe   *11*

Chapter 2:
Gaining Cultural Competence in the Classroom and Beyond
by Leland Harper   *25*

Chapter 3:
The Three *P*'s of Culturally Relevant, Responsive, and Sustaining Education
by Kenneth Gyamerah and Doreen Bonsu   *37*

Chapter 4:
Affirmation, Allyship, and Action for 2SLGBTQIA+ Students
by Sarah Stapleton and Rob Grant   *54*

Chapter 5:
Using the Tools You Have to Dismantle Racism
by Canute Lawrence   *67*

Chapter 6:
Disrupting Racism from Within
by Marie Green   *80*

Chapter 7:
Being Intentional about Diversity, Equity, and Inclusion
by Shelita Walker   *91*

Chapter 8:
Cultivating, Sustaining, Protecting, and Celebrating Joy in Our Classrooms
by Tanitiã Munroe   *105*

Chapter 9:
Creating and Sustaining Spaces of Belonging in Our Schools
by Nancy Cargioli and Jaclynn Devaux   *117*

Chapter 10:
Fostering Intellectual Curiosity in Marginalized Students
by Karen Murray and Rasulan Q. Hoppie   *130*

Chapter 11:
Strength-Based Approaches to Eliminate Deficit Thinking in Schools
by Michael John Daniels   *143*

Chapter 12:
Working with Parents to Establish Everyday Equity Practices
by Matthew Sinclair   *161*

Chapter 13:
A Seat at the Table
by Camille Logan and Shelby A. E. McPhee   *174*

Chapter 14:
Holding and Supporting High Expectations for Black Students
by Veronica Montague, Keisha Evans, Kai Gordon, Sheldon Dixon, and Jason Brissett   *187*

Chapter 15:
Collective Care While Doing the Work
by Michelle Forde   *202*

References and Resources   *220*

Index   *231*

Introduction

I have been privileged to engage in transformative conversations with educators for nearly three decades. Whether in workshops, round tables, or school staff rooms, these discussions have been foundational to my evolution as a teacher, leader, disrupter, advocate, and lifelong learner. When I began this work years ago, I always started with the teacher. No matter the topic, I would ask teachers: *Who are you in this work*? Too often, we underestimate or avoid the fact that who we are profoundly shapes how we teach and lead in schools. Our identities, lived experiences, and biases are not separate from our practice—they inform it. That is why, for me, self-reflection is not optional; it is the foundation to all of my work.

I grew up in Jamaica as an expressive child in a low-income working-class community, where navigating daily life required resilience and constant self-awareness. I remember witnessing other children being treated unfairly at school, in church, and in the streets, though at the time I didn't have the language to name those moments as injustice, inequity, or oppression. But I could sense that something wasn't right—something felt deeply unfair. Even as I faced my own experiences with bullying, I could still see the injustice being done to others. From a young age, I found myself speaking up, sometimes getting scolded by adults, older siblings, or teachers for challenging what didn't feel right. Before I ever heard words like *equity* or *advocacy*, I was already moving through the world guided by a deep sense of fairness, empathy, and care. I often say now that I learned how to advocate long before I knew what advocacy was. Back then, it was just about doing what felt kind, what felt respectful, what felt right. It was about showing care to those who were pushed out of the circles and excluded from the tables.

My professional teaching career began in 1995, when I earned my teaching diploma at the Mico University College in Jamaica and was selected by my first principal, Barbara Reid, to attend a UNICEF Reading Specialist workshop. There, I sat among more than 120 educators working with students who had been held in deficit; streamed, labelled at-risk, and marginalized by the system.

I was a young teacher then, but I had something to say. To my surprise, I was invited to say it. I shared my ideas on teaching children to read, but I also encouraged educators to care, to see each child as deserving of a quality education, to look beyond their present circumstances, and to offer them the hope to dream. That moment of being welcomed into a space where honesty and transformation were possible defined the course of my life and solidified my commitment to the work I now do.

Since then, I have facilitated workshops in various countries and contexts, including the Special Education Unit of Jamaica's Ministry of Education, Youth, and Culture, as well as schools in The Bahamas, private career colleges, and public school systems across Canada. In Canada, my collaborations span multiple school boards, as well as organizations across sectors, such as financial institutions, non-profits, municipal offices, and provincial and federal agencies. These sessions have never been merely professional development days; they have been ongoing conversations—spaces for truth-telling, deep listening, reflection, and courageous growth. Time and again, educators have expressed gratitude, saying, "Thank you for articulating what we have been thinking." These gatherings transcended traditional workshops, becoming brave conversations that fostered powerful connections and understanding.

Active Brave Conversations serves as a natural extension of this lifelong endeavor. It weaves together powerful themes rooted in my personal experiences and enriched by the voices of a vibrant community of educators, storytellers, and artists. I have always believed in the extraordinary power of collective energy, and this book embodies that spirit. Brave conversations flourish only when diverse voices are invited to share their perspective and stories. Reaching out to others was not merely a choice—it was essential in crafting something authentic and transformative.

This work transcends a mere collection of ideas; it is a compelling invitation to explore. It calls upon all educational stakeholders—teachers, leaders, staff, administrators, and community partners—to embrace discomfort, foster courage, and cultivate growth. Brave conversations are challenging. Many educators and stakeholders hesitate to initiate difficult discussions, often convinced they need more preparation or the perfect words to express their thoughts. Yet the truth is that we find readiness through engagement, because silence does not shield us—it keeps us stuck. Brave conversations demand that we confront what we have avoided, unlearn what we have accepted, and voice truths that might disrupt the status quo. For decades, I have had brave conversations in schools, offices, and communities, as these open dialogues are the catalysts for genuine change.

How to Use this Book

What follows in the ensuing chapters are bold reflections and urgent provocations grounded in lived experience, deep listening, and shared learning. They are thoughtfully designed to guide the reader from vision to action, from awareness to impact, and from conversation to transformation. They offer practical tools and gentle reminders to support educators in doing this essential work with purpose and care.

Chapter 1: Becoming a Champion for EDIA and Anti-Oppressive Practices is a call that should echo through our schools, playgrounds, homes, and communities.

We each have a responsibility to be champions in the face of oppressive practices. Advocacy is not optional; it is part of our shared duty in education. We must show up, speak out, and commit to justice, wherever we are.

In Chapter 2: Gaining Cultural Competence in the Classroom and Beyond, we explore the ongoing need to grow through intentional learning and unlearning. Gaining cultural competence means confronting the assumptions, stereotypes, and biases we all carry, consciously or unconsciously, at different points along the continuum of our lives. It prepares us to engage with others, celebrate difference, and navigate the complexity of a global world. This chapter reminds us that becoming culturally competent is essential, not only in our classrooms, but also for becoming responsible, compassionate global citizens.

In Chapter 3: The Three P's of Culturally Relevant, Responsive, and Sustaining Education, the discussion centres around the preparation, planning, and practice required to build classrooms that are culturally relevant, responsive, and sustaining. We cannot simply walk into a space and hope for inclusion. This work demands intention and ongoing commitment. When we lead with care and clarity, our classrooms become spaces where students are affirmed, seen, and supported. Ultimately, these are the kinds of learning environments that intentionally cultivate a deep sense of belonging for all.

Chapter 4: Affirmation, Allyship, and Action for 2SLGBTQIA+ Students speaks to the importance of affirmation, allyship, and action as ongoing practices within our schools. Affirmation isn't symbolic; it's structural, it's lived, and it's deeply tied to justice. Allyship must move beyond gestures into accountability and transformation. As the chapter reminds us, one meaningful way we create safer and more courageous spaces is by deepening our understanding of what it truly means to affirm and stand beside our students—especially those whose identities have long been marginalized in our schools.

In Chapter 5: Using the Tools You Have to Dismantle Racism, we are invited to expand our anti-racist toolkit and add new strategies to the work we are already doing. I often say there are many ways to disrupt, and this chapter reminds us that we don't need to wait for permission or perfection. We begin with what we have, stay open to learning, and commit to taking action. As disruptors and change agents, we must keep sharpening our tools, deepening our awareness, and using every resource available to challenge racism wherever it shows up.

In Chapter 6: Disrupting Racism from Within, we are reminded that we often work within systems that uphold the very racism we're trying to dismantle. The question becomes this: *How do we disrupt spaces we benefit from, especially when our careers, our security, and our reputations are tied to them?* This chapter challenges us to hold institutional knowledge, learn how to navigate and negotiate complex systems, and still act with courage and clarity. A certain kind of advocacy is required here—one grounded in honesty, skill, and the belief that change from within is not only possible, but also necessary.

Chapter 7: Being Intentional about Equity, Diversity, and Inclusion centres the power of intentionality and reminds us that nothing just happens. We can create equity plans, action plans, strategic goals, performance improvement plans, IEPs, and more. But plans alone don't change schools. Without real commitment and follow-through, they remain words on paper. This chapter calls us to move from intention to action, to lead with purpose, consistency, and a deep belief that transformation happens only when we act on what we say we value.

Chapter 8: Cultivating, Sustaining, Protecting, and Celebrating Joy in Our Classrooms reminds us that joy is not a fleeting moment or just a sign of a good day. It's something we must cultivate, protect, sustain, and celebrate. Joy is part of the work. It nourishes our spirit, fuels our teaching, and helps maintain spaces of belonging. For our students, joy creates room to breathe, to feel safe, to be seen, and to learn without fear. Joy is not a distraction from justice—it's part of how we build it, and part of what keeps us all going.

Chapter 9: Creating and Sustaining Spaces of Belonging in Our Schools helps us see that belonging is more than being included; it's about being recognized, valued, and held. When students walk into a classroom and feel like they matter, everything shifts. They participate more fully, take risks, and trust the space around them. Belonging is built through consistent care, affirming relationships, and the choices we make about whose stories, languages, and identities are made visible. It is a commitment.

In Chapter 10: Fostering Intellectual Curiosity in Marginalized Students, curiosity is seen as a form of resistance. When we create classrooms where students feel safe, affirmed, and seen, they ask powerful questions that connect learning to justice. Curiosity isn't extra—it's essential. It grows when teachers reflect, build trust, hold high expectations, and let students lead their own inquiries. Our role is to nurture that spark, not control it, because when students are curious, they are empowered.

In Chapter 11: Strength-Based Approaches to Eliminate Deficit Thinking in Schools, we disrupt deficit thinking and seek to challenge the harmful stereotypes, assumptions, and cultural ignorance that show up in our schools. Too often, our students are held in deficit—defined by what they lack, misunderstood, and offered less. This chapter reminds us of the power that comes when we see our students through a strength-based lens, a strength-based approach, and strength-based imagining. How we see our students shapes how we serve them, and that shift can change everything.

Chapter 12: Working with Parents to Establish Everyday Equity Practices is a strong reminder that parents are an integral part of the teaching and learning equation. This chapter challenges educators to move beyond seeing families once a year at parent–teacher night or reaching out to caregivers only when something goes wrong. Communication and collaboration must be intentional and ongoing. Parents are not just supporters of the school—they are co-educators, culture builders, and critical partners in shaping student success. When we embrace that, we begin to build something that looks and feels like a true community.

Chapter 13: A Seat at the Table calls us, as teacher leaders, to take up the space necessary to bring about change. Too often we forget the power we walk in every day. Our voice matters, our choices matter, and our presence can shift what's possible. We are not helpless or passive participants in this system—we are active agents of change. We have a seat at the table of education, and how we choose to use that seat can influence policy, practice, and culture. We are transformational leaders, influencers, and impactors. This chapter is a reminder that we have always had the ability to lead, and now is the time to use it.

Chapter 14: Holding and Supporting High Expectations for Black Students centres our Black students and the urgent need to disrupt anti-Blackness at every level of our education system. Written by a team of graduate coaches, professionals who both serve Black students and come from the very communities they write about, this chapter is full of reminders, strategies, and truths. We are called to change the narrative, change trajectories, and challenge the pervasive low expectations placed on Black children. And we must equip all teachers—

regardless of identity—to build classrooms where Black students are seen, supported, and able to thrive.

Chapter 15: Collective Care While Doing the Work reminds us that, in all we do and all we are called to do, we must engage in real self-care. As I often say, you have to be well enough to be good enough. Educators, especially those doing equity and advocacy work, are constantly expected to take on more, often without recognition, compensation, or support. Self-care is not a luxury. It is a necessary act of preservation, resistance, and gratitude. It's how we stay grounded in the work without burning out or breaking down.

Let us begin.

Dedication

To educators who are learning and growing—don't stop. The best teachers are also the best students. We must continue to acquire the tools to do better.

To the disruptors who stand up, speak up, and show up in a world where so many still struggle to be seen and heard.

To all the brave people doing the work with heart, intentionality, and passion. And to those who pour into the lives of our children so they can flourish.

Throughout my career, I have genuinely appreciated the power of collaboration and learning within community. The invaluable lessons I learned from my colleagues at Waterford Primary School—Ms. Hussy, Ms. Ferron, Ms. Waite, Ms. Myers, and Ms. Barbara Reid (RIP)—remain etched in my heart. Similarly, in the Bahamas, I flourished alongside Ms. Archer, Ms. Romer, and Ms. Hunt-Wilson. Here in Canada, educators such as Mr. Crichton, Mr. Travers, Ms. Floria, Ms. Esposito, and Mr. Skios have influenced my educational journey and fostered my belonging. This is not simply a list of names; each one reflects a meaningful relationship and a shared commitment to the teaching profession, representing the essence of our collective dedication to education.

Andrew B. Campbell (DR.ABC)

1

Becoming a Champion for EDIA and Anti-Oppressive Practices

Andrew B. Campbell (DR.ABC) and Saffiyyah Waithe

> "Every child needs a champion"
> — Dr. Andrew B. Campbell (2025)

Saffiyyah Waithe is an emerging scholar with a Master's degree in social justice education. She is pursuing a PhD in social justice education with a special focus on Black futurity at the Ontario Institute for Studies in Education (OISE). Her scholarship is focused on the intersections between Islam and Blackness, and the experiences of African, Afro-Caribbean, and Black (ACB) diasporic youth and their families in Canada. Specifically, her research focuses on the lived experiences of Black Muslim girls.

Who Is a Champion?

A *champion* is often defined as someone who has defeated or surpassed their competitors. The notion of *champion* is not one we typically associate or think about in the educational context in this way. However, what we are inviting you to do is explore the definition of champion as one who fights for a cause or on behalf of someone. As a teacher, you are always acting on behalf of your students. And this chapter is a reminder that, as educators and stakeholders in education, we all have a duty to fight for our schools and classrooms being spaces of belonging. They must be spaces that are safe for *all* students.

The reality is that not all our students are safe in our schools, due to systemic inequalities and discrimination, such as anti-Black racism, that prevents some students from attaining their full academic potential. There are many roadblocks that exist in our education system on a systemic level that create barriers to full participation and involvement for all students. To address this, many educators have worked toward dismantling and reshaping pre-existing education models in which competition, hierarchy, and what Freire describes as "banking education" (Freire, 1970) have been prominent barriers towards inclusivity and accessibility. Having educators actively involved in reshaping how education is approached, from a theoretical to a practical level, is critically important. However, to make our classrooms a safe place of belonging for all students, we must all become involved champions of Equity, Diversity, Inclusion, and Accessibility (EDIA). EDIA work calls on society to become more inclusive and equitable for all social groups and communities. This ideology is especially important for teachers who deal with vulnerable and diverse communities every day. Teachers provide the care and support our students need and help them shape their classroom spaces to become safer and more inclusive. A true champion is a "flag bearer, defender and supporter of not only their students' rights but more importantly, someone who upholds principles of EDIA and social justice" (Campbell, 2022). It is our duty and responsibility to ensure that we are on the front lines, fighting for equity and inclusion in our classroom spaces and beyond (Campbell, 2023). In this book, the various chapters will, among other things,

- refer to issues surrounding equity in schools and in wider society
- help you identify your position in the equity journey and what actions you can take to ensure your own learning and unlearning
- offer you tools to use to engage in courageous conversations and brave spaces to speak up, show up, and stand up
- provide activities to help you think through ways to become a champion in your classroom space, and what success and victory look like in that context

We have been exploring the concept of *educational champion* in our work and in the workshop format. For example, in workshops with school boards, we ask participants *Why do we need champions? Why do we need champions in equity work?* and *Why do we need champions in education?* The responses include the idea that people see champions as role-models, and those who do the "heavy lifting." To be an educator who believes wholeheartedly in principles of social justice and EDIA is to be someone who believes they have the power, potential, and possibility to create change.

Activity: Why Do We Need Champions?

This exercise can be a journal reflection for you or a whole-class activity for students.

1. Consider/discuss the definition of champion as both "a winner" and "someone who fights for a cause or on behalf of others." Brainstorm a list of people who are considered champions.

13

2. Write (journal) or post (classroom) the question: *Why Do We Need Champions in Education?*
3. Write down responses. For classroom use, create a Champion Board using sticky notes.
4. Think about/discuss the list of responses and how they might have changed the way you/your students think about champions.

Winners and Losers

When we consider championing EDIA in education, the opponents are obvious: the traditional systemic ideas and discriminatory practices that keep our students from learning in a safe, equitable space, from feeling a sense of belonging in school, and from reaching their full potential.

As educational leaders, we find workshops one of the most effective ways to uncover social issues that affect marginalized communities. For example, we find that one of the primary recurring challenges teachers face is the disparity related to the hierarchy that exists in education. We are told about tensions between the grassroots level and the higher-ups, rooted in promises that have been made related to EDIA without the correct action and steps needed to follow through. In these instances, the losers are teachers like you, who might be frustrated in your efforts to make their classrooms places of belonging and learning success; however, the true losers are your students.

We want teachers to show up, step in the ring, and go through the fight. We hope to help you discern and identify the opponent, and also to combat hopelessness and self-doubt in relation to your potential and power. We want you to feel that you are empowered and confident to proclaim that you, too, can be an EDIA champion. The title of champion is not reserved for board leaders, superintendents, directors, or high-profile keynote speakers. The term and its applications are for all of us, especially for teachers, parents, and students—the true educational stakeholders. We believe that we must all be involved and active to make meaningful change happen in our educational environments.

Definitions and Terminology

The last thing we want is for you to get caught up in or feel overwhelmed by the usages and various acronyms and definitions being used. As educators ourselves, we understand that, although these terms are critical and important, they often become nothing but buzzwords to placate or direct away from actual meaningful action and social change. We present a table here of various acronyms used in the social justice and educational environments, to emphasize the importance of each of these terminologies, and to show how interwoven these terms and the themes threaded through them are.

DEI	Diversity, Equity, and Inclusion
DEIB	Diversity, Equity, Inclusion, and Belonging
EDIA	Equity, Diversity, Inclusion, and Accessibility

EDIB	Equity, Diversity, Inclusion, and Belonging
EDIDA	Equity, Diversity, Inclusion, Decolonization, and Accessibility
IDEA	Inclusion, Diversity, Equity, and Accessibility
JEDI	Justice, Equity, Diversity, and Inclusion

In our chapter we focus on the terms *champion*, as well as EDIA. However, we want to draw your attention away from the often-mechanical application of these terms and instead encourage you to root your pedagogy and teaching practice in the core concepts of care, love, empathy, and kindness. This is what is at the core of being an EDIA champion, and this is one of the threads that connects these terms and terminologies together.

Voices from the Field

As a visible Black Muslim woman, my story is one of overcoming systemic barriers and obstacles related to Islamophobia and Anti-Black racism, both within and outside of the Muslim community. Growing up in the GTA, my educational journey primarily took place in a private Islamic academy. This experience shaped me in many ways, because I was one of the few Black students in a predominately Arab and South-Asian Muslim-identified space. I felt powerless in a system where I was a racial minority, with all my teachers as well as the administration being a close-knit community of Arab and South Asian descent.

Experiencing this in my childhood was transformative. It ultimately inspired my goal to go into education myself. Pursuing a Master's of Social Justice Education at OISE was an empowering phase of my educational journey, because I felt like my toolbox as an educator expanded to become more critical, to embody principles of decoloniality, and to centre "other ways of knowing," such as Afro and Indigenous educational practices. Moreover, through other educators and theorists, I was able to find the language that accurately gave color to my experiences and the experiences of others who fall outside of the margins of what is considered the norm and the status quo. My journey has allowed me to imagine other ways of knowing and education rooted in radical and liberatory practices.
— Saffiyyah Waithe

As a teacher, I believe every student deserves the chance to succeed, no matter their background. I work hard to make my classroom a place where students feel respected, supported, and ready to learn. I use education to help students build a better future. In my role, I try to be more than just a teacher—I want to be someone who helps students grow, both in school and in life. Being a Muslim woman who wears the hijab in the classroom is interesting and shapes my teaching experiences, especially within a diverse environment, as I teach students from all over the world—North America, South America, Asia, Europe, and Africa. Wearing the hijab means that I often stand out in ways that allow me to connect with my students on a deeper level. Many of my students come from backgrounds where cultural and religious differences can create feelings of isolation or misunderstanding. I have experienced first-hand how it feels

to be seen as "other," and I bring this awareness to my classroom. It helps me create a space where students can feel safe to express themselves and explore their identities without fear of judgment. I encourage my students to embrace their diversity, while fostering an atmosphere of mutual respect and understanding among all learners. My empathy has shaped the way I teach, helping me create a classroom where all students have equal access to learning. I use diverse materials that reflect my students' cultures. I work hard to build an inclusive, respectful classroom where every student feels seen, valued, and supported.
— Tayba Hathiyani, MEd and ESL instructor

To be a champion means to be oneself
Championship creates an energy surrounding the need for success
The need to be something, or someone in the eyes of society,
In the eyes of the other.
Black championship is held hostage often times,
Tied up with the ideal of Black excellence.
To be excellent means to be extraordinary,
To be extraordinary means to be a champion.
No?

My Blackness and my being in itself is championship.
My Blackness means resilience,
It means tenacity, strength, beauty, courage,
It means survival.
There is no need for me to overachieve as my being in itself is an achievement.
I wear the dreams and the achievements of my ancestors on my sleeve.

To be a champion means to be oneself.
It is being the past, the present and the future all at once.
This is what makes up me and my Blackness
And
You and yours.
Championship cannot be taught,
It is an inherent attribute which can be found within us all.
It is simply a matter of finding it within.
Championship means being your most authentic self.

Teach what cannot be taught in the spirit of storytelling.
Keep our stories, our communities and your ancestors' dreams alive.
Championship cannot be taught,
As a teacher it is your duty to remind those who look to you of this.
As a student it is your duty to remember to look.
As a champion, it is your duty to both remind, and remember.

To be a champion means to be oneself.
Grow,
Learn,
Teach,
Speak,
Remember,
Remind.
You are and always have been a champion.
— KALM (Keianah Alexis Linton-Madray), MT candidate

The Journey of Becoming: Learning and Unlearning

The act of learning has always been a journey that leads to growth. As educators and teachers, as acutely involved as we are in maintaining our students' learning, we must also be as involved and invested in our own learning/unlearning and growth. This is vital. The journey of education never ends. In particular, EDIA issues and tensions about topics around EDIA are ever-changing. We are constantly presented with new vocabulary, new ideas, and, most of all, shifting political thoughts and beliefs that either challenge or reinforce EDIA ideology. It is necessary for us to equip ourselves against these rolling waves. Moreover, we need to maintain our growth, because often we find ourselves in spaces where educators and administration fear the brave courageous conversations that surround EDIA issues, inside and outside of the school environment. It is our duty to maintain these brave conversations and have the courage to speak up for our students and to champion conversations. The more we invest in our learning and build our awareness, the less fear we feel as we go into our growth.

Growth within the education field can come in different ways. For example, there are many valuable opportunities we should seize, such as workshops, conferences, summits, etc.; however, we also need to maintain our growth, as our reading, reflections, and speaking to others who are different from ourselves are part of that learning journey. This is how we can ensure that the investment in our growth is constant and meets the criteria needed to care for our students.

There are those who do, and those who don't (Campbell, 2022). Action is derived from a process of "do's," and the journey of becoming a champion of anti-oppressive practices in education is through a mindset shift of a series of beliefs and actions.

These actions are especially important for teachers who work with racialized and marginalized communities, or who are themselves members of these social groups. It is critical for us to adopt an EDIA and champion stance and mentality because of the ways in which our interactions shape our students and their futures. It is important not only to be an ally, but also to become a champion.

Equity is a critical notion in EDIA work. As noted by Carol Campbell (2021), "Canada prides itself for being multi-cultural and valuing diversity especially in education settings" (p. 409). However, the ideal is far from the norm. The issue of educational equity is an equally complex history and present of serious and persisting inequities, especially to historically racialized and marginalized communities, such as Black and Indigenous peoples. Therefore, to support our students' diverse needs, one of the most critical and important notions toward becoming a champion for anti-oppressive pedagogies is to have the foundational groundwork and understanding of what EDIA is and why it matters.

As EDIA educators, we are also actively working against systemic oppression and oppressive ideologies that limit our students' potential and their power, and we strive to move toward other ways of rethinking and redefining what education is and how it can be used a tool for liberation and resistance. Part of the framework for emancipatory pedagogy asserts that we should challenge systems of oppression, like racism, sexism, heteronormativity, colonialism, and classism. Emancipatory pedagogy is a theory derived from Paulo Freire's (1970) teachings and ideologies, and is characterized by themes of social justice, teaching/learning to raise awareness about power structures in society, and the cognition occurring within social contexts (Omodan, 2022).

Master Teacher candidate contributors for the case studies in order:
- Vanessa Gayle
- Afnan Musa
- Chloe Jones-Westgarth
- Dasia Jeffery
- Layla Khani-Mohammed
- Shaheem Harris
- Mohamed Rage

Emancipatory pedagogy allows for us not only to unlearn harmful policies and practices that have been ingrained on a systemic level but also to reimagine what is possible through a dialogic relationship with our students. In this way, we can implement an equity framework and give voice to those who have systematically been silenced, working in spaces and places that directly have an impact on their everyday lives. When we come to this work with intention and purpose, our central focus is not only that we help the students in our immediate care, but also that we are deeply connected and concerned with the welfare of generations to come.

STORY FROM THE CLASSROOM

In a Kindergarten-to-8 school, there is a Grade 8 girl named Jade, who has recently transitioned. In gym class, students are being assigned groups to practice volleyball drills. The teacher, Mr. Brown, pairs all the girls together and all the boys together, but the only two left without a partner are Jade and another boy in the class named Anthony. Mr. Brown says, "Sorry, Jade and Anthony, you'll have to be a pair. But Jade is basically a boy anyway, so it really shouldn't matter." Anthony sighs, "I guess," and walks away, sulking. Jade freezes in front of the class and stands in place, not knowing what to do. Mr. Brown goes to apologize to Anthony, while Jade leaves the class crying.

- How do you think Mr. Brown's comment about Jade being "basically a boy" might have made Jade feel?
- What are some ways teachers can be more mindful when assigning groups or making comments about students, especially those who might be navigating their gender identity?
- How might Jade's classmates have reacted to the teacher's comment? Do you think any of them noticed or were affected by it?
- If you were a principal, what might you say to Mr. Brown about his comments?

STORY FROM THE CLASSROOM

Ayesha, a Grade 12 Muslim student who wears a hijab, is preparing to compete in a track and field championship. Before the race, her coach pulls her aside and suggests she remove her hijab, saying, "I'm just worried that it might slow you down or make you uncomfortable during the race." Ayesha feels conflicted and uncomfortable with the request. She has trained for months while wearing her hijab, and never felt it hindered her performance. The comment makes her feel singled out, and she questions if her religious identity is truly accepted in the athletic community at her school.

- What cultural or ethical challenges are present in this scenario, and how do they affect Ayesha's experience?
- In what ways could the coach have demonstrated greater cultural awareness and inclusivity when addressing their concern?
- What actions could the coach have taken to affirm and support Ayesha's identity and performance as an athlete?
- If you were in Ayesha's position, how might this experience affect your sense of belonging, confidence, and relationship with the coach?

STORY FROM THE CLASSROOM

Tommy is a Grade 12 student who identifies as gay. He is a member of the 2SLGBTQ+ club. Tommy has supported the club year-round, volunteering time as a mentor to younger students, supporting fundraising events, and organizing events for the club and the larger student community. All the club members and Tommy are excited to attend an outing at the local library for a book signing by a famous drag queen. Tommy has not submitted the permission form required to attend the club outing. He has been very excited about this event and shared that meeting this author is the highlight of his year. When the teacher leading the club asks Tommy for the permission slip signed by a parent or guardian, he tells you that he doesn't want his parents to know about his sexual orientation or involvement in the club.

- Given Tommy's reaction to his parents' possible disapproval of his sexuality and involvement in the club, could this suggest an emotionally unsafe or potentially abusive home environment? Do you believe it is the teacher's responsibility to ensure Tommy's safety and security in this situation?
- What could be the implications of contacting Tommy's parents to ask them to fill out the consent form?
- How could the teacher make Tommy aware that he will not be able to attend the event without the form?
- What could the teacher offer Tommy to support him in his circumstances and disappointment about not being able to attend?

STORY FROM THE CLASSROOM

Laylah, a Black student in Grade 10, attends a predominantly white high school in a small town. She is one of the few Black-identifying students, and there are no Black teachers or administrators on staff. In February, she notices that her school and teachers have done nothing to acknowledge or celebrate Black History Month—not even a mention during the morning announcements. Bothered by this, Laylah works up the courage to approach one of her favorite teachers, someone she considers a friend and mentor, to ask why. "Well, it's not that we don't care," the teacher responds, "but it wouldn't make sense to make a big deal of it when there are only, like, ten of you in the whole school anyway." Laylah walks away from the conversation feeling dismissed, unseen, and more isolated than ever. Over the following days, she begins to question whether her voice and experiences truly matter in a school culture that consistently overlooks them.

- What explicit and implicit messages does the teacher's response send to Laylah about the value of her identity and culture within the school community?
- How might this interaction affect Laylah's sense of trust, safety, and belonging—not just with this teacher, but within the school as a whole?
- What does this scenario reveal about the difference between performative and authentic allyship in educational spaces?
- How could the teacher have responded in a way that acknowledged Laylah's concerns, while demonstrating a commitment to allyship and fostering an inclusive environment for all students, regardless of their number or background?

- What concrete steps can schools take to ensure the cultural identities of marginalized students are recognized, valued, and celebrated consistently—not only during heritage months?

STORY FROM THE CLASSROOM

Hazel is a female student with high academic achievement and a passion for science. Many of the science-based clubs at her high school are filled predominantly with male students. Despite her high academic achievement, she often finds herself ignored and ridiculed when she presents ideas to her male club members in her after-school robotics club. They make hurtful comments toward Hazel, claiming she does not know what she's talking about because she's a girl. The attitude from her male counterparts often makes Hazel feel excluded, and she struggles to find a way to express her ideas without fear of mockery. Hazel confides in her teacher, Ms. Waters, about the ongoing situation, hoping to receive support from someone who might understand and help resolve the problem. Her teacher refuses to intervene, and says to Hazel, "Boys will be boys." This conversation leaves Hazel feeling dismissed and unsure if she should continue participating in the club.

- What are the long-term consequences of not addressing gender-based discrimination in educational spaces?
- What are the ethical responsibilities of educators in addressing gender-based discrimination, and how might similar experiences in educational spaces affect a student's perception of the teacher–student dynamic and their trust in authority figures?
- What potential effects could the normalization of phrases like "Boys will be boys" have on impressionable youth?
- Why is it important to have diverse perspectives and representation in STEM clubs and fields?

STORY FROM THE CLASSROOM

Karan, a 15-year-old student of South Asian descent, reports that he has been facing repeated instances of racial discrimination by his peers on the soccer team. He has informed his coach about the issue several times but was told to "shake it off," as it is normal for new players to be intimidated by senior players on the team. One day in the locker room, Karan is held down by two of his peers and kicked numerous times in the abdomen. He approaches his coach once again to report the bullying, but is dismissed, with the coach brushing it off as a typical hazing ritual following a rookie player's first game. Karan seeks acceptance from his new peer group and fears that speaking out further might lead to greater isolation. Over time, the scrutiny intensifies, as he continues to endure both physical and emotional abuse.

- What could the coach have done differently to make sure Karan feels safe, both on the field and in the locker room?
- Why might Karan be hesitant to inform others about this instance of bullying? Is there any risk associated with disclosure? How might his teammates react?

- In your opinion, is this discrimination able to continue due to ineffective safeguarding and reporting mechanisms?
- How might this locker-room abuse affect other areas of Karan's life? Could it lead to academic struggles or trigger social anxiety? How might his sleep patterns be affected as a result of the experience?

STORY FROM THE CLASSROOM

Mr. Ahmed, a dedicated high school teacher, has grown concerned about the academic performance of several students in his classroom who have been diagnosed with learning disabilities. Although he has dutifully followed the school's pre-established accommodation measures, such as extended test times and differentiated assignments, he notices that these measures fail to meet the needs of his students. Many of his students continue to fall behind, growing increasingly disengaged and overwhelmed by the pace of instruction. Determined to meet their educational needs, Mr. Jefferson gathers academic data, student feedback, and recent research on inclusive practices. He presents this information to the school's administrative team, advocating for additional supports, such as a learning support teacher, smaller group instruction, and assistive technology. Despite his efforts, Mr. Ahmed's attempts are met with polite resistance. The administration team maintains that the current curriculum and accommodation protocol meet provincial requirements and caution against altering established systems without district approval. Now at a crossroads, Mr. Jefferson must decide whether to quietly continue operating within the limitations of the current system or to persist in his advocacy, knowing it could cause tension with leadership but potentially lead to meaningful change for his students.

- What are the potential consequences, both positive and negative, of Mr. Jefferson challenging the existing system?
- How can Mr. Jefferson balance his professional responsibilities with his ethical obligation to support all learners?
- What strategies could Mr. Jefferson use to build support among colleagues or allies before re-approaching the administration?
- In what ways might systemic barriers be influencing the administration's reluctance to change, and how can Mr. Jefferson address those constructively?
- What role can student voice or data play in strengthening Mr. Jefferson's advocacy efforts?

Teacher Activity: Creating Your Own Case Study

You are invited to develop your own case study. Base it on a real experience or on a situation observed in the classroom or wider school community that highlights issues of equity and belonging. Reflect on the following guiding questions to shape your case study:

1. What specific incident or situation did you observe, and how did it affect the students involved?

2. Which aspects of equity and belonging were most prominent in this experience?
3. How did the school culture or policies influence the outcomes of this situation?
4. What strategies could be implemented to foster a more inclusive environment for all students?
5. What would you have done differently today? Why?

Student Activity: Writing Ourselves In

Encourage students to do the same activity. This is a way for them to tell their story. Encourage the use of pseudonyms. Explain why we use them.

Champion Toolbox

In order to make lasting social change, the fix will not be a bandage solution, nor will it happen overnight. Dismantling harmful ideologies and practices in education will take time, as well as renewed investment and deep commitment across the board from all levels.

You can implement effective change into your teaching practice, change that can transform your classroom environment and provide you and your students with the scaffolding needed to get to larger social change. But first you must undertake a shift in attitude. One of the barriers that inhibit action, both for teachers/administrators and students, is an *Us vs. Them* mentality. This attitude is divisive, in that it creates division and perpetuates it. We must be unified in order to accomplish our goals and also provide lasting meaningful change.

In order to assist your journey of becoming, we have identified some ways that champions of EDIA can create the power of change in their classroom space:

- Create opportunities for students to practice and develop empathy, through guided activities and by encouraging more open dialogue on social issues and critical conversations on global affairs.
- Create opportunities for all students to exercise and practice their voice, by encouraging them to speak up, and to write and reflect.
- In moments of conflict or disagreement, validate each student's experience while also firmly modelling an equitable approach.
- Create a communal set of classroom rules, in which students democratically decide the rules for a *safe space* for them.
- Encourage more group-based learning.
- Expand what you define as a *learning environment* and *classroom space* by making use of materials and ideas like oral histories and narratives, and geographical land-based knowledge.
- Involve the community in your teaching practice; allow for students to expand their ideas of who and what are "knowledge keepers" and where their education comes from.

By implementing these practices and strategies, you will positively influence how your students engage with their educational environments and start to dismantle harmful ideologies and practices at their root. This form of social change is critical, because it creates a harmonious and unified space that allows for learning, growth, and action.

Final Thoughts

To end this chapter, we want to leave you with three questions to reflect on:
1. What can you do?
2. What are you willing to do?
3. What have you done?

We use these questions to end our equity workshops as a take-home and reflection point; they have been asked hundreds of times over the span of 10 years to various educators and advocates. What has consistently stood out was that students were at the centre and heart of their responses. Teaching and being champions means centring our students and their needs in our teaching practice. At the core of these reflection questions is the central principle of action.

As educators who are interested in implementing championship and victory in our educational spaces, we know that this will not happen unless we all cross the finish line together. Our goal is to bring our students with us across the finish line and allow for them to leave our classrooms feeling encouraged, empowered, and enlightened. That is at the heart of being a champion. This is what we hope you will be able to take away from this chapter. As a teacher, your voice matters; your representation, especially of those who are racialized and part of a marginalized community, matters. Fighting against systemic oppression, implementing an anti-racist pedagogy that invites in all students, matters. We hope you are willing to answer the call: *Our students need champions. Are you willing to be one?*

> ### Progressive Reflection: Using this Book
>
> As you read each chapter in this book, you are encouraged to come back to these prompts:
> - One thing I am learning
> - One thing I am unlearning
> - One question I have
> - One tension/struggle I am having
> - One action I will take

Sample word clouds on page 24 are made from responses to these prompts after workshops on Becoming a Champion of EDIA.

Also reflect on these questions:
- What has shifted?
- What is new in your learning/unlearning journey?

Activity: Looking Back on Learning

Present these prompts and questions to your students after a challenging lesson. Create a word cloud of their responses. This can be done as an individual worksheet, or taken up as a whole class. Please ensure that each student participates and responds to each question!

Word cloud 1: grow cultural competence, importance, care, community, situation, stop, happens, s, okay, Moral courage, advocate, matter, include, also, continue, right, means, Disruption, Don t, make, every, use, see, belonging, things, say, better, people, s, classroom, feel, need, call, kids, want, stand, even, important, **learning**, actions, speak, educator, voice, class, seat, table, kindness, way, **disrupt students**, joy, teacher, lead, much, work, unlearn, looks, disruptive, going, thinking, kindness, empathy, Ask, question, hard, biases, harmful, language, uncomfortable

Word cloud 2: unlearning, cultural, Unconscious bias, Continue, classroom, Big, assumptions, comes, t, don t, stereotypes, feel, unlearning, need, Challenging, know, **biases**, learn, thought, action, people, culture, may, make, teaching, **students**, speak, voice, way, things, approach, understandings, reflect, place, racist

Word cloud 3: show students, table, allow, Use privilege, afraid, class, families, comes, ask, will continue, use, included, people, cultural, spaces, kids, actions, take, teaching, think, something, work, right, inequities, Stand, speak, disrupt, make, see, aware, listen, going, others, know, **students**, Call, way, unlearn, step, wrong, address, feel, Reflect, said, will, Continue, learn, needs, children, injustices, want, make sure, hear, cultures, classroom, open, read, books, Continue, learn, understanding, challenge, everyone, bring, conversations, Interrupt, educators, moral courage, Continue advocate

24

2

Gaining Cultural Competence in the Classroom and Beyond

Leland Harper

Leland Harper is Associate Professor of Philosophy and of Race, Justice, and Equity Studies at Siena Heights University. Dr. Harper grew up in Vancouver, BC, and received a PhD in Philosophy from the University of Birmingham (UK). He founded Leland Harper Consulting to assist organizations in being more just, equitable, diverse, and inclusive to and for their stakeholders; he sits on the Board of Directors of AI4BK, whose mission is to empower and elevate Black youth through Artificial Intelligence and innovation.

As educators, we are often seen as, or expected to be, *the* subject-matter experts, and not just by others, as this perspective can sometimes be internalized. The simple fact of the matter is that, while we may be subject-matter experts in one or more areas, there are still many areas where we are not. We have all heard the old adage of the teacher as "the sage on the stage," and many of us now understand that this approach no longer represents best practices for reaching learners in meaningful and effective ways. The transmission model of education has given way to more collaborative, student-centred approaches. We no longer see our students as empty vessels waiting to be filled with knowledge. Rather, we acknowledge that they have rich lives, complex thoughts, deeply held beliefs, and valuable lived experiences. Our task is not simply to teach content, but also to help students navigate it critically and contextually, and to do so in ways that recognize and incorporate who they are, where they have been, and where they are going. Considering this in relation to our ever-evolving teaching practice, Vanessa Rodriguez notes, "Teachers must constantly change themselves based on the interactions they have with their learners in order to produce intellectual and behavioral success" (2012, p. 177). As educators, it is incumbent on us to model lifelong learning that extends beyond textbooks and the classroom. Whether you're a new teacher navigating your first classroom or a seasoned educator with decades of experience, you likely know that doing this (or anything, for that matter) well, and doing it equitably, inclusively, respectfully, and effectively, is much easier said than done. But it is necessary work if we are to make the kind of impact we hope to make on our students. In this chapter, we explore what cultural competence is, why it matters in education, and how to develop it in ourselves.

Before moving much further, it is important to note that this chapter is not going to contain a bunch of extra or busy work for you to add to your already full work–life schedules. Just as I share with my students that there are plenty of ways to learn that do not necessarily require the old-school, formal, stereotypical vision of studying and learning, the same holds here (Boschee, 1990). Of course, spending time in libraries and reading encyclopedias is a fine way to learn (if that's your jam), but it is certainly not for everybody. Nor is it the only option available. Instead, the aim of this chapter is to empower you to embrace learning in nontraditional methods, in nontraditional places, and from nontraditional resources that you already (or can) engage with on a regular basis. It is about providing you with a lens through which to view some of the things you encounter and experience, and ways to recognize, expand, and utilize the world outside your classroom in ways to improve your cultural competency and, ultimately, your teaching practice.

Defining Cultural Competence

Loosely defined, cultural competence is "the ability to understand, appreciate and interact with people from cultures or belief systems different from one's own" (DeAngelis, 2015, p. 64). In the context of education, it is not about having an exhaustive understanding of every culture your students might identify with. Rather, it is the ability to recognize, understand, respect, and appropriately respond to the cultural differences and similarities that exist among your students. What exactly this looks like in any given situation will vary, but a definition provided by Eden et al encapsulates the underlying foundation of the concept in educational spaces:

> Cultural competence in education refers to the capacity of educators to recognize, understand, and appreciate the cultural diversity present in educational settings. It involves not only acknowledging cultural differences but also actively integrating them into teaching practices, curriculum development, and institutional policies. (2024, p. 384)

Of culturally competent educators, they go on to say that these are educators who "strive to create inclusive classrooms where students from diverse backgrounds feel safe, supported, and engaged in their learning experiences" (Eden et al., 2024, p. 384).

Given increasing globalization, migration trends, and various geopolitical and socio-economic considerations, our classrooms today often look very different than they did even just a few years ago, and so should our approach to teaching. We all know that the likelihood of our teaching making an impact on our students is largely dependent on our ability to connect with those same students, and to do this effectively it is essential to develop not only our understanding of the content we teach, but also of the students to whom we teach it. Developing cultural competence involves a continuous process of learning, self-awareness, interrogation, and action, and can yield incredible benefits for us and our students.

Why Cultural Competence Matters

The research is unequivocal: students are more likely to thrive in educational environments where they feel welcome, safe, seen, and valued. An educator's cultural competence helps create these environments (Hamdan and Coloma, 2022). When educators understand and affirm their students' identities, they build trust. That trust becomes the foundation for academic risk-taking, deeper engagement, and ultimately greater knowledge acquisition, practical skills, academic success, and student satisfaction (Arruzza & Chau, 2021). But, contrary to some beliefs, culturally competent teaching doesn't just benefit students from marginalized, underrepresented, or equity-deserving communities. It benefits all students. In a diverse and equitable classroom, each learner has the opportunity to build empathy, challenge assumptions, and expand their worldview. Unfortunately, that kind of classroom isn't typically one we inherit, and it doesn't emerge by accident. Creating and maintaining it requires intentionality.

Other chapters in this volume will discuss specific ways to create a culturally responsive teaching environment within your classroom, so that is not the focus of this chapter. Here, we focus on *you* and developing *your* knowledge and understanding of identities different from your own, helping to form the foundation from which you will build your culturally responsive pedagogies and learning environments.

Developing Cultural Competence Outside the Classroom

Too often, professional development in education focuses almost exclusively on in-classroom strategies. But cultural competence isn't something you can fully cultivate during a Tuesday afternoon staff meeting, by completing an online asynchronous course, or by attending a professional development workshop. To be fair, none of these things are inherently bad (if done properly), but they are certainly insufficient to get us to where we need to be in terms of developing our cultural competence to its full potential. Proper development of cultural competency requires time, space, and experiences outside your typical teaching and learning environments.

Assess Your Position

One of the first, and most helpful, things to do when embarking on this journey is to determine your level of progression down the cultural competency path. Just as we use any number of diagnostic assessments to help identify a student's strengths, weaknesses, and existing knowledge before instruction, we can do the same here for ourselves. While there are various formal tools available online or via private consulting groups to help assess your current standing (whether they are accurate or not is another question), informal yet focused introspection can be sufficient for our purposes.

Set aside some dedicated time to devote to your introspection and reflection, and consider where you might be situated in relation to the different stages of cultural competency on the diagram below.

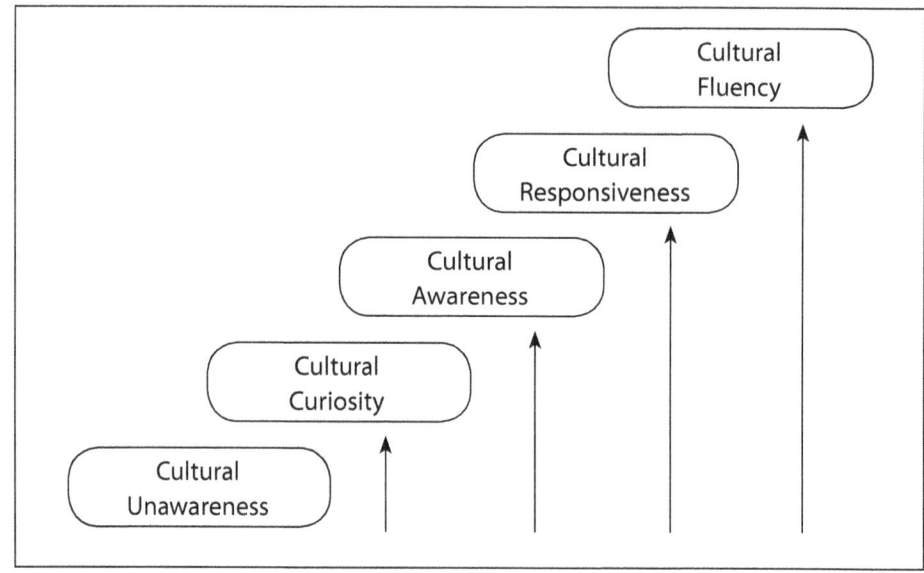

Cultural Unawareness

"I don't see the need." At this stage, individuals are largely unaware of how culture influences experiences and interactions. They might see the dominant culture as "normal" and others as deviations or exceptions. Biases and stereotypes often go unexamined.

Cultural Curiosity

"I know there's something I don't understand." Here, individuals recognize that differences exist and begin to express interest in learning more. They might seek out information, but often rely on surface-level knowledge or make assumptions based on limited exposure.

Cultural Awareness

"I see how culture shapes perspectives." Individuals at this stage understand that their own worldview is culturally influenced and that others' experiences are equally valid. They recognize systemic inequities but might not yet know how to address them effectively.

Cultural Responsiveness

"I adjust my actions with cultural understanding." These individuals actively adapt their behavior, communication, and decision-making to be inclusive and affirming of diverse cultural identities. They seek ongoing feedback, advocate for equity, and work to dismantle biases—both their own and those within systems.

Cultural Fluency

"I skillfully navigate and honor cultural complexities." At this most-advanced stage, individuals deeply integrate cultural competence into their daily practice. They mentor others, engage in courageous conversations, lead systemic change, and approach cultural differences with humility, respect, and strategic insight.

Moving Toward Cultural Fluency

Based on the different experiences we have each had, we have different starting points on our journey. Where I start is probably different from where you start, and that is completely fine. Knowing where to start helps you better understand where you need to go. Moving from one level to the next is not about speed, but about taking progressive steps forward, and we need to be deliberate about our steps.

Here is an analogy for the athletes and sports fans out there. Just as many of us cannot go directly from playing Little League baseball to playing in the Major Leagues, many of us cannot go directly from Cultural Unawareness to Cultural Fluency. In the baseball example, we would need to go from our Little League team to a local representative (rep) team, from our rep team to a post-secondary team, from the post-secondary team through the ranks of the professional minor leagues, and ultimately up to the Major Leagues (or some variant of that path). Similarly, if we want to progress to Cultural Fluency from wherever our starting point is, we must work through the other levels first. Not only does this help build the foundation from which we step up to the next level, but this "baby steps" approach also prevents us from making bigger mistakes that could cause harm to our students and others around us.

Once you have determined your starting point, you now have a destination for your next step. To revisit our baseball example, if you are currently on a Little League team, it would not be the most prudent action to start preparing for your transition to the Major Leagues. There is still a lot of work to do before that point, so you will cross that bridge when you get to it. Similarly, if your self-assessment places you at the level of Cultural Curiosity, there is no need to worry about how things might look at the Cultural Responsiveness level. Instead, keep your focus manageable and goals attainable, and work toward moving from Cultural Curiosity to Cultural Awareness. Once you reach Cultural Awareness, you can then start to think about and work toward reaching Cultural Responsiveness, and so forth. Remember, it is about progress, not speed.

Now that you have an idea of where you are and where you are headed, the work of strengthening (or building) the foundation can begin. As mentioned above, this does not mean that you need to take a semester off to do a literature review on race and ethnicity in the 21st century, try to watch every documentary available on CBC Gem (not the worst idea), or spend thousands of dollars to go on long trips to foreign countries and learn about their cultural practices (I'll take it if I can get it, though). Again, there is nothing wrong with any of that, but that is simply beyond the means (financial and otherwise) of many of us. There are more accessible ways that many of us can set off to improve our cultural competency to ultimately create better learning environments for our ever-evolving student population.

STORY FROM THE CLASSROOM

> If you are having trouble getting started, it might help to frame your first-action steps toward building your cultural competency as a kind of homework assignment for yourself. To help get you started, try the assignment on page 30 from my Introduction to Justice, Equity, Diversity, and Inclusion course; I have received great feedback on this assignment from students over the years. Of course, some of the particulars might not apply to your specific

> situation, needs, or goals, but this is just an example that you can feel free to take, adapt, and utilize it as you see fit.
>
> Some of the questions I use to prime my students for this assignment, and that you can consider asking yourself, include
> - What aspects of your identity do you most often take for granted or rarely think about?
> - When you reflect on your upbringing, what cultures or communities were absent or rarely discussed?
> - Are there communities in your city or region that you know very little about?
> - What identities, histories, or traditions do you feel curious about, but hesitant to engage with for fear of making a mistake?

Assignment: Engage with an Identity

This assignment requires you to engage with a cultural, social, or demographic identity different from your own. Through an activity of your choosing, you will immerse yourself in an experience that allows you to learn first-hand about perspectives, traditions, and practices that are distinct from your personal background. After participating in the activity, you will reflect on your experience and what it has taught you about justice, equity, diversity, and inclusion.

Objectives
- To encourage personal growth through experiential learning.
- To foster empathy and understanding of identities different from your own.
- To critically reflect on the role of diversity, equity, and inclusion in society.
- To apply course concepts to real-world interactions.

Instructions
1. Choose an Activity
   Select an experience related to a demographic identity other than your own. This identity can be based on race, ethnicity, gender, religion, ability, age, sexual orientation, immigration status, or another identity factor. Examples include but are not limited to
   - Reading a book by an author of a different gender or cultural background
   - Attending a cultural or religious event (e.g., a festival, a service, a celebration)
   - Dining at a restaurant serving cuisine from a culture different from your own
   - Visiting a museum exhibit focused on a historically underrepresented community
   - Engaging with a community organization that serves a demographic you are unfamiliar with

2. Participate and Take Notes
   While participating in the activity, observe how it relates to issues of justice, equity, diversity, and inclusion. Consider, for example,
   - How were you made to feel as someone from outside that demographic?
   - What did you learn that you did not previously know?

Whatever activity you choose, ensure it is meaningful, respectful, and allows for genuine engagement with the selected identity.

- How did this experience challenge or reinforce your existing views and beliefs?
- How might this experience help you understand broader societal issues related to justice, equity, diversity, and inclusion?

3. Reflect

   After the activity, reflect on your experience in relation to the course themes. Consider, for example,
   - Why you chose this particular activity.
   - What surprised you, made you uncomfortable, or deepened your understanding.
   - How this experience connects to the ideas of justice, equity, diversity, and inclusion.
   - What lessons from this experience could be applied to fostering justice, equity, diversity, and inclusion in other areas of your life, including any professional spaces you hope to enter in the future.

Building Your Cultural Competence

Expand Your Media Diet

Read books, watch films, and listen to radio stations and podcasts that reflect perspectives and experiences different from your own. Don't consume only content that is designed for or caters to your cultural background. Choose works by authors and creators from marginalized, underrepresented, and equity-deserving communities. And don't just stop at passively consuming content—engage critically with it. Reflect on what surprised you, what challenged you, and what moved you.

Expand Your Literal Diet

Step outside your culinary comfort zone to explore foods and food traditions from cultures different from your own. Seek out restaurants, markets, and recipes that reflect diverse cultural practices and histories. Food is deeply connected to identity, migration, resilience, and community, and learning through cuisine can offer insights you might not encounter otherwise. Approach new flavors and dishes with curiosity and respect, and take time to learn about the cultural significance behind what you're eating.

Attend Community Events

Make an effort to attend cultural festivals, art exhibits, public lectures, or local events in communities that differ from your own. Being physically present in these spaces—with humility and an open mind—can help build a deeper understanding of the social and cultural contexts beyond your own lived experience. Many municipalities and community organizations host cultural events throughout the year that are free to attend.

Engage in Ongoing Learning

Take courses or attend workshops on equity, anti-racism, decolonization, and inclusive education. Look for opportunities to learn from scholars and practitioners with lived experience and academic expertise. The internet is a great resource, and web conferencing technology has dramatically improved access to diverse voices and engaged academics. Often, colleges and universities host events, sessions, and learning opportunities that are free and open to the community. Seek out these opportunities, and make it a habit, not a one-time event.

Build Relationships Outside Your Identity Group

Form meaningful, lasting, and genuine connections with colleagues, community members, and mentors from different racial, cultural, linguistic, religious, and socio-economic backgrounds. These relationships can be powerful learning experiences in themselves. And they can offer perspectives that challenge your assumptions and broaden your worldview.

Travel with Purpose

If you have the means, travel not just as a tourist, but also as a learner. Visit museums, heritage sites, and communities that offer insights into histories of colonization, migration, culture, resistance, and resilience. Do not limit yourself to the confines of your hotel room or resort property—get out and experience the space around you. Prioritize ethical and community-based tourism when possible.

Approaching the Work

The list of activities mentioned above is not exhaustive, and there are many more things you can do to build up your cultural competency. I encourage you to take some time to consider what resources and activities are accessible to you, and what you hope to learn by engaging yourself with them. Of course, before setting out to engage in any of the activities listed above or that you've identified on your own, it is essential that you consider how to do it respectfully.

In anything you choose to do to try to advance your cultural competence, it is necessary to approach it with respect and humility, otherwise you risk harming others and damaging the integrity of what you are trying to accomplish. An essential component of cultural competence is cultural humility—the recognition that we can never fully know or master someone else's lived experience, no matter how hard we try or how knowledgeable we think we are. Cultural humility requires us to approach our work with a learner's mindset, to remain open to being corrected, and to acknowledge the limits of our own perspective. It emphasizes relationship-building over expertise and centres mutual respect, accountability, and lifelong reflection. Where cultural competence provides the tools, cultural humility provides the attitude: one of openness, receptivity, and a deep respect for the lived experiences of others. If ever in doubt about whether you are approaching a learning opportunity respectfully, it is essential to exercise your cultural humility and do some individual research or speak to some trusted friends or colleagues about helping to keep you in check. Often, devoting even just a few minutes to finding and reading online articles, or having a quick conversation with somebody, can help identify potential oversights before you start whatever you've chosen to do. It is also important to note that this—identifying, acknowledging, and understanding the limits of your own knowledge—is an essential part of the process.

Dealing With Discomfort

Part of developing cultural competence is learning to sit with discomfort (DiAngelo, 2018). As educators, we are often trained to be in control—to have the right answers, to maintain authority, to create stability in our classrooms. But cultural competence invites us into spaces of vulnerability, uncertainty, and sometimes even loss of control. It requires us to confront the limits of our own knowledge and assumptions, and to acknowledge that there are ways of knowing, being, and teaching that fall outside our own lived experiences.

We will make mistakes. We will get things wrong. We will mispronounce names, misunderstand references, misinterpret histories. We will be called out or called in—sometimes gently, sometimes bluntly. That is not a reason to retreat or shut down. It is an invitation to do the work, and we should welcome it.

What matters most is how we respond. Can we reflect without defensiveness? Can we apologize without centring ourselves? Can we sit with the discomfort long enough to truly hear what is being shared, rather than rushing to repair our own feelings? Can we model humility, openness, and resilience for our students and colleagues? These are the moments that often have the most powerful, lasting impact—not only on our personal growth, but also on the learning environments we create.

Discomfort is distinct from danger, and it is not failure. It's growth. It's where transformation lives. It is the heat that forges new understanding. When we allow ourselves to stay present in uncomfortable moments—rather than avoiding, minimizing, or rationalizing them—we exercise our neuroplasticity and build the muscle memory necessary for deep, lasting change within ourselves and beyond. We also live what we preach every day to our students: that learning is not always smooth, that important lessons often feel uneasy, and that mistakes are a natural, even necessary, part of the journey toward justice and equity.

Building cultural competence demands courage, and courage is not the absence of fear or uncertainty, but the willingness to act even in their presence (Aristotle, 1998). Sitting with discomfort, reflecting honestly, taking responsibility, and striving to do better next time: these practices are not optional add-ons. They are at the very heart of becoming a culturally competent global citizen. In fact, many academics and practitioners working in spaces of diversity, equity, inclusion, anti-racism, and decolonization (myself included) will say unequivocally that discomfort is necessary for growth, and even that our best opportunities for growth are found precisely in those moments of discomfort (Creswell, 2023). As Aristotle says, "We become just by doing just acts; temperate by doing temperate acts, brave by doing brave acts" (1998, p. 29). So we must practice what we want to become.

The Importance of Being Present

The work of building cultural competence has been laid out above in terms of action: attending workshops, reading books, forming cross-cultural relationships, participating in community events, even just going out for dinner! These activities are vital, but their impact depends not just on the fact that we complete them, but how we show up to them. Being present—being deliberate, engaged, and reflective with our body and mind—is essential to translating these experiences into meaningful growth.

When attending a cultural festival or community event, for example, there is a difference between being there as a passive observer and being there as a humble learner. The former might allow us to check a box; the latter asks us to slow down, to notice what is unfamiliar, and to reflect on what we see, hear, and feel. Being present in this context means going beyond surface-level participation. It means getting involved. It means asking ourselves: *What can I learn from this community's expression of identity? How does this challenge or expand my understanding of culture, identity, power, purpose, resistance, or belonging?*

Similarly, when we read a book by an author from a marginalized background or engage with a documentary that explores systemic inequality, presence means doing more than simply consuming the content. It involves pausing to reflect on what makes us uncomfortable, asking questions about how the work relates to our own social positioning, and allowing our worldview to be reshaped. Presence means resisting the urge to skim or fast-forward through difficult material and instead sitting with its implications.

Even professional development opportunities, such as equity seminars, antiracism workshops, or public lectures, require presence to be truly transformative. It is easy to show up physically while mentally staying detached. But presence demands more. It asks us to take notes not only on what we learn, but on how we respond internally. It invites us to grapple with what lingers long after the session is over. It pushes us to ask: *How will I carry this insight into my daily life? What do I now feel compelled to change?*

Presence is especially important when engaging with people and communities whose lived experiences are different from our own. Whether building relationships with acquaintances across lines of difference or stepping into unfamiliar social spaces, presence requires humility. It means not dominating conversations with our own reflections and unfounded assumptions. It means being open to discomfort without demanding, or even expecting, emotional labor from others. It means showing up with the intention to learn, not to fix, rescue, correct, or extract. Keep in mind that this is not a Disney movie, and you are not a knight in shining armor.

Without presence, any activity you choose to engage in risks becoming performative. By being present, however, your new knowledge and experiences become fertile ground for transformation. A podcast becomes a portal into someone else's truth. A conversation becomes a moment of mutual recognition and understanding. A community gathering becomes a site of shared humanity.

Much of this likely sounds similar to what you might tell a student about engaging with course content, or a tip you might provide about getting the most out of a course, and it is. Ultimately, being present means resisting the pressure to rush through building cultural competence (or anything, for that matter) as a task to be completed. It asks us to step away from physical and cognitive multitasking to get the most out of information exchange (Baires et al., 2021, p. 1046). It reframes the work as an ongoing journey, as one that asks us to notice, to reflect, and to return again and again with greater openness, focus, and intention. In doing so, we can create not only a more just and inclusive teaching practice, but a more expansive and humane way of being in the world.

Final Thoughts

Gaining cultural competence is not an end point; it's an ongoing commitment. It is a practice rooted in humility, curiosity, empathy, and justice. It calls on us to be lifelong learners—not just in our academic and professional disciplines, but in our relationships with others, in our understanding of systems and histories, and in our capacity to self-reflect and grow. Cultural competence is not about achieving a fixed set of skills or becoming an expert in someone else's experience. Rather, it is about cultivating a mindset that stays open to complexity, that honors difference, and that recognizes the humanity in every student we encounter.

This work is neither quick nor easy. It requires time, effort, courage, and humility to confront our own biases, honesty in acknowledging the ways we might have contributed to exclusion or harm, and patience with ourselves as we challenge our own deeply ingrained assumptions. It demands that we engage, not just intellectually, but also emotionally, ethically, respectfully, and genuinely. And while the work might often feel uncomfortable, messy, or incomplete, it is some of the most vital work we can do—not only for our students, but for the integrity of our profession and the well-being of our communities, and for ourselves.

You won't get it perfectly. None of us will. But perfection is not the goal. What matters is the willingness to try, to listen, to reflect, and to keep showing up with intention and care. What matters is that we continue to move forward, imperfectly, perhaps, but purposefully.

Our students are watching us more than we recognize. They are learning not only from what we teach, but from how we live out our values. When we develop and demonstrate cultural competence through our presence, our openness, and our actions, we model what it means to be both educators and engaged citizens. We show students that lifelong learning isn't a slogan, but a practice. We show that learning doesn't end when the bell rings or at the edge of the curriculum, but extends into how we treat one another, how we show up in the world, and how we imagine a better future together.

> **Essential Questions for Reflection**
>
> - Whose perspectives do I prioritize in my teaching?
> - How do my own identities shape my assumptions and expectations?
> - What steps have I taken to understand the cultural contexts of my students? Of my colleagues? Of those around me?
> - How often does the media I consume centre equity-deserving voices, experiences, and perspectives?
> - How intentional have I been in learning about other cultures?

Voice from the Field

While I enjoyed the experience [of participating in a sweat lodge], it felt more personal than reading *Finding Refuge* did. A lot of my revelations were about my life, my experiences, more than it did make me feel like I learned about Native American culture. Reading *Refuge* made me feel more immersed in Iranian American culture, as opposed to where the sweat lodge made me feel more connected to myself. I didn't feel like I left myself and experienced something new, to me, it felt like I went deeper into myself within the new experience. Writing out this assignment, I'm realizing that I did have a Native American experience and I seem to be judging its value against what information I got out of it. For the sweat lodge, I didn't gain much "information," but it is obvious that it afforded me knowledge and a connection to Native American culture that I never had before. I will never again forget that learning takes on many forms.

— Student reflecting on their participation in a sweat lodge and comparing it to reading *Finding Refuge: My Journey from the Middle East to Michigan* by Shirin Kambin-Timms

3

The Three P's of Culturally Relevant, Responsive, and Sustaining Education

Kenneth Gyamerah and Doreen Bonsu

Dr. Kenneth Gyamerah is an Assistant Professor at Ontario Tech University. His research explores Black youth experiences in K–12 and post-secondary education, focusing on anti-colonial education policy, STEM equity, and epistemic justice. He brings international experience from Canada, the UK, and Ghana, and previously served as a research coordinator at the Toronto District School Board.

Doreen Bonsu, a proud Ghanaian-Canadian and award-winning educator, holds a Master's degree in Social Justice Education from the Ontario Institute for Studies in Education (OISE). Passionate about equity, she centres Black narratives and uses culturally responsive pedagogy. With teaching experience in Ghana, Italy, Greece, and Costa Rica, she emphasizes experiential learning and global perspectives in her high-school classroom.

The Three P's of CRRSE:
1. Preparing
2. Planning
3. Practice

Culturally relevant, responsive, and sustaining education (CRRSE) draws on educational theories that begin with Gloria Ladson-Billings' seminal work on culturally relevant pedagogy. Ladson-Billings' work identified three interdependent dimensions of culturally relevant teaching: academic success, cultural competence, and critical consciousness (Ladson-Billings, 1995). Since this foundational work, the field has expanded through the contributions of numerous scholars and educators. Geneva Gay (2000, 2010) offered culturally responsive teaching, emphasizing pedagogical care, affirming relationships, and responsive curriculum design. Django Paris and H. Samy Alim (2017) introduced culturally sustaining pedagogy, which challenges educators not only to acknowledge students' cultures, but also to authentically protect, sustain, and centre them in the face of ongoing systemic erasure in our society. Many others have expanded the field, connecting culturally relevant and responsive education to critical multiculturalism, constructivist teaching, culturally responsive leadership, equity-focused pedagogy, culturally responsive assessment, and critical pedagogies.

In this chapter, we position CRRSE not as something for educators to add to their teaching practice, but as a pedagogy, a stance, a way of being, and a set of ethical relationships that educators continually build, sustain, and maintain in their work with students and families. Andrew Campbell's (2022) work reminds us that culturally responsive teaching is not just about strategies educators share in their teaching, but also about their disposition. The culturally relevant and responsive teacher is someone who holds high expectation of their students, sees students through a lens of capability, and teaches from a place of empathy, emotional intelligence, relational care, and responsibility. Further, a culturally relevant and responsive educator is an active agent of change. In their practice, they are committed to dismantling barriers and sustaining the cultural and intellectual lives of students through liberatory and dynamic practice.

This chapter speaks directly to all educators. As an teacher, you might already be engaged in this work or you might be unsure where to begin. Also, you might be wrestling with questions about how to integrate CRRSE into everyday classroom practice. Wherever you are, this chapter is designed to meet you there and support you in moving forward with actionable strategies. In this chapter, we frame CRRSE not as something you complete, but as a relational commitment to your students, your colleagues, your communities, and to a future where all children can learn in the fullness of their identities, voices, and potential.

The chapter begins with our voices, then is organized into three sections: preparation, planning, and practice. It features case studies from educators and testimonials from students that remind us that culturally relevant and responsive education is alive in lesson plans, classroom discussions, hallway check-ins, and communities. We close each section with reflective activities and guiding questions to help you carry this work into your school, classroom, and community.

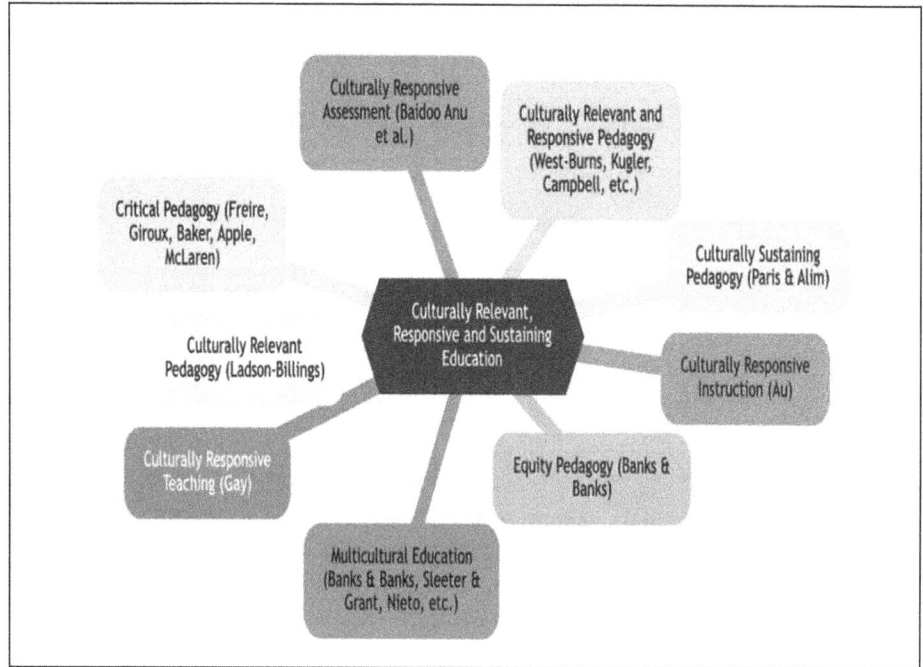

This infographic summarizes the different bodies of work that are constituents of CRRSE.

Adapted from Campbell (2022)

Voices from the Field: Centring Our Stories

My journey through education has never been one of neutrality. I studied in classrooms shaped by the tension of carrying my culture into spaces that were not created with me in mind. As a student, I learned early that success in Western educational institutions was often conditional on assimilation and leaving parts of myself at the door. Yet I carried with me the teachings of home: wisdom passed through stories, African proverbs, and kitchen-table conversations with my grandmother. I knew I held histories, languages, and ways of knowing that Western schooling rarely recognized as valuable. Now, as a University Professor, I bring those stories and teachings with me. In my classroom, I teach my students not to fit into a broken system, but to interrupt it to make space and plant seeds that will bear good fruit. I draw from relational, culturally grounded, and justice-oriented pedagogies in my teaching. Also, the things I continue to do in my teaching are centring storytelling, holding my students to high expectations, creating room for critical thinking. I know what it means to be misread, underestimated, or rendered invisible in institutions that see cultural diversity but fail to dismantle systems of oppression. I know how dangerous it can be when students internalize these distortions. That is why I refuse to replicate that harm. Instead,

I strive to reimagine my teaching by co-creating classrooms where students are not asked to erase themselves but are affirmed and welcomed in the fullness of who they are and who they are becoming.
— Kenneth Gyamerah

In my early years of teaching, I worked in a predominately white school. As the only Black educator on staff, I was aware of the lack of representation among teachers, but I hadn't yet considered the absence of diverse voices in the curriculum or its potential impact on students.

In the English Department where I taught, it was common practice to focus on texts from the traditional literary canon. At first, I thought nothing of it. I abided with the rest of the department, as I wanted to be a collaborative member. As I began to engage in culturally responsive teaching, I felt an urge to challenge the texts that were being used—but I didn't. In hindsight, I wish I had had the confidence, the language acuity, and a deeper practice of self-reflection to process the discomfort I felt.

Early in my career, I viewed myself simply as a Black teacher focused on building strong relationships and serving as a positive role model for all students, especially those who were Black and racialized. It was not until I became a student in Dr. Andrew Campbell's Special Issues in Curriculum and Pedagogy: Black Educator Identity and Practice course that I thoroughly reflected on my positionality in relation to my work as an anti-racist educator, and how my lived experience as a Black student in K–12 education influenced me. It allowed me to reflect on my pedagogical practice and the classroom setting I wanted to foster for my students.
— Doreen Bonsu

Preparing for Culturally Relevant and Responsive Teaching

Voice from the Field

As a former high-school English literature teacher who worked in Catholic schools, I witnessed the positive impact of culturally relevant and responsive pedagogy and practice on Black learners. Witnessing a Black child be themself, see and bring their people and heritage, and have it affirmed at school evokes fond memories of prideful smiles, heads held high, and confidence taking root. Now a mother of two Black boys in elementary school, my determination is driven by an undercurrent of fear and fierceness. As my children's first teacher, I am hyper-reflective as I think (some might say overthink) about how we will navigate our way through the education system that has proven to be quite damaging and harmful to Black children, especially to Black boys. What will it require to sustain, to maintain, and to fight for the dream of all Black children flourishing at school? My hope is that, by the time my children graduate from high school, there will be many educators who are strong and steady in preparation, planning, and practice of culturally relevant, responsive, and sustaining education. It is well past time.
— Tia Duke, Mother and educator

When thinking about preparation, educators often focus on unit planning, gathering materials to create an inclusive classroom, or ensuring that students have the resources they need to succeed. While these actions are important, it is necessary to reassess what preparation truly means. Preparation begins with self-reflection. Culturally relevant, responsive, and sustaining educators must acknowledge their positional power in the classroom and recognize that there is no neutral stance in education. Lived experiences, biases, and assumptions inevitably shape teaching practices. Engaging in authentic introspection is essential, as it sets the tone for meaningful and transformative classroom experiences.

Positionality and Your *Why*

Adapted from Harrington (2022)

When reflecting on a teacher's positionality, the following considerations are important:
- What groups—race, gender, sexual orientation, age, social class, religion, ability, etc.—do you identify with and how does your connection to each group relate to your actions as an educator?
- In what ways do your identities represent privilege or marginalization, and how might they compare to those of your students? How might you be engaging in actions that marginalize or discourage students?
- How has your upbringing influenced your perspective on education?
- What beliefs or values and characteristics do you have, and how do they affect your identity and related actions as an educator?

While reflecting on positionality, use the opportunity to examine your own educational philosophy. For example, a teacher's commitment to anti-racist practices might stem from personal experiences within an education system that failed to provide adequate representation in staffing, course materials, or the curriculum. In many cases, these gaps can shape a deeper understanding of the need for inclusive and affirming learning environments.

Sharing your positionality and educational philosophy can serve as a catalyst for others to conduct their own internal audits, assessing how they interact with students and their caregivers:
- Are you committed to removing barriers that are present for your students? What does that look like?
- Are you operating from a place of critical care within your classroom, a place that combines high expectations with empathy and compassion?
- Are your students, regardless of socio-economic status or background, being held to high standards?
- Has your past interaction with a particular race of people affected your ability to communicate with parents?

When engaging in culturally relevant and reflective teaching, the core tenets include high expectations, critical consciousness, and cultural competence. To understand your students, you must first understand yourself. It is critical for educators to "examine who they are and articulate how they should use their power and privilege to disrupt and dismantle the increase in deficit thinking seen in so many of our schools" (Campbell & Watson, 2022):

> If educational leaders are going to commit to the process of eradicating deficit thinking in schools, they need to first engage in authentic self-reflection, where they can examine their power, privilege, biases, stereotypes, and assumptions about diverse marginalized students. Only after this self-reflection can they genuinely tackle the best practice approach to culturally relevant responsive pedagogy, which stems from their dispositions as educators (Campbell & Watson, 2022, p. 113).

Reflection Activity: Positional Power Inventory

The goal of this activity is to support teachers in translating ideas into actionable self-awareness and pedagogical commitment through structured self-inquiry. See page 51 for a reproducible template of this activity.

1. Reflect on Your *Why*
   Write a response to the following prompts:
   - What brought you into education and how has your purpose evolved?
   - How have your lived experiences shaped your understanding of what your students need most from you?
   - What assumptions might you be making about your students' families, values, or motivations?
   - Have you ever witnessed or participated in deficit-based language or thinking in your school community? How did you respond (or not) and why?

2. Commitment Checkpoint
   One belief I need to challenge in myself: _____
   One small but meaningful shift I can make this month: _____
   One colleague I can engage with for accountability or shared learning: _____

3. Reflect on Your Identity

Identity Category	How I Identify	Areas of Privilege	Areas of Marginalization	Impact
Race/Ethnicity				
Gender				
Sexual Orientation				
Socio-economic Background				
Religion/Spirituality				
(Dis)Ability				
Language/Culture				

Planning for Culturally Relevant and Responsive Education

Before planning any lesson, it is essential not only to align with curriculum expectations but also to ensure that the content is relevant to students' everyday lives. Here are three strategies teachers can implement when planning culturally responsive and sustaining lessons: getting to know your students, creating a sense of belonging, and utilizing responsive course materials.

Getting to Know Your Students

Questions should be tailored to grade level.

Getting to know your students, whether through student profiles at the beginning of the school year or informal class conversations that help gauge their interests and experiences, is crucial for building positive rapport with students. Setting up confidential student profiles at the beginning of the year is a helpful way to get to know your learners. By gathering key information, it provides for a starting point for educators to connect with their students. See page 52 for a reproducible Student Profile Questionnaire.

Creating a Sense of Belonging

While the idea of creating safe spaces has long been emphasized in education, there is a growing need to shift toward cultivating brave spaces and environments where students, particularly those who are marginalized and under-represented, feel empowered to share their perspectives, challenge dominant narratives, and engage in critical dialogue. As bell hooks articulated: "Rather than focusing on issues of safety, I think that a feeling of community creates a sense that there is a shared commitment and a common good that binds us" (hooks, 1994, p. 40). A brave space is not about comfort; it is about fostering courageous conversations that centre marginalized voices, promote authentic participation, and actively dismantle barriers to inclusion and belonging. The infographic below features quotes from three high school students in response to the question: *What does Brave Spaces mean to you?*

Responses by high-school students

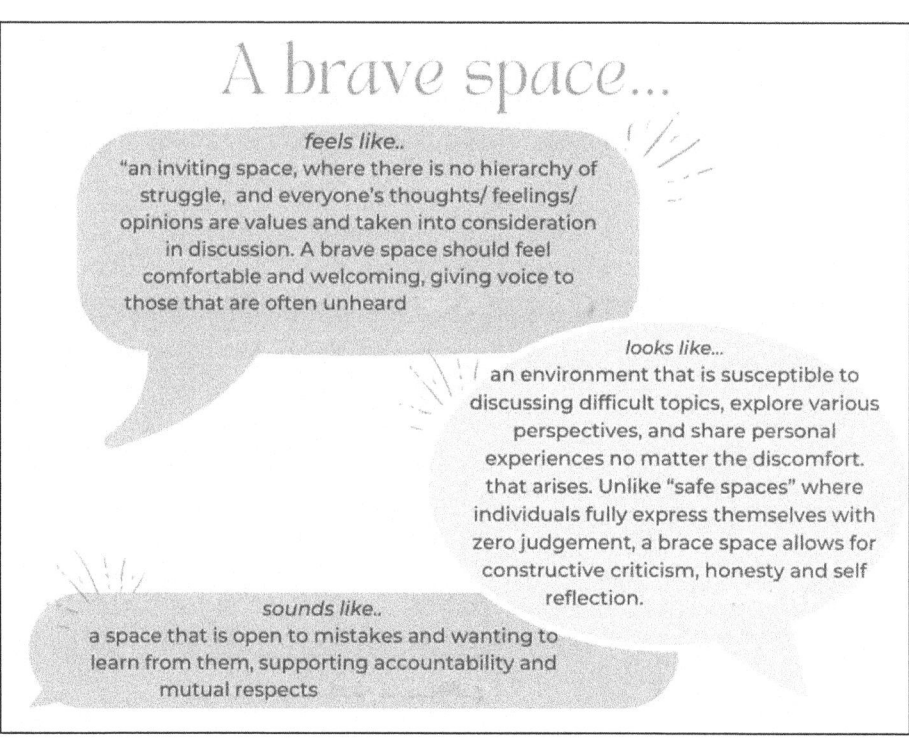

Responsive Materials

Activities can be adapted for different racialized groups.

All students, not only our Black students, must be made aware of the joy experienced within Black communities. Unfortunately, the media depicts far too many examples of Black trauma that Black folks face every single day. Our students have access to this information as well, and that is why it is essential that we highlight Black joy to parallel such heavy subject matter. Black joy is resistance. It is music, love; it is art. Centring Black joy in schools must go hand-in-hand with culturally relevant, responsive, and sustaining pedagogy; they are interdependent. To truly support students, educators must hold high expectations (encouraging personal connections in learning), demonstrate cultural competencies (building authentic relationships and interrogating biases), and nurture critical consciousness (continually asking: *Am I championing my Black students?*)

Voices from the Field

Student were asked, "What does Black Joy look like in a classroom?"

- Being proud of being Black and having a fair and racist free environment
- Black joy is when Black students are not being left behind as if that is what is meant for them.
- Being able to connect our experiences and find happiness in our blackness without judgement and feelings of hate.

Instead of…	Try this…
Black History Month	Black History 365!
The "same" guest speakers	Black guest speakers (speaking on a variety of topics)
Going on customary field trips	Request experiences that cater to the needs of your Black students

Mirrors, Windows, and Sliding Glass Doors was coined by Rudine Sims Bishops, and it highlights the importance of representation in any text that enters the classroom. It is essential that students see a variety of texts that look like themselves or reflect their lived experiences:

Mirrors: Students see themselves and their lived experiences reflected in texts.

Windows: Students are able to learn about the experiences of others through texts.

Sliding Doors: Texts that allow students to enter a world. To create an authentic experience requires knowledge of a particular culture or group of people to understand and appreciate the importance of perspective.

"The problem with stereotypes is not that they are untrue, but that they are incomplete. They make one story become the only story" (Chimamanda Adichie, 2009)

Marginalized students need affirmation, while students who are typically represented must also encounter diverse perspectives. Exposure to all three provides an opportunity for the affirmation, representation, and empathy that is essential to fostering an inclusive and empathetic learning environment.

Questions to ask yourself when choosing materials:
- Am I providing a single story?
- Does that story portray trauma or deficit representation?
- Have I considered the impact on students whose identities align with the representation?
- Have I considered the impact on students whose identities do not align with the representation?

Ways to incorporate Black Canadian history into classrooms and school communities:
- Engage students' creative art skills to produce artefacts that commemorate prominent Black Canadian individuals.
- Highlight key Black Canadian figures on a bulletin board

STORY FROM THE CLASSROOM

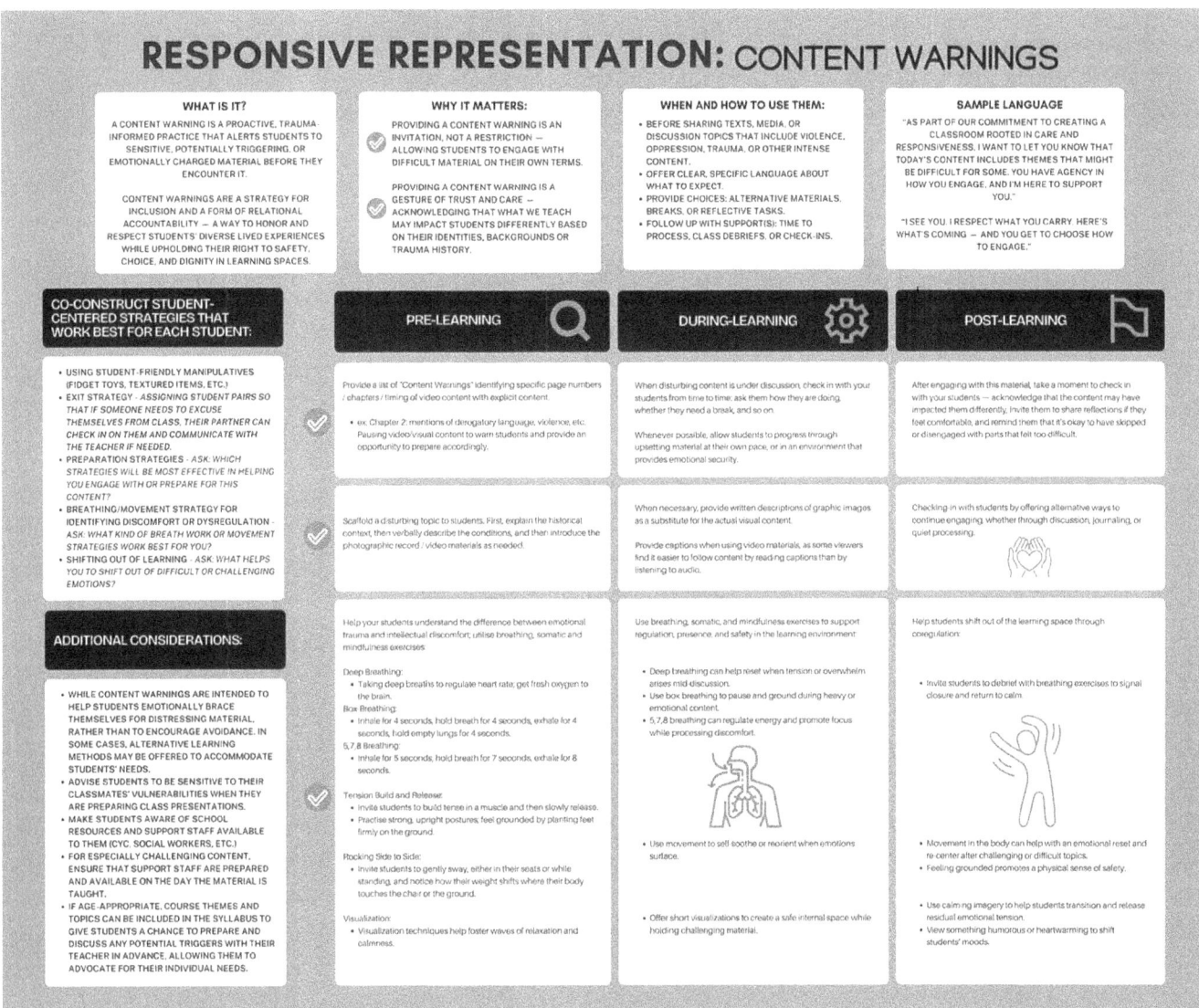

This strategy was created by Amanda Gonsalves, Curriculum Consultant: Equity and Inclusive Education (K–12).

- Which pre-, during-, or post-learning strategy would be most effective with your students, and what one practical step can you take this week to implement it with challenging content?
- What potential challenges might arise in offering consistent content warnings and how can you proactively manage them?
- How can you offer content warnings and learning choices in a way that supports student agency without making students feel exposed or singled out?
- How will you recognize and respond to emotionally charged content that might not involve explicit trauma but still negatively affects students based on their identities or lived experiences?

Reflection Activity: What Has Shifted in Me?

The goal of this activity is to guide you in putting into action what you have learned from planning for CRRSE.

- What surprised me most as I engaged with these CRRSE strategies?
- Which assumptions or habits of mine are no longer aligned with the relationships I want to nurture?
- Where do I feel tension, discomfort, or resistance? What might that be teaching me?
- On a blank sheet of paper or in a digital document, draw three concentric circles like a ripple:
  - Circle 1 (Inner): What is one small shift I can make in my classroom environment to better honor a given student's identity?
  - Circle 2 (Middle): What is one change I can make in how I relate to students' culture, in broader social context, or in responsive materials?
  - Circle 3 (Outer): How might this ripple outward affect how my school community, colleagues, or curriculum practices evolve?

Practice of Sustaining Education

STORY FROM THE CLASSROOM

Centring Identity

by Jamie Philip, Indigenous Education Consultant K–8

In our Kindergarten classroom, identity is centred in all learning experiences. Early in the year, we begin by learning about the land we are on. Students learn that people lived on this land long before we did. Students respond to this learning with curiosity and respect: "Who lived here before us?" While students' understanding of who the Anishinaabe people are is developing, they will continue to learn more.

We extend this learning by exploring where our families come from. We map out our roots, using our classroom world map. We discover where we live and how near and far away from what is now Canada our ancestors come from. Families are encouraged to engage in discussion of their family roots, languages, culture, food, climate, family stories, and more.

Students learn about and color flags of their heritage. These flags, along with students' pictures, are displayed around our world map. Using twine, we connect students' pictures and flags to the corresponding countries on the map. We learn that everyone comes from somewhere, and that these places, and the land we are in now, matter.

We talk about treaties in simple terms: promises made and often broken: "How do we feel when someone breaks a promise?" We ask what it means to be a good relative to the land, to each other, and to Indigenous Peoples who still live here and whose land we share.

Through these layered conversations that continue throughout the school year, children begin to see themselves, each other, and the land as deeply connected. They begin to reflect on their role as citizens of the world and their communities, the gifts they share with each other, and how to treat others with dignity and care.

- What messages does your classroom environment send about whose histories, cultures, and contributions are valued?

- In what ways can you create space for students and their families to share their cultural identities, languages, and stories as part of our collective learning?
- How do you continue your own learning about the treaties that cover the land where you teach, and how does this learning shape what and how you teach?
- In what ways are you introducing young learners to the histories and ongoing presence of Indigenous Peoples and the land we are on; and how can you make this learning more meaningful and ongoing in your classroom?
- How can you help students understand that we are all treaty people, with shared responsibilities to care for the land and one another?

Image Source: Jamie Philip

One way to put culturally relevant, responsive, and sustaining education into practice is by designing multiple ways to engage student learning. Learning stations are an effective approach that offers students a more interactive and engaging experience, allowing them to explore different aspects of a subject at their own pace while deepening their understanding of the material. When designed thoughtfully, learning stations allow students to see themselves reflected in the curriculum, engage in meaningful, student-driven learning, and explore diverse perspectives. To be successful in using learning stations, do the following:

- Determine learning objectives.
- Set up stations based on key topics/concepts/learning.
- Differentiate media sources.
- Explain instructions/facilitation.
- Debrief and discuss (assess the learning).

Lesson: "We Built this Too"

1. To help students get started, create a strong guiding question to help students see how it can connect to a bigger idea:

    Whose stories have shaped Canada and whose have we missed?

    Post this question at each station and encourage students to jot connections as they go along
2. Prior to the lesson, create a reflection booklet or a learning passport made of five pages. This will be used as an assessment piece and an exit ticket where students can share their takeaways from the lesson.
3. Invite students to visit the stations and complete their tasks in their booklet/passports.

Station 1 Hidden Stories: Communities that Built Canada Students explore the histories of different communities that are often left out of textbooks	Sources • Indigenous Communities • Ukrainian immigration to Canada • African and Caribbean immigration to Canada • South Asian immigration to British Columbia Task: Students create a history spotlight card that shares what these communities did, the challenges they faced, and why their stories matter
Station 2 Voices of Resistance: Advocating for Justice Students examine different voices of folks who have been marginalized and use their voice to stand for justice	Sources • The town of Dresden, Ontario standing against segregation • The introduction of the *Accessibility for Ontarians with Disabilities Act* (AODA) • Indigenous groups (e.g., Louis Riel and the Red River Resistance) Task: Students discuss *What happens when people advocate for equity and fairness in Canada's history?*

Station 3 Taking Up Space: Sources of Pride Students analyze visual primary sources that show accomplishments of marginalized individuals/ groups	Sources could include • A video explaining the installation of Canada's first mosque, the Al-Rashid Mosque • A document explaining the emergence of Chinatowns across Canada • 2SLBTQIA+ pride (e.g., Jackie Shane's impact on the R&B music scene in Toronto) Task: Students explain the importance of these historical moments and their impact on Canadian culture
Station 4 A More Inclusive Canada	Task: Students create a museum exhibit poster that tells a story that should be taught in schools that focuses on a marginalized group (Asian community, Black Canadians, 2SLGBTQIA+ or the Muslim community)

Questions for Reflection on Implementing CRRSE in Your Practice

- How do I create opportunities for students to bring their lived experiences, cultural and linguistic backgrounds, and identities into the learning process?
- In what ways do my instructional strategies and assessment practices honor multiple ways of knowing and demonstrating understanding?
- How do I foster a classroom environment in which students feel empowered to challenge dominant narratives and engage in critical conversations?
- What mechanisms do I have in place to ensure ongoing feedback from students about the relevance and inclusivity of my teaching practices?
- How do I sustain the principles of culturally relevant, responsive, and sustaining education beyond a single lesson or unit, ensuring it is embedded in the culture, curriculum, and assessment of my classroom year-round?

Final Thoughts

> "I realized I could not serve two masters. I could not serve the children and the system. The system was not about helping children; it was about helping the system. If you are a part of the system, by default, you are helping to maintain the system."
> — Bettina Love (2019)

The truth captured in Love's quote can be unsettling for many educators. However, if teachers are willing to engage critically, they will realize that they cannot transform education without first transforming themselves. Also, as educators, we cannot claim to serve justice while protecting the very structures that perpetuate harm. The system is not a distant entity made of buildings and policies; the system is us. We are all part of the system, and this system includes the teachers, administrators, leaders, and staff whose everyday actions, decisions, and silences either sustain the status quo or disrupt it. Therefore, culturally relevant, responsive, and sustaining education (CRRSE) demands more than symbolic gestures. CRRSE is not a checklist or a singular initiative teachers do in a term. It is a lifelong relational commitment and opportunity to engage in critical reflexivity; to unlearn internalized biases, stereotypes, and deficit ways of thinking; to surface and interrogate the unseen assumptions that shape teaching; and to reimagine teaching practice as a living, liberatory relationship with students, communities, and the wider world.

Throughout this chapter, we have shared learnings on the Preparation, Planning, and Practice of CRRSE as dynamic, interconnected ways of being with students and not isolated tasks to be completed. We have emphasized that true preparation begins with critical self-reflection: facing the ways our own histories, identities, biases, and positionalities shape the classroom. Also, we unpacked how planning rooted in CRRSE requires more than aligning with standards. Planning for CRRSE demands intentional creation of brave spaces, student-centred learning pathways, and cultural sustaining curricula. CRRSE challenges us to move from performative gestures toward transformative, liberatory, and social action.

In conclusion, we provide these questions for you to carry into your everyday work:

- How will you centre the diverse lived experiences, knowledge, and dreams of your students, not just during special months, but every day?
- How will you stay present to discomfort and let it sharpen your relational imagination, rather than seeking quick resolutions or fixes that often reinforce the very patterns of exclusion, erasure, and inequity that culturally relevant, responsive, and sustaining practices seek to dismantle?
- How will your practice continue to question and disrupt the everyday normalizations of colonialism and racism within educational spaces?
- How are you creating and sustaining spaces within your professional learning communities that centre critical reflexivity, foster brave dialogue, and advance the principles of culturally relevant, responsive, and sustaining education?

It is important to always remember that this work is never finished. It is a practice of preparation, planning, and practice at every moment. It is a cyclical, spiraling process of reflection, reorientation, and re-commitment.

Reflection Activity: Positional Power Inventory

1. Reflect on Your *Why*
   Write a response to the following prompts:
   - What brought you into education and how has your purpose evolved?
   - How have your lived experiences shaped your understanding of what your students need most from you?
   - What assumptions might you be making about your students' families, values, or motivations?
   - Have you ever witnessed or participated in deficit-based language or thinking in your school community? How did you respond (or not) and why?

2. Commitment Checkpoint
   One belief I need to challenge in myself: _____
   One small but meaningful shift I can make this month: _____
   One colleague I can engage with for accountability or shared learning: _____

3. Reflect on Your Identity

Identity Category	How I Identify	Areas of Privilege	Areas of Marginalization	Impact
Race/Ethnicity				
Gender				
Sexual Orientation				
Socio-economic Background				
Religion/ Spirituality				
(Dis)Ability				
Language/ Culture				

Student Profile Questionnaire

- What is your full name? Do you go by another name? What are your preferred pronouns (she/her, he/him, them/theirs, etc.)?

  _____

- Would you like me to address you using your preferred pronouns? If so, when? For example: when referring to you individually, when referring to you when speaking with your guardians/parents. You can tell me as much or as little as you feel comfortable with.

  _____

  _____

- Is there anything you would like me to know about you as a student? For example: sometimes I need extra time to process written instructions; I prefer to work independently; I prefer to work in groups; positive feedback helps to motivate me; it's been a while since I have interacted with people in real life so I think I am a little socially awkward, etc.

  _____

  _____

- After reviewing the syllabus, is there any topic of study that you would like to opt out of because it causes you distress? If the answer is yes, please identify the specific topic(s). You don't need to explain why you are opting out.

  _____

Reflection Activity: What Has Shifted in Me?

- What surprised me most as I engaged with these CRRSE strategies?
- Which assumptions or habits of mine are no longer aligned with the relationships I want to nurture?
- Where do I feel tension, discomfort, or resistance? What might that be teaching me?

On a blank sheet of paper or in a digital document, draw three concentric circles like a ripple:

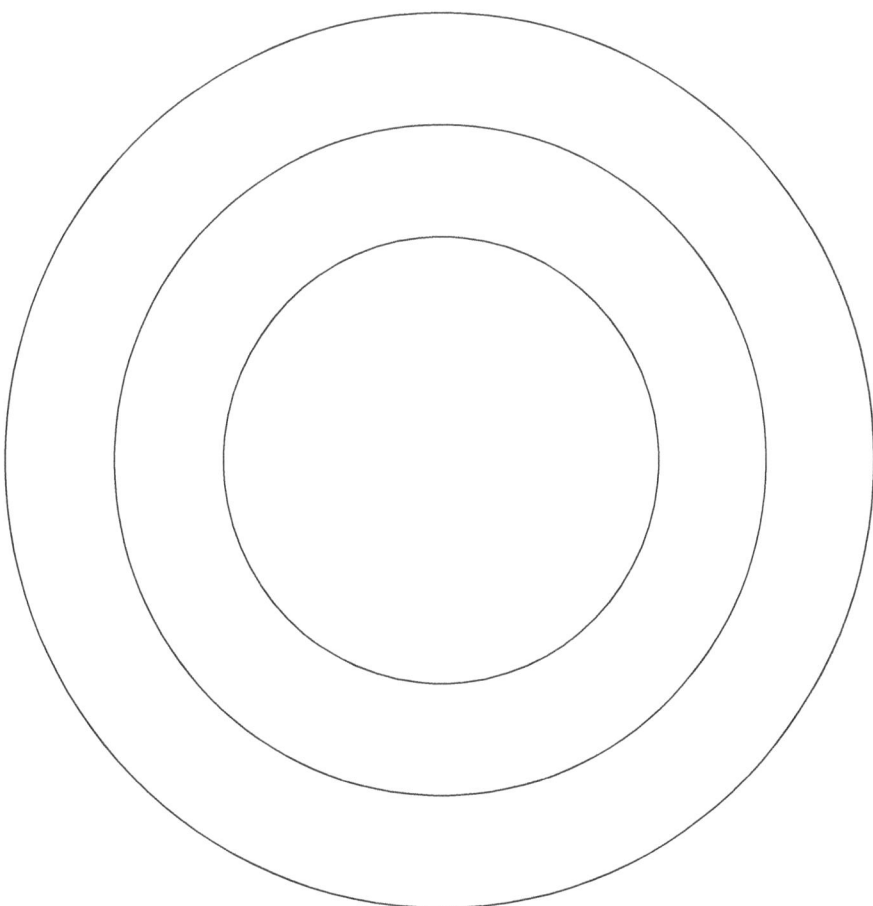

- Circle 1 (Inner): What is one small shift I can make in my classroom environment to better honor a given student's identity?
- Circle 2 (Middle): What is one change I can make in how I relate to students' culture, in broader social context, or in responsive materials?
- Circle 3 (Outer): How might this ripple outward affect how my school community, colleagues, or curriculum practices evolve?

4

Affirmation, Allyship, and Action for 2SLGBTQIA+ Students

Sarah Stapleton and Robert Grant

Sarah Stapleton (she/they) is a Community Music PhD candidate at Wilfrid Laurier University and holds a Master of Teaching from the Ontario Institute for Studies in Education (OISE). Sarah is an avid performer, researcher, psychotherapist, and educator with more than a decade of experience teaching music. Sarah aspires to develop more accessible, inclusive, trauma-informed, and community-oriented vocal pedagogies throughout her studies.

Rob Grant is a PhD candidate at the Faculty of Education, University of Ottawa. Rob is a part-time instructor at the University of Ottawa, as well as a teacher with the Toronto District School Board. His research interests include inclusive French as a second language education, queer identities in schools, and the experiences of queer educators.

As a teacher —regardless of the subjects, grades, or divisions you teach—you have to create equitable and inclusive learning environments to enable all your students to succeed academically and socially. This is especially true for Two-Spirit, Lesbian, Gay, Bisexual, Trans, Queer, Intersex, Asexual, Plus (2SLGBTQIA+) students, who often experience harassment, bullying, and discrimination at school because of their gender identity or expression and/or their sexual orientation. A concrete way to create safe(r) spaces (or brave spaces) is through developing a deeper understanding of affirmation and allyship. In this chapter, we define both terms, provide examples of how they manifest in the hallway and in the classroom, offer space for you to reflect on your experiences as an educator, and finish with actionable ways you can begin integrating affirmation and allyship into your classroom. Our hope is that you will walk away from this chapter with a few more tools to support all learners, especially 2SLGBTQIA+ students. We also want to acknowledge that building an affirming and allyship-focused practice is a learning process. You will make mistakes (just like we have!), but you will grow from them.

A Note on Language

In considering the tenets of affirmation, allyship, and action, we must first acknowledge the importance of language through association and connotation. As we progress through this chapter, we will be referring to affirmation and allyship as two distinct, yet interconnected, terms. We also engage with a range of queer-focused terms that might be useful to support shared understanding. These definitions might not fit all folks' understandings of these terms, and should be used primarily to contextualize our work. We humbly propose the following tentative definitions for these terms, used for the purposes of this chapter; likewise, we appreciate that language is a continually evolving tool shaped by context, experience, and history. Before you read our proposed terms, take a second to think about how you might define *affirmation*, *allyship*, and *action*, based on your own understanding and experiences.

Affirmation: A process of supporting, upholding, defending, encouraging, and supporting a person's identity

Allyship: Intentional and active support offered marginalized communities to support their much-deserved voices and seats at the table

Cisheteronormativity: The societal belief that cisgender and heterosexual people are the "norm" or default person, positioning diverse identities as invisible, invalid, or unacceptable. Discrimination, exclusion, fear, misunderstanding, misrepresentation, and marginalization are potential outcomes of this stance.

2SLGBTQIA+: An acronym created to represent and include myriad queer and trans identities, including, but not limited to, Two-spirit, Lesbian, Gay, Bisexual, Trans, Queer, Intersex, Asexual, Plus (and other identities). We use this term interchangeably with *queer* and *trans* as umbrella terms to acknowledge the multiple and varied sexual orientations and gender identities that exist in our schools and the world at large.

We will explore these terms in greater detail as we proceed through this chapter, giving context to these working definitions and linking both concepts with actionable steps to achieve them.

Questions for Reflection

Combining your definition of *affirmation* and *allyship* with ours, consider the following:
- What are some ways you have already offered affirmation and allyship in your personal life and in schools?
- How does your role as a teacher empower you to offer affirmation and allyship on a larger scale?
- How do you think being a teacher committed to 2SLGBTQIA+ allyship and affirmation might affect the next generation of youth in schools?

As a teacher, you have the power to be a changemaker in these areas. No matter how small or simple a change may seem at first, allyship makes a big impact!

STORY FROM THE CLASSROOM

When Sarah (she/they) was in teacher's college, they worked with a six-year-old girl. This student was clever, brave, intelligent, creative, curious, and, like many children, not raised in a family where gender expression and identity were discussed. At that time, as a closeted non-binary woman, Sarah was careful to lean into conventionally femme presentations—wearing dresses, having long hair, and leaning into feminine social norms. As a teacher, Sarah ensured that their gender expression never deviated too far from societal expectations, for fear that they couldn't have an open conversation about gender with children.

When Sarah walked this child to the girl's bathroom one day, she told Sarah that they couldn't go in there. "Why not?" Sarah asked, taking in their outwardly femme-presenting dress. "Well, you're not a girl," the student replied. "You're in between. Not really a boy, or a girl. Right?" As a closeted non-binary person, Sarah was shocked. How did this girl know? And how was she okay with it, especially as a child without much exposure to conversations around gender, in a world where Sarah had learned that it wasn't okay to be themself?

In the days that passed, Sarah realized how much sense gender fluidity made to a person who had never been exposed to the harsh realities of stereotyping and hate. This child was quick to tell her friends that, when they played games, Sarah should be allowed to play the king and the queen equally, and began using a range of pronouns for them without Sarah needing to ask. Without knowing it, this child painted an incredibly vivid picture of what affirmation and allyship could look like if more people were simply open-minded, curious, caring, and kind.

- What stereotypes do you associate with different genders? How might you make assumptions about a person's gender based on their physicality or appearance before getting to know them?
- How can we interrupt cisheteronormative conditioning around gender assumptions, both in the classroom and in our daily lives?
- What fears do you have about introducing gender diversity as a topic in classrooms with young children? How might you create support for yourself to face those fears?
- How might you show up as an ally if a young child expressed to you that they felt they were a different gender than assigned at birth?

Affirmation

As we consider best principles for affirmation in practice as educators, it is useful to consider how affirmation has been defined. Oxford University Press (2024) offers the following definition for the word *affirm*:

> state as a fact; assert strongly and publicly...declare one's support for; uphold; defend...offer (someone) emotional support or encouragement.

Through these definitions, we see the multifaceted nature and nuance of affirmation. Affirmation might begin with a clear and public assertion of the existence and prevalence of 2SLGBTQIA+ identities, followed by a message of support for our students. This affirming work in our classrooms can be done explicitly through statements, discussions, and announcements, as well as implicitly through the resources and material selected for courses and classwork. When we observe a deficiency in acceptance and safety for our students, it is our mission to defend their rights and create more affirmative spaces. At the same time, when we witness our students and colleagues taking active steps to affirm themselves and others, it is our responsibility to celebrate and encourage these moments.

When someone is a part of the 2SLGBTQIA+ community, their personal identity and interpersonal relationships alike are perceived as "different." Sexuality, relationships, and gender identity are deeply intertwined with one's relationality and therefore must be considered when working with the queer community.

Such consideration is particularly crucial for youth, whose identity formation and need for acceptance are integral to their healthy development.

As teachers, we need to move beyond being queer-informed or queer-friendly, and instead adopt queer-affirming teaching and activist stances. For example, being a queer-affirming educator goes beyond learning about 2SLGBTQIA+ labels and historical contexts or acknowledging the presence of queer folks in the classroom. Instead, affirming someone's identity could involve an awareness of what the identity conventionally means, understanding what the identity means for the person to whom it belongs, and advocating for rights and supports that align with that person's identity. Affirmation involves fostering, cultivating, and sustaining a sense of belonging for all sexual orientations and gender identities, inside and outside the classroom. Among many others, 2SLGBTQIA+ students should be able to hold the following expectations for us as their teachers:

- An open-minded, accepting, and non-judgmental classroom space
- The availability of a wide range of media, literature, authors, and resources that feature many different genders and sexual orientations
- A classroom culture that is explicitly supportive of diverse identities
- Time taken outside of class for us as teachers to personally educate ourselves about queer identities, lifestyles, and orientations
- Respect for the privacy of students and colleagues surrounding their identities, pronouns, and who they wish to have them shared with
- Active advocacy for the rights and well-being of queer and trans people, including boldly standing up to instances of discrimination and hate
- A practice of holding high expectations—both personally and academically—for all queer and trans students, believing in their ability to flourish and achieve their dreams.

While we affirm our queer students' identities, we are also affirming their lived experiences and everyday existence. An increasingly prevalent example of this affirmation—or lack thereof—that we often hear at school, arises during conversations about correct name and pronoun use.

STORY FROM THE CLASSROOM

We invite you to consider a hypothetical teaching colleague named Jennifer. On your first day of working together, Jennifer lets you know that she goes by Jenn. From that day forward, you refer to her as Jenn, both in front of her and when referring to her with your colleagues. This feels natural to you, just as you might call a Nicholas "Nick" or Alison "Allie," as per their request. A few years later, when Jenn gets married, she decides to change her last name from Patterson to Smith, matching her partner's last name. Now, you let students know to refer to their teacher as Mrs. Smith rather than Ms. Patterson, and they adjust quickly. Jenn's paperwork is updated to reflect these name and title changes, and the staff also quickly adapts to this change. If they ever make a mistake and misremember Jenn's name, they gently apologize and move on, making the effort to correct themselves in the future. Jenn feels welcomed and present at work, knowing that her colleagues not only are respectful towards her, but also have actively acknowledged and celebrated this new phase of her life.

Next, please consider a hypothetical student. On your Grade 8 attendance sheet, the student has a male gender identifier with the legal name Benjamin,

> but they introduce themselves as Sophia, and a girl. You notice your administration constantly refers to her by the incorrect name and pronouns; if they do make the effort to refer to her correctly in person, they often use her legal name behind her back. When addressed incorrectly by her peers, Sophia corrects them, only to be met with awkwardness, over-apologizing, or blatant ignorance. Sophia's school forms for home identify her Benjamin, and she never quite feels comfortable using the bathroom at school, leading to regular incidents of indigestion and an upset stomach. In these contexts, naturally, Sophia doesn't thrive. She often feels sick, uncomfortable, and unwelcome, making it increasingly challenging for her to learn. Since she doesn't have a trusted adult to talk to at school, when bullying occurs, she skips classes and falls further behind. Sophia will likely have a much harder time graduating middle school than she should.
> - Why are Jenn and Sophia treated so differently?
> - If you arrived as a new teacher with the aforementioned environment as the existing school culture, what would you do?
> - What would you do if this culture was so strongly established that no one wanted to listen to you?

Constructive Conversations for Affirmative Spaces

Difficult conversations are likely to arise when we fight to create more affirmative spaces for 2SLGBTQIA+ people in our schools. These challenges serve as important reminders that critical conversations are still necessary. Just as Jenn faced no backlash surrounding her name changes in the Story from the Classroom, there is space for queer students to have the same experience when they introduce themselves and their pronouns.

Inviting all students and staff to share their correct names and pronouns during initial introductions offers an opportunity to affirm identity and begins to normalize the sharing of pronouns in daily life. However, it is important to never force someone to share this information: some people might not feel comfortable sharing their pronouns, especially if they're at different stages of navigating and understanding their gender identity and expression; sometimes, people feel emboldened to say hurtful things in response to pronoun sharing, which can create harmful and discriminatory spaces. These challenges are exacerbated by the emotional and mental labor required to continually explain and enforce one's identity, as is the case for far too many queer youth. The Yale LGBTQ Center (2025) describes the process of coming out as "[not] something you do once—it's a journey that LGBTQ people make every day of their lives." By normalizing and actively affirming the process of offering names, pronouns, and any other preferences around identity—for example, asking to be called by one's first name rather than by specific pronouns—we can reduce the need for students to constantly other themselves by "coming out," thereby reducing barriers to them living and learning as their full selves.

We also wish to acknowledge the systemic barriers rooted in colonialist ideologies that arise surrounding intersectionality between queerness and other identities. While *2S* has been increasingly prevalent as an addition to the traditional LGBTQ+ acronym, Two-Spirit folks are rarely discussed or acknowledged in queer spaces or education. Two-Spirit folks are Indigenous people who embody

> Both authors of this chapter experience immense white privilege as queer folks, privilege of which we must constantly remain aware when we enter queer spaces. Our experiences cannot reflect the experiences of all queer people, particularly those who are racialized. We are both on continuous journeys of learning and unlearning, and our writing reflects our current thinking and stage of knowing.

both masculine and feminine spirits, transcending beyond the gender binary and offering a connection to gender and sexuality rooted in Indigeneity. They could hold additional important roles within their communities due to the spiritual nature of their identity, such as healing or caregiving responsibilities (Beaudry et al., 2024). The intersectionality of Indigeneity and queerness can often result in unjust systemic barriers and hate directed toward this population. While trans folks are already targets for hate-based violence as a result of deviation from the gender binary, this danger is magnified when Indigenous and racialized folks also exist outside of socially accepted norms.

In light of these systemic imbalances, it is equally important for us to recall that affirmation must transcend boundaries and hierarchies; we must not only affirm our students, but also our 2SLGBTQIA+ colleagues, our administrators, our community members at large, and, of course, ourselves. As active affirmers, we must take care to fill our own cup through self-care, rest, activism, and surrounding ourselves with other loving and affirming folks. Affirmation gains staying power and presence when we cultivate affirming communities and environments.

When we strive to affirm all our students' identities and gender expressions, we create spaces where queerness belongs. When we choose to affirm someone, we choose to stand by them as their supporter and their champion. When we tell our students that we believe in who they are, as they are, we show them that we believe in their fullest potential as human beings. To affirm our students is to allow them to see their brilliance and their power—aspects others have relegated to the sidelines. Affirmation is an experience of transformation, empowerment, and healing.

Creating an affirming space involves offering an invitation for students to take up space as their full selves and acknowledging their experiences of navigating a system that privileges cisheteronormativity (see Moore et al., 2024, for examples of how cisheteronormativity is challenged in the language classroom). In affirming spaces, we must be intentional about recognizing the inherent challenges of surviving as a queer person within a colonized and patriarchal system (Lugones, 2007). We continue to hold high expectations for our queer students and colleagues, acknowledging that their success and excellence can show up in unique or less conventional ways when working in a system that was not designed with them in mind. We must welcome our queer students into our spaces, letting them know that they are valued and belong in our classrooms, in spaces of learning and progress, and in the wider community. As educators, the most powerful lesson we can offer is the same lesson that Sarah learned from a six-year-old girl: that it is possible to offer unconditional care, love, and kindness in a world filled with hate.

Allyship

Use of the term *allyship* has skyrocketed in recent years, both in theoretical and practical senses (De Souza & Schmader, 2025). While terms similar to *ally*—such as *accomplice*—are often used interchangeably, we use the term *allyship* purposefully throughout this chapter to maintain the necessity of being and becoming allies. Building on the work of other scholars, like Campbell and Swartz (2023) and Trinh (2024), we see allyship as the intentional, purposeful, and active support for equity-deserving groups who create actionable change. In a school setting, such allyship might mean interrupting homophobic or transphobic comments heard in the hallways, reminding someone of the importance of using correct pronouns, or advocating for more inclusive learning materials that honor and validate the myriad identities that students embody within our schools.

Within allyship, we need to remember that our actions are not static, not a "one and done" endeavor (Trinh, 2024). Instead, allyship is an ongoing process of (un)learning and resisting injustices that occur in and beyond a school's four walls. Allyship is a continual process of growing "despite facing resistance, frustration, disappointment, and exhaustion sometimes" (Trinh, 2024, p. 4). Allyship can appear daunting at first, but it is critical to fostering deep inclusion, respect, and empathy within schools.

How can we, as teachers, engage in allyship? Taking a moment to consider the different types of allyship can be a helpful first step. Campbell (2023) distinguishes four ways that allyship can manifest in schools:

- Convenient allyship: You are an ally, but only when the timing and the context suit your needs.
- Performative allyship: You are an ally, but only through talk and not through action.
- Optical allyship: You are an ally, but only when people are watching you.
- True allyship: You are an ally.

As queer educators, we encourage all teachers to move beyond convenient, performative, or optical allyship to true allyship. Intertwining our teaching with true allyship demands us to first think from within. In other words, we have to reflect on our positionality, our biases, our lens, our vantage points, our potential blind spots, and our personal baggage.

Four types of allyship:
- convenient
- performative
- optical
- true

Reflection Activity

Take a few moments to collect your thoughts, sit, and think about the identities and lived experiences of students in our schools, as well as your own school experiences.
- How do you think any of your biases show up?
- Do you have any assumptions about students, colleagues, parents, other community members, or even yourself?

STORY FROM THE CLASSROOM

When planning to co-facilitate events for Pride Month in June, a student declared they were "afraid of gay people," and "didn't want to learn about *this* stuff." As a queer teacher, Rob felt frustrated, and even a little angry. However, he took a few seconds to consider the lived experiences of his student: *What were the students' prior beliefs? What might he have learned from the media or from others? Were there any cultural implications at play?* Rob used these guiding questions to assess his own biases around the situation. Rob thought about his blind spots, too, and attempted to leverage this situation to ask students why we engage in Pride Month events.

In a hopeful moment of being an ally for his community, Rob engaged in discussion around why we celebrate Pride in particular. While these conversations went in a few different directions, students began to understand some of the overlapping and marginalizing factors that are at play for the 2SLGBTQIA+ community, as well as some of their successes. Reproaching the students' comment and channeling it to help dissect students' understanding, Rob was ultimately able to shift the classroom environment.

- Reflect on a time that you and a student clashed because of beliefs. What were the outcomes?
- [a] What do you think was done well in the situation described here? What needs more work? How might you approach this situation differently?
- Celebrating students and their identities is key to a safe classroom and allyship. Think back to a time that you've celebrated a student. How did this affect the student, if at all?
- Try to think of one or two sentences you could say to a colleague, administrator, or student who was using homophobic or transphobic language. Write it down, and then say it aloud. Doing this could help you interrupt or question their language in the future!

Allyship in this instance meant confronting the situation and our own biases—not letting homophobic or transphobic comments slip away—to help bring actionable change for students. Addressing these comments also meant that we worked toward creating brave spaces, so that "students know they do not need to hide parts of their identity for fear, shame, exclusion, or bullying" (Campbell & Swartz, 2023, p. 44–5).

Diving deeper into true allyship means continuously fostering these brave spaces through our actions. Allies are powerful people. They recognize the injustice against marginalized people and do not sit quietly while injustices occur and reoccur. They actively listen to their 2SLGBTQIA+ students, colleagues, and community members to better understand their experiences and perspectives—and their needs. This allyship manifests from the beginning of each year or semester.

For example, Rob sends out a Google form or distributes a paper survey, asking all students the following question: *How can I support you? What do you need from me?* Responses from his 2SLGBTQIA+ students in particular often emphasize their need for teachers to use correct pronouns and/or names, to check in with them occasionally about their experience within the school's climate, and to call out homophobic or transphobic language clearly within the classroom. Allyship here required taking an intentional stance. Rob remembered that when he was beginning his teaching career and heard this language, even as someone from within the community, it felt daunting to call out. However, if we don't, we run the risk of creating unsafe environments for all our students. Now, if and when Rob hears this language in the classroom, he asks students to either

1. clarify what they had said, or
2. confirm whether they understand the impact of their words

Rob attempts to approach these situations through a humanistic lens and give students the opportunity to learn from these moments.

Calling out harmful language can be a bit of a balancing act. On one hand, we need to be clear and firm in our approach. On the other hand, we have to be educational and kind. If we grow angry with students for using this language, then we might lose them. Our goal with allyship is to transform students' thinking and actions, giving them the knowledge to understand how harmful this language is so they do not (re)use it in the future. This serves as a reminder that our words hold immense power and that we need to be mindful about what we say.

Think about a time when you noticed the power of your words, and the accompanying challenges of this power. There can be difficult moments in light of resistance that can make it hard to remember we're doing important work. It's important, in these moments, to affirm ourselves as queer teachers or as allies. For example,

- Acknowledge the power and influence that we have as educators.
- Think about the impacts we have already made with our students and in our communities.
- Come back to the *why* of our teaching philosophy and our goal to support and uplift all students.
- Make sure to engage in self-care practices regularly.

Allyship in Your Teaching Practice

> When you've had queer students in your classroom, how much queer educational responsibility have they shouldered?

For us as educators, allyship requires that we do additional learning ourselves about the 2SLGBTQIA+ community. There are plenty of publicly available resources (e.g., https://egale.ca/) to support this learning. Understanding the hostile reality within some of the experiences faced by queer students, as well as becoming equipped with information about this community generally, can help us avoid relying solely on students to do the work for us. Indeed, while 2SLGBTIQA+ students tend to be activist and knowledgeable about their own communities and lived experiences, we cannot expect them to have the answers for everything or be the spokesperson for queer-related identity questions or issues (Cole & Surette, 2024).

Just as important as holding these brave spaces and disentangling our entrenched beliefs with our students—and perhaps more challenging—is holding these conversations with our colleagues. Rob recalls overhearing a fellow teacher becoming increasingly frustrated because one of their students used they/them pronouns. As a new teacher, Rob felt that his only option at the time was to remain reticent and let the conversation unfold around him. However, this option misaligns with an allyship approach. In hindsight, he could have probed further, asking why these pronouns caused such internal turmoil for the teacher. Having one-liners, such as how language is in constant evolution and defines us as people, might have helped transform the situation.

As it has likely become clear now, allyship requires action. Allyship demands that we ensure "curriculum is reflective of many genders, sexualities, and family structures that exist in the world, to celebrate diversity" for both students and ourselves as educators (Campbell & Swartz, 2023, p. 46). There are many different ways that teachers can embed various genders, sexualities, and structures throughout all their curricula.

Voice From the Field

In my first year of teaching, posters advertising the GSA (Gay-Straight or Gender-Sexuality Alliance) I facilitated were being torn off the walls. My co-facilitator and I would post new ones, for them to be torn down again hours later. Attendance in our club started to dwindle when students stopped feeling it was safe to show up. With homophobia on the rise, our staff called a meeting to workshop different actions of solidarity. The art teacher crafted a new rainbow design of our school's logo, alongside a message of *[Our school] is for everyone and everyone belongs at [our school]*. Students in the art program assisted with screenprinting it on shirts for staff and student leadership. Wearing the shirts regularly created a visible wave of allyship. It sparked conversation through our entire school about allyship and, crucially, how visibility does not always equate to safety for marginalized students. These shirts challenged our school's assumptions about identity and allyship more broadly. I was moved by my colleague's willingness to approach difficult questions: *What makes a space safe and to whom? Who gets to be visible? At what cost?* The shirts were a catalyst to think beyond rainbows and slogans to consider new ways of making our school a safer and more inclusive place. I learned that true allyship isn't just making a T-shirt. It happens in community, through conversations, reflection, and discomfort. As a queer and trans teacher early in my career, being out can feel risky. This moment made me feel that meaningful change in our profession is possible.

— Macaulay Mauro (he/they), Queer/trans educator

Action

With a solid understanding of affirmation and allyship, we pivot to think through how we can actively support our 2SLGBTQIA+ students in specific contexts. In the following sections, we offer strategies that we have used in our classrooms and personal practices to affirm and act as an ally for our students.

Many curricula do not contain a lot of prescribed activities to do, authors to read, or texts to analyze (Carroll, 2018). While this fluidity can lend itself to flexibility, it sometimes limits teachers, leaving them wondering how to support their 2SLGBTQIA+ students without particular guidelines. Due to our cisheteronormative society, Western ways of knowing and learning are often prioritized by default, including the promotion of heterosexual and cisgender creators, authors, and resources. We argue that the inclusion of 2SLGBTQIA+ students and identities should not be limited to one time, occasion, or month—Pride Month in June, for example. Instead, it should be an integral and regular part of our materials, lessons, and activities, alongside other diverse representations. One way to bring in this representation is through listening to different 2SLGBTQIA+ musicians at the beginning or end of class. After the song of the day finishes, teachers and students alike can discuss the musician, their biography, and some general themes of their lyrics. In these moments, 2SLGBTQIA+ students' identities are affirmed, and other students in the room begin to understand that the community is flourishing.

Actionable Activity

Examples of texts to be used:
And Tango Makes Three by Justin Richardson and Peter Parnell
Julián is a Mermaid by Jessica Love
Love, Violet by Charlotte Sullivan Wilde

For teachers who want to dive deeper with action, we propose an activity with the goal of showing students the diversity of lived experiences within their communities and the benefits offered by these differences. This activity can be customized per school subject by tailoring the questions asked to surround topics of history, science, or careers, or by adjusting the focus, such as involving interview statistics in math class.

Options with younger students:

1. Invite them to imagine becoming friends with the protagonist (or another character they choose) and consider what questions they might ask to get to know them better.
2. Students can write a few sentences or a short story all about their new friend and how they would make them feel welcomed at school.
3. Students can also draw a picture of themselves with their new friend doing an activity they would enjoy together.

Options for older students, depending on your community contexts:
1. Invite them to interview a member of the community (see page 66 for a reproducible list of questions) or engage in a more in-depth imaginary interview with a queer literary character.
2. After the activity, students will draft and share a 200-word article or blog post about their interviewee and how they might affirm their identities in the school and beyond.
3. Students can find photos that represent the interview subject online or in a magazine and combine them to create a collage that affirms their experiences.

The goal of this activity is to encourage learning about the lived experiences of queer folks and proactively consider how to include and welcome diverse community members at school and beyond. We find that taking action with the 2SLGBTQIA+ community and becoming an ally follows suit after learning about their lived experiences with kindness and empathy, in contrast to the dehumanizing societal norms of a cisheteronormative world.

> **Reflection Activities**
>
> - Think about school-wide initiatives or efforts that uplift 2SLGBTQIA+ students in your school and/or community. What do these look like? Feel like? How could you get involved (if not already)?
> - What are your main concerns or tensions about bolstering inclusivity for 2SLGBTQIA+ students in your school right now?
> - Reflect on the types of opposition you might receive in linking 2SLGBTQIA+ identities to your teaching practice (from parents, other colleagues, students, administrators, etc.). Write a few sentences down and work with a colleague to brainstorm ways to work against these forms of opposition.
> - What are some current successes you have experienced with affirming your students' identities? In what ways have you shown up for your students recently?
> - Take a minute to dream about a fully inclusive environment. What does it look like? Feel like? Sound like?

Final Thoughts

Throughout this chapter, you have encountered the nuanced ways in which affirmation and allyship can materialize to create inclusive spaces for 2SLGBTQIA+

students. Affirming our students will include celebrating their identities, uplifting their voices, and centring their experiences in our classrooms. We will carve out intentional space to name and locate queer perspectives in our teaching materials and practice. We will seek to provide active support alongside equity-deserving groups of students to ensure our affirmations are backed by concrete actions and advocacy. The journey toward creating inclusive spaces within all our classrooms is an ongoing process: one where we (un)learn, reflect, and think through the ways that we can make small changes to our practice to support all students.

The examples we've shared from the classroom serve to show that affirmation and allyship can take many forms. These practices can be integrated into a variety of curriculum subjects and activities, as well as beyond the classroom. Most importantly, these practices should be integrated into our daily interactions and conversations with students, so they walk away with the understanding that they belong and are loved for who they truly are.

We leave you with an invitation to reflect on your own practices and consider how you might begin or continue your affirmation and allyship work in your classroom. This reflection might involve examining your own personal biases, expanding your knowledge base on 2SLGBTQIA+ identities and experiences, advocating for inclusive language in the school, or simply being willing to listen and learn from students themselves. It is important to highlight that creating safe(r) spaces for 2SLGBTQIA+ students not only benefits queer and trans students, but also enriches the learning environment for all students. When students feel seen, validated, and supported for who they are, they can bring their full selves to the classroom, deepen their learning, and have more meaningful experiences in school.

Interview Questions

What does forgiveness look and feel like to you?

What did it feel like when someone helped you?

What does it mean to stand up for someone? How have you done this in the past?

What does it mean for you when you're in a good/healthy relationship?

What does it feel like to be affirmed by a friend/teacher/community member?

What inspires you to consider helping others and standing up for others?

What does it mean for you to belong? How do you make others feel like they belong?

How can you make school a better place to be for everyone?

Describe a time you felt safe at school.

What is your favorite thing about yourself?

5

Using the Tools You Have to Dismantle Racism

Canute Lawrence

Canute Lawrence is a secondary teacher of English at the Toronto District School Board, and has been an educator for four decades at the secondary and tertiary levels in Jamaica, the USA, and Canada. His bestselling *Pathology of a Pandemic: a collection of poems* won the International Impact Book Awards in 2024. Canute's recent research article, "Reflections on the History and Intergenerational Trauma of Using the 'N' Word" appears in the Handbook of Anti-Discriminatory Education.

Racism continues to be a pandemic around the world, despite laws and policies in the education system that seek to promote diversity, equity, and inclusion of all students. Many students and parents have shared their experiences of being discriminated against, oppressed, and excluded from educational opportunities that could and would have benefited them. I have listened to the stories of many Black, Indigenous, and People of Color (BIPOC) staff who have experienced blatant racism that was so violent and insidious that it caused them to go on stress leave, despite having satisfactory appraisals and no disciplinary letters in their files. Some people claim that racism no longer exists because they have never seen or experienced it, which is one of the ways to discount and deny the experiences that individuals have. Claims to never have experienced racism does not mean racism does not exist, just as never witnessing or experiencing road rage does not mean road rage does not exist and that others have not experienced it.

What Is Racism?

Racism is any form of prejudice, discrimination, or antagonism by a person, community, or institution against another person or persons, on the basis of their skin color or ethnic background. According to a scholarly article:

> Systemic and structural racism are forms of racism that are pervasively and deeply embedded in systems, laws, written or unwritten policies, and entrenched practices and beliefs that produce, condone, and perpetuate widespread unfair treatment and oppression of people of color. (Braveman et al., 2022, p. 171)

Racism is the belief that different ethnicities inherently possess distinct characteristics, abilities, and qualities that distinguish them as being inferior or superior to another. Over the last several decades, racism, like other beliefs, has evolved into a deadly monster that marginalized people can see but can have difficulty proving at the workplace or in a court of law. Braveman et al. also articulate clearly that "Racism is not always conscious, explicit, or readily visible" (2022, p. 171). Because of anti-discriminatory laws, persons who harbor racist beliefs have created deceptive ways and practices to execute their racist agenda against those they deem inferior to them or not worthy of enjoying success. It is easy for negaters to claim that BIPOC individuals are "playing the race card," as these negaters intentionally do not use the "N-word" or make any specific reference to skin color, racial, or ethnic background, but persist in exclusionary practices that seek to devalue, denigrate, and dehumanize others.

Racism is not only practiced by individuals, but is entrenched into large organizations. "Systemic racism emphasizes the involvement of whole systems" (Braveman et al., 2022, p. 172). Some examples are the political, legal, criminal justice, health care, and education systems. "Structural racism emphasizes the role of the structures" such as laws, policies, institutional practices, and entrenched societal norms that form the steps and scaffolds of the various systems (p. 172).

Active Racism

Many people have witnessed and experienced active racism, which can come in many forms: racial slurs hurled at them, racist jokes told in their presence, hate crimes, racial profiling, police harassment, hiring discrimination, housing discrimination, and other forms of microaggressions. Canada has had a history marked by discriminatory policies and practices against Indigenous peoples, Canadians of African descent, Asians, and other racialized groups. Racism remains throughout society, and schools are not immune to it. Laws in Canada, such as The Indian Act of 1876, sought to regulate and control the lives of Indigenous peoples, one way that formalized and normalized blatant racism against communities of people.

Passive Racism

Passive racism is arguably more dangerous than active racism because it is harder to see and prove. It is pretentious, deceptive, and diabolically dangerous. It is more difficult to dismantle racism when those who are guilty of upholding structures, racist notions, and values purposely deny any existence of such, despite repeated evidence; for example, a Eurocentric curriculum in a school system where there is ethnic, religious, and cultural diversity, denial of racism, denial of white privilege, tokenism, racists mascots, and more.

Ripped from the Headlines

Headlines: Global News, October 19, 2021; November 30, 2020; February 19, 2021

Over half of Canadian students see racial bullying in their schools, survey finds

CBC News carried a headline: "Serious racism problem" in 2021, which focused on an annual report released by the Toronto District School Board's human rights office that highlighted hate activities among its 245, 000 students and 40, 000 staff over a two-year period from 2018–2020 (Gunn, 2021).

An astonishing report by Ali Raza of CBC News titled "Being Black in School: Peel students open up about the racism they face in the classroom" interviewed a number of Black students, one of whom said, "I've had teachers talking about the history of racism, say that it was a myth about how bad Black people were treated during slavery, and how of course, slavery is wrong, but they weren't actually treated that badly" (Raza, CBC News, 2022 April 13).

> ***School curricula haven't represented the Black perspective, says Winnipeg principal***

> **Prince Andrew students walk out of class to protest racism within Nova Scotia school system**

All these headlines are strong anecdotal data that racism is still a huge issue in schools across Canada. It is shocking to learn that there are educators who continue to downplay the horrors of Black enslavement, which took place over several centuries, articulating to children that enslaved Africans were not treated "that badly" (Raza, CBC News, 2022 April 13). In an article titled, "Reflections on the History and Intergenerational Trauma of Using the "N" Word" published in the Handbook of Anti-Discriminatory Education, I report that "There are many Canadians who pretend that Canada never participated in the enslavement of African people and downplay the trauma of slavery" (Lawrence, 2025 as edited by Eizadirad & Trifonas, 2025). The existence of structural and systemic racism in Canada is not a myth. They permeate the education system and play out in the classroom. Teachers must become more aware and reflective of their values, attitudes, and impact on students. Teachers are mandated to show care and compassion to all students, despite their racial or ethnic backgrounds, religious persuasions, genders, and sexual orientations.

> **Questions for Reflection and Discussion**
>
> - As a teacher, what can you and your colleagues do in your classrooms to minimize and eventually dismantle racism and anti-discriminatory practices to create a more welcoming classroom environment for all your students?
> - Are you aware of school board policies that make it challenging for Black, Indigenous, and People of Color (BIPOC) students to feel welcomed and wanted?
> - What are some strategies you currently use in your practice to dismantle racism and promote anti-discriminatory education?
> - If you need professional development in anti-Black racism and anti-oppression strategies, are you comfortable asking your instructional leader/principal for that support?

How Can We Dismantle Racism?

Dismantling racism takes work. It takes courage and tenacity. Dismantling racism takes purpose and intentionality. To do the work of dismantling racism in a system whose players have benefited and continue to benefit significantly from it, you need to be prepared to experience challenges, pushbacks, and, sometimes, being alienated. Dismantling racism is not glamorous work, and it is not for the faint of heart.

To dismantle racism, you truly must understand the many ways in which racism morphs and disguises itself at the workplace and in the classroom. If you believe calling someone the "N-word," and criticizing their accent, hair, or skin color are the only evidentiary demonstrations of racism, you are not ready to take on the job of dismantling racism. To take on the work, you have to be genuine, honest, authentic, and compassionate toward those who are marginalized and under-served.

Being open to having difficult and uncomfortable conversations is another marker of your readiness to do the work, which can become emotionally, mentally, and physically draining. So, before embarking on this long, laborious endeavor, which may take a lifetime, it is critical to regularly engage in self-care practices or regimens to recharge, refuel, retool, and return to do the work. If you are drained and exhausted when doing the work, your efforts will be counterproductive and in vain.

What Tools Do You Have?

Everyone does not have the same set of tools for accomplishing anything, and you are not expected to have the same tools as anyone else to carry out anti-racism work. However, there are some basic tools everyone should have:
- An inquisitive and inquiring mind toward the different ethnicities in your classroom. Because you might not be familiar with every student's culture, ask them about their background and how they best learn. Be culturally inquisitive! When your students see that you are genuinely interested in their success, they are more likely to show interest in class.
- Every teacher cannot be culturally competent with respect to all cultures represented in their classroom on the first day of school. However, it is incumbent on you to grow your cultural competency skills by learning about the diverse student demographics, by expanding your cultural knowledge and cultural awareness.
- Having and demonstrating genuine care, concern, and compassion for your students as personal tools can make your job more fulfilling.
- Use your talents, skills, lived experiences, and privilege as tools to dismantle racism. With intentionality, turn your position to a purpose. If you are good at public speaking, use your voice to raise concerns about an anti-Black, anti-Islamic, or anti-Indigenous policy that hurts even one student.
- Encourage students to advocate for themselves and speak out whenever they see injustice. Encourage students to hone and develop their own skills and experience to present stories that are missing from the existing narrative. When there is only one story about a group of people, it perpetuates negative stereotypes and seeks to trap them in a box. Writer Chimamanda Ngozi Adichie articulates the many dangers of only one story in her TEDGlobal talk, "The Danger of a Single Story" (Adichie, 2009 July). Encourage your

students to share parts of their lived experiences and their culture through writing tasks, such as descriptive narratives and short memoir pieces. Tasks like these allow students to express themselves, empower them to own their stories, and provide opportunities to share and learn about each other while improving the cultural awareness and empathy for others within the classroom and school community.
- As a teacher, you can use your position of authority to advocate for vulnerable and marginalized students. Teachers have a responsibility to teach and model for students how to self-advocate, and to demonstrate action if the student is unable to advocate for themselves.

STORY FROM THE CLASSROOM

I recall teaching a student who was a recent immigrant from the African continent. The student was placed in a Grade 11 Workplace English course, and worked hard to do well. I realized the student was capable of doing Grade 11 College Preparation English, but neither the student nor the parent was confident about that pathway. The parent, knowing very little English herself, felt she was not in a position to request a switch from Workplace- to College-pathway English for her child. When I saw the student's potential to go into a more rigorous program, I decided to advocate on their behalf. I gathered a collection of the student's work and other evidence, and made a strong case on behalf of the student to the Guidance and Special Education departments. The evidence was overwhelming, and the student was placed in the college stream the following semester. I repeatedly checked in with the student and the English teacher, and received positive reports of the student's progress. The student graduated and was accepted into college. It is through acts like this that we can use our privilege and position of authority to advocate for students who are not able to do it for themselves. Every teacher should advocate for students, despite their ethnicity, religious persuasion, socio-economic status, sexual orientation, or gender. This is how you can dismantle racism, bigotry, and oppression from within.
- Have you had recent immigrant students join your class?
- If yes, what strategies or welcoming practices do you use to help them transition to an entirely new educational system?
- If a student's first language is not English, and they are a new English as a Second Language (ESL) learner or a Multilingual Language Learner (MLL), what strategies have you used to support their language acquisition skills in English?
- Can you share an instance when you intentionally advocated for a racialized or minority student who was not confident enough to do so for themselves?

Collaborate with Community Agencies

Other useful tools can be acquired as you intentionally work to dismantle structural and institutional racism. There are community agencies that can provide useful resources and materials to assist you in the dismantling work. Research to find data and reports on anti-racism work carried out by different organizations to see how you can learn more about the nature of the work and how you can become part of the solution; for example, community organizations support, promote, and celebrate Black history and culture through year-round programs, not just in February; community agencies build relationships with other racialized groups in efforts to creating a more inclusive community for everyone. You are encouraged to find community agencies that partner with district school boards to work to dismantle racial inequities and racism. As teachers, you should never feel like you are working by yourselves. Dismantling racism is not a one-person endeavor; it is hard work that involves members of the school community as well as community organizations and agencies.

There are agencies that you can contact, and collaborate with, and from which you can receive diversity and inclusion training, diversity workshops, and resources on diversity from. Some of these agencies provide interactive workshops, virtual training, and customized programs for teachers, administration, parents, caregivers, students, youth, and other community workers to equip them with the tools to challenge prejudice, stereotypes, and discrimination, and to make real change in the workplace, in schools, and in the wider community. Search for organizations that provide support for district school boards to equip staff and the entire school community to effectively address racial slurs and discriminatory language in their spaces.

Our classrooms and schools do not operate in a vacuum. Partnering with BIPOC agencies to enlighten and educate fellow staff members on cultural awareness, as well as to inform students about opportunities that are available to promote student success, is a strategy you can take advantage of throughout the school year.

Use Affirmations

Practicing affirmations in your classroom empowers students to affirm and celebrate their identity, be it Afrocentricity, Indigeneity, ability, gender, neurodiversity, or other. Having students read positive words at the beginning of each class can be a powerful activity.

The saying, "Sticks and stones can break my bones, but words can never hurt me" is a myth. Negative words uttered from one's mouth can inflict emotional, mental, and psychological harm to students, especially pre-teens and teenagers. When a child is perpetually fed hateful, damaging words, over time they can come to believe what they are told, and might also use those words to describe themselves; for example, when a child is repeatedly told they are "good-for-nothing," they might eventually believe it, and that belief can cripple their confidence and self-esteem, restricting their overall psychological growth and success. Daily or regular affirmations are effective tools because positive words are powerful and can change mindsets, attitudes, and actions.

STORY FROM THE CLASSROOM

A Teacher Candidate I mentored wrote a quote on the board for each class and would ask a volunteer to read it aloud, after which the entire class would read it together. The quotes were from individuals of diverse ethnic, religious, and cultural backgrounds, as reflected in the class demographics. After reading the affirming words, the student-teacher would invite students to share what the words meant to them and how the words affected them. I noticed how this activity engaged students and how much they looked forward to the daily affirmations. I have seen videos of students repeating the words, "I am smart. I am intelligent. I am beautiful," and the confidence with which the children say those words with conviction and affirmation is remarkably empowering.

Practice and model affirmations with your students in different ways. Encourage them to write and share their affirmations with the rest of the class. Be the teacher who affirms when students do something positive and are worthy of commendation by saying words that encourage, inspire, and celebrate them. A teacher who does not regularly use words of affirmation to and with their students is restricting the potential of the students, especially those with low self-esteem. Words carry with them energy and have the power to uplift or tear down. Words do have power. Unleash the power in daily affirmations to empower your students.

- How often do you use words of affirmation with your students?
- Do you intentionally incorporate lesson materials that reflect the ethnic diversity in your classroom?
- How can you incorporate affirmations in your lessons to inspire all your students?

Address Racial Slurs

Racial slurs are used in school hallways, classrooms, and school cafeterias regularly. Students who identify as Black or who appear to be of African descent are heard using the "N-word," sometimes in friendly situations and also in tense situations. Students who are of different ethnic backgrounds or non-Black are also using the "N-word" quite casually among themselves. There have been instances where it has been written on desks, classroom doors, and washroom walls and stalls, which is quite unsettling. Quite often, teachers tend to ignore the racial slurs heard in the hallways. They will retreat into the classroom or staff room and pretend they did not hear the slur. Some teachers who are non-Black say they are not sure how to address the issue of racial slurs and are hesitant to intervene, because the students who are heard using the slurs belong to the same ethnic group, and they (the teachers) feel it is "out of place" for them to challenge the students on it.

Schools are supposed to be welcoming and safe spaces for all students and staff. There are students and staff who are triggered when negative and hateful slurs are hurled around the school space, regardless of their use and intentions. Racial slurs of any kind should never be tolerated in a school environment. All staff need to show courage and care whenever any student or staff uses a racial, ethnic, antisemitic, or homophobic slur on school premises. There must be no withdrawal or hesitation to address the issue, because it perpetuates and normalizes the use of such language and, by extension, causes psychological harm. I recommend that administrators, teachers, and community workers access my research paper, "Reflections on the History and Intergenerational Trauma of Using the 'N' Word" (Lawrence, 2025). It examines the genesis, use, intentions, and impacts of the use of the "N-word" through historical, social, political, and psychological lenses.

There should never be a situation where some slurs are promptly addressed and others are not. Students from the Roma community are often called unpleasant names by others, one of which is the "'G-word." I recall, decades ago, watching movies where the word *gypsy* was used regularly. At that time, I never thought the word was pejorative. Today, members of the Roma community, whose ancestors were originally from the Punjab region of northern India, have declared it is offensive to call them the "G-word."

Students who belong to the 2SLGBTQIA+ community complain of feeling unwelcomed in some school spaces. "That's so gay!" is a common phrase used by students in the hallways and in the classroom to suggest an action is unacceptable or "weak." And students whose physical appearance does not meet certain expectations of beauty are subtly or explicitly taunted for their weight, hair, complexion, and other physical features.

All slurs must be treated with the same level of urgency and energy if we truly want to create a welcoming and respectful space for all. Your responses to slurs are critical for creating a welcoming environment where every child feels safe. Teachers, other staff, and students should not make any racial slur the norm in the educational space or in other public spaces.

Create Cultural Learning Opportunities

You have the power to create many opportunities for students to not only learn, but also to feel empowered and grow in cultural awareness, empathy, and respect for others. In subject areas like English, History, Social Studies, and Art, encourage students to research different ancient kingdoms in Africa and Asia, to dispel notions that persist about people from non-European continents, especially Africa. The North American education system and its curriculum are historically Eurocentric. Over the last three decades, most of what pre-teens and teenage students learn have been through a Eurocentric lens. Many people still believe all of Africa is enveloped in poverty without signs of civilization and modern technology. Many students and teachers alike would be amazed to find out that many African and Asian kingdoms thrived for centuries in trade, art, architecture, and political organization. The Mali Empire, the Kingdom of Benin, Ancient Egypt, the Songhai Empire, and the Ghana Empire are a few examples that teachers can assign as individual or group projects for students to research advancement in particular fields. This is one of the ways teachers can approach and correct the deficit mindset that is perpetuated by the educational system.

Teachers need to realize that highlighting the history and conquests of only Europeans subliminally teaches or communicates the message to students of non-European backgrounds that their history and that of their ancestors is not significant to learn about or talk about. This is practically what inequality looks like in the school system. Learning about the Zhou Dynasty, the Maurya, and Gupta empires in India, and the Srivijaya, and Majapahit kingdoms in Southern Asia can be game-changing. You can transform your classroom into a creative cultural hub, where not just one story is seen, but stories and narratives from different parts of the world are celebrated. Think of how empowering a project like this would be in any classroom where one Black, South Asian, or First Nations student feels seen and appreciated when their culture is acknowledged and celebrated for others to see.

Some schools celebrate the diverse cultural groups represented in the student and staff demographics with an international show. If there is no international show at your school, be that teacher, be that leader that makes it happen! This is a great opportunity for you to exercise your transformational leadership skills.

> Do you know where the majority of the over three thousand (3,000) bronzes from the ancient Kingdom of Benin are? The largest collection of the Benin Bronzes, which includes brass plaques and leopard sculptures, are housed in the British Museum in London. Other collections of Benin masterpieces are held in Germany, Austria, Switzerland, North America, and Nigeria. Can you imagine the delight and pride an immigrant student from the Caribbean or Africa feels knowing that their ancestors came from royalty and wealth?

Collaborate with a few other teachers, talk with parents, students, and the school administrators, and set your initiative in motion. With an international show, students have opportunities to showcase talents and skills that otherwise might never have been seen, within their cultural domains. Events like international shows can transform students into success stories: confidence-boosters that transform the school environment into culturally vibrant, eclectic, and welcoming spaces. Providing students with opportunities to showcase their singing and dancing, their spoken-word, acrobatic, culinary, and other skills is one of the most beautiful and magically empowering things that schools can do to create a culture of inclusivity and respect for all peoples.

Use Your Creative Talents

> "Art should comfort the disturbed and disrupt the comfortable."
> — Banksy

You have an abundance of talents and skills beyond your pedagogic abilities and expertise. These talents can be used for the common good of humanity, not just for yourself. If you are good at photography, use your photographic skills to showcase and highlight the horrors and destructiveness of racism against the beauty of inclusion and diversity. Those of you who paint, draw, or sculpt, can channel these skills into impactful art pieces that tell a thousand stories of creativity intersecting with social justice activism for meaningful diversity, equity, and inclusion in classrooms. Yes, dismantling racism in the education system is no easy feat, but using art is a creative way to challenge yourself (and others) to think differently when social issues are presented. Art should stimulate, challenge, and move you in powerful ways to engage with new ideas and to create space for those persons who have not been privileged to occupy seats and sit at decision-making tables.

> "Poetry is a political act because it involves telling the truth."
> — June Jordan

If you are a writer or a poet, use your craft as a vehicle to carry and deliver stories of the oppressed, the marginalized, and the disenfranchised. Poetry carries with it the power to capture the imagination, challenge societal norms, and offer new perspectives, all of which make it an apt tool for self-expression, empathy building, and making meaningful connections with each other.

STORY FROM THE CLASSROOM

"I'm in Love With My Hair" is one of the poems in my book, *Pathology of a Pandemic: a collection of poems* that resonates with countless students and adults, regardless of racial background (Lawrence, 2021, p.33). I have read this poem at several schools, community events, and academic spaces, where it sparked much spirited conversations around issues of identity, the politics of hair, and using one's natural hair as Black resistance and rebellion against the status quo. I have developed lessons around the poem to teach my own students, and the discussions, perspectives, and shared experiences that resulted have been nothing short of inspirational and beautiful. Poetry is indeed a powerful tool that enhances critical thinking, fosters empathy and

understanding, boosts reading comprehension and overall literacy skills, and helps individuals process difficult emotions and experiences, giving them a platform to express themselves and share their own experiences and perspectives. Ask students
- How important is your hair to you?
- How much do you love or dislike your natural hair?
- Would you like to elaborate/share your feelings about your hair?

Lesson: Identity and Self-Esteem

Remember to model and encourage respectful discussions.

I'm in Love With My Hair
by Canute Lawrence

After months of solitary confinement
Staring at myself and who I've become
My hair declares its roots run deep and strong
I've denied it, fried it and even maligned it
But my hair, like an ever faithful friend
Calmly reminds me that we are one
That we belong together forever
Despite your disapproval and celebration of Bether
My hair is Kilamanjaro
Why do you stare? I'm in love with my hair.
You bar me from school, you deny me the job
You say my hair is unbecoming
But the real reason is: my hair is a muse
For creativity and upliftment
Its curls are tight like inseparable lovers
Its texture thick like fine wool
I don't need your replacements
Promising me some other thrix
For my hair is my strength – my crown jewel
I love my afro, my braids, my Nubian knots
I love everything my hair dares to express
Because my eyes are wide open to who I really am.
I'm in love, so in love, with my hair.
(Lawrence, 2021, p. 33)

Anticipatory Set
- Capture students' attention by reading or playing a recording of "I'm in Love With My Hair."
- Instruct students to take out their notebooks and make notes of anything that resonates with them during a second reading.
- You might do a third reading so that every child has the time to write something in their notebook. (6 minutes)

Discussion and Building Oral Communication Skills
- Ask students: What does your hair mean to you?
- Allow as many of them as possible to share their perspectives.
- If a student didn't write notes or a response to the poem, use prompts to build a conversation/discussion about hair. (15–20 minutes)
    - How does your hair influence your identity?
    - Are you 100% satisfied or in love with your hair? Explain why or why not.
    - How do you relate to this poem?

Exploring Themes
- Ask students to briefly explain the main message in the poem. (5 minutes)

Identifying Literary Devices
- Ask students to identify three figures of speech used in the poem and explain their usage or effectiveness. Students can take a few minutes to look for them and write their responses in their notebooks. (10 minutes)

Vocabulary Development
- Ask students to identify three unfamiliar words in the poem:

    Find words you never saw or heard before today. Let's do a mini research and find their meanings.

    (6 minutes)
- Ask students why they think the poet used *Kilamanjaro* and not the correct spelling of *Kilimanjaro*. Examine how the sound of "Kil-a-man-jaro" alludes to the many historical crimes and injustices against enslaved Africans and people of African descent because of their physical features. Discuss how poets can deliberately alter words to expand their meaning and significance. (3 minutes)

Spoken Language
- Assign individuals, pairs, and groups to read different lines of the poem as a choral speaking activity. Let them practice a few times, experimenting with different volumes, intonations, pace, and pitch. (20 minutes)
- Have volunteers share how they feel after the choral speaking exercise. (5 minutes)

Voices from the Field

I have gathered perspectives from students, colleagues, and hallway safety monitors to hear their take on how racism can be dismantled in the classroom and schools. It is important that teachers, principals, superintendents, other system leaders and community partners listen keenly to these voices as their voices matter too.

Questioning and challenging curriculum sharpens students' critical thinking and problem-solving skills.

- Teachers should teach lessons specifically on empathy.
- Teachers should ensure that empathy is an ability that is modelled and taught not just once, but throughout the year. This is a good suggestion, and district school boards should also demonstrate this leadership by providing workshops to teachers on teaching empathy. The poem, "Jamie" by Elizabeth Brewster is an ideal poem to teach both middle and high school students empathy, especially toward persons who are living with a disability and those who are social outcasts.

- Constantly check your bias. Some teachers have false assumptions about some students. For example, asking a student about their life in the Philippines when in fact, the student and their parents are not from the Philippines.
- Teachers should treat every student like a human being. Don't be color blind.
- Telling students, "I don't see color" is in essence denying the student of their identity as Black, Brown, or any other ethnicity.

Teachers should encourage students to question the curriculum. Students should be encouraged to challenge the contents of the curriculum and ask what is missing. For example, are there individuals and groups whose lives and experiences are visibly missing from the curriculum?
— Muslim student

Engage In and Encourage Self-Reflection

Self-reflection is a process of assessing and evaluating oneself—one's feelings, thoughts, actions, and motivation—in as honest and objective a way as possible. It is a mental exercise that helps you understand yourself better as a professional and a person. When self-reflection becomes part of your praxis, you gain perspectives on your areas of strength and areas of need and are better able to make more informed decisions moving forward.

Self-reflection is a critical part of metacognition, which involves thinking about one's own thinking, and reflecting on one's actions, experiences, teaching, and learning strategies. This is a practice that both teachers and students should adopt because, when it is honestly done, individuals learn how to become better teachers, learners, students, and empathetic people. Students should be taught that it is okay to question their own biases, as constant self-reflection is one way to keep oneself in check and hold oneself accountable.

Whether it is teacher or students self-reflecting, guiding questions can elicit powerful ideas:
- When have I felt "othered"?
- How did it make me feel?
- What assumptions do I have about someone who is different from me?
- How did my assumptions about others influence my behavior toward them?
- Did I ever have a conversation with that person afterward in order to get to know them despite the assumptions held?

Voices from the Field

I fielded feedback from teacher colleagues and a hallway safety monitor, and they shared similar comments to those of students.

Teachers who build rapport can serve as positive role models for marginalized students, demonstrating the value of empathy, respect, and understanding across cultural divides.
—Teacher

Regularly check-in with students to build rapport. It is important so that you can highlight the importance of and encourage engagement among racially marginalized individuals.
— Hallway safety monitor

Strong relationships between teachers and students can lead to improved academic performance. When students feel understood and supported, they are more likely to be motivated to go to class and not idle in the hallways.
— Member of school support staff

Final Thoughts

Dismantling racism and anti-oppressive classroom practices is not a one-time thing; it is an ongoing effort that you should incorporate into your daily practice. Dismantling racism takes purpose, intentionality, empathy, and a significant amount of work. While engaging in anti-discriminatory work—against discrimination historically embedded in institutional practice and rooted in systemic racism—connect and collaborate with colleagues, students, parents, and community agencies. And always remember to make time to take care of your own physical and mental health. Positive teacher–student relationships can empower marginalized students to build confidence and resilience. A confident student is more likely to take ownership of their education and future—a powerful strategy to dismantle racism from within.

6

Disrupting Racism from Within

Marie Green

Marie Green (OCT) holds Master's degrees in theology and adolescence education, and a PhD from the University of St. Michael's College at the University of Toronto, with a fellowship at Harvard. She teaches history and law at the secondary level and anti-discrimination, religion, and research courses at the Master of Teaching program at the Ontario Institute for Studies in Education (OISE). She coauthored a chapter in *Handbook on Caribbean and African Studies in Education*.

With this chapter, I hope to disrupt the idea of disruption and what it means for anti-racism in education. I lament that some of my fellow academics, many of whom have never set foot in the classroom as a teacher, appear to be shouting from the lofty windows of ivory towers about "burning down" the education system. I lament even more that they are often not willing to light the match. Their ideas of disruption frequently remain in theory, never coming into practice. They seem to forget that *disrupt* is a verb, an action word.

As someone who has the privilege of being in a schools on a regular basis and to witness what is happening in the education system, I want to offer up tangible ideas about how we, as teachers, can disrupt systems of oppression and racist structures by empowering our students and positioning them to become agents of their liberation. We do this by believing our students can achieve, by warmly demanding the best from them, by challenging the master scripting of curriculum, and by being willing to go outside of our classrooms to do what is necessary for them to succeed. Most importantly, I wish share how, in order to disrupt racism from within our schools and educational institutions, we must first disrupt the racism within *us*. Having done a fair share of street marching, I have come to the realization that sometimes the warmth of the sun is more powerful and effective than the harsh force of a cold north wind. Ultimately, if in fact schools are, as Connie Wun (2017) asserts, part and parcel of a "logic of punitive carcerality," if they are to "operate as multilayered sites that do more than funnel students into prison or prime them for incarceration," then every student helped to overcome the system and thrive must be considered a disruption of the order of things.

This chapter includes activities that can be implemented with junior and intermediate senior students. They are meant to facilitate active, brave conversations with and between students. I explore how teachers can navigate institutional constricts and disrupt racism from within, one classroom and one student at a time, as a micro-level approach within the framework of warm demander ideology (Delpit, 2012; Irvine, 1998). I am joined in this quest by three excellent educators disrupting the system in their way and brilliantly ensuring the success of their students. Nigel Hunter gives us an example of how to navigate when questions or comments from students catch you off-guard. Craig Christie shares how he meets the needs of students inside and outside the classroom; Michelle Muir details in striking prose how our mere presence as Black teachers in educational spaces is, in itself, already a disruption.

Voice from the Field: Marie's Story

I was called to teach. And by that I mean the kind of burning-bush calling that stopped Moses in his tracks. I consider my career to be a ministry. Born and raised in the Pentecostal *retranchement*s of the beautiful island of Jamaica, I am a living testimony of what it means to become the teacher that students need, no matter the indoctrination you have been exposed to your whole life—what it means to grow, to undergo the archeology of self (Sealey-Ruiz. 2021), to not only blossom but also to bloom where you are planted. I teach and research at the intersection of Christianity, education, race, and indigeneity. Applying the lens of emancipatory pedagogy and Unapologetic Black Inquiry (Clark and Brooms, 2021), I make the case for what I term *Black site-ation*; that is, viewing the experiences of Black people as a site of learning and justice building. By extension, I engage the "incommensurability of antiblackness" (Jung and Vargas, 2021, p. 7) in my academic work. As such, my work centres on Black experience with a strong belief that it can illuminate what Charles W. Mills terms "the darkness of whiteness" (Jung and Vargas, 2021, p. 18), ultimately informing policy and practice to positively affect everyone.

What Is Disrupting Racism?

A really in-depth understanding of the concept of disruption can be gained from grasping the difference between it and the closely aligned term *interruption*. The two are often conflated, used interchangeably, and thought to be one and the same. Though they bear the same etymology, they are quite different. *Oxford Languages* identifies a stem found in the Latin *rumpere* or *ruptura* and the Old French *rupture*, which means "to break." The root word is *rupt* which means "to burst." When the prefix is added in either case (*inter-rupt/dis-rupt*) the inflection is the same, but a new meaning is derived. *Oxford Languages* offers the following definitions:

> *Interrupt*: (verb) stop the continuous progress of (an activity or process)
>
> *Disrupt*: (verb) cause a disturbance or problem; drastically alter or destroy the structure of

To interrupt something is to impose a temporary break, usually with the view that things will continue after the interruption. An interruption does not put an end to the thing that was interrupted; it pauses it, but the conditions for it to continue after the interruption remain in place. To disrupt something, however, is not to merely put a stop to that thing, but to do away with the conditions necessary for that thing or activity to continue to occur. The conditions that facilitated the event are shifted so that it cannot possibly continue, be revived, or be sustained. When we disrupt racism, we unseat it, we displace it, we render it placeless, so that it cannot continue to take root. Furthermore, unlike the seemingly more polite and unprovocative term *interrupt* (imagine the newscaster saying, "we interrupt the scheduled program to bring you the following news..."), *disruption* means disturbing something, causing problems, and even potentially causing destruction. It is by no means polite in the true essence of the word. That said, what we are discussing in this chapter can exist on a spectrum ranging from varying degrees of interruption to disruption.

This chapter started out with a challenge to the idea of disruption and what it looks like. It does not always have to resemble a burning building. However, as educators, we are constantly discerning what is necessary for us to address racism. I propose warm demander pedagogy as a disruptive action, because of its potential for helping students overcome a system that they are often set up to fail in. Disruption might look different from one educator to another educator and from one educational experience to another. In *Disrupting Hate in Education: teacher activists, democracy, and global pedagogies of interruption* (2021), Rita Verma and Michael Apple feature a wide range of ways in which various "isms" are being disrupted around the world. In their article "Disrupting Structural Racism: Counter-Narratives of Pride, Growth, and Transformation" (2018) Rosann Tung and Adriana Villavicencio identify convergence on how best to disrupt the color-blind posture and practice of some educators. I suggest this useful checklist, drawn from their work, that can be applied to any initiative, including lessons and activities in the classroom:

☐ See people of color as experts on their communities, not just as blank slates to be molded.
☐ Take responsibility for being responsive to race and gender, instead of assuming a "color-blind" stance.
☐ Focus initiatives on changing the adults in the system, rather than trying to change students.
☐ Employ asset-based and intentionally anti-racist positions, instead of deficit-based language.

STORY FROM THE CLASSROOM

Teachers in the Parkdale neighborhood of Toronto stood up for their students, who were showing up to school with many of the signs that come with living in poorly managed rental properties focused only on profit. They determined that not only can a child who, for example, has bed bugs bring them to the classroom, but also living conditions can negatively affect the child's learning. In June 2017, these teachers donned signs and joined residents on the streets in a rent strike protest. Their participation was carried by major news outlets in Canada and drew attention to the housing crisis being faced by so many Torontonians, especially newcomer and immigrant families.

- Are there students in your classroom whose home lives negatively affect their ability to learn? What conditions are they living in?
- What can you do to identify those students?
- What can you do in the classroom to offer help to these students, without bringing undue attention to them from their classmates?
- Are there ways you can advocate—in the school and in the community—to help students in your classroom?

> ### Giving Teachers Tools for the Work
>
> In recent conversations with veteran teachers, I have found an overwhelming concern about fragility among new teacher cohorts and their seeming unpreparedness for what Molyneux (2021) terms *emotional labor*. Also of concern is the alarming turnover rate (Garcia and Weiss, 2019; Clark and Antonelli, 2013), and the pacifier posture adopted by many of those who decide to stay. Systemic racism and incidents of racism, those experienced personally and those witnessed, further compound the issue of teacher retention (Mawhinney, Cabral & Pierce, 2025). There are days when it can feel like the education system is one giant insurmountable infrastructure that is too big to fail, yet quietly fails so many. Still, many teachers want to be the exception needed when the norm is acceptable and even lauded. They want to keep calm and carry on when it would be so much easier to lose their cool and abandon the colossal ship that is education.
>
> I worry that the future teachers who hear my lectures will leave so overwhelmed by the theory they encounter that they decide to abandon any attempt to make a difference and stick with the status quo. As eye-opening as it all is, and as much as they might embrace the theoretical opining of Paulo Freire, Gloria Ladson-Billings, Kimberle Crenshaw, Lisa Delpit, Wayne Au, Eve Tuck, George Dei, and others, I can't help but wonder what they will do when they get into the real world of the classroom. I worry that they will succumb to pressures, fall in line, toe the line, simply adapt the department rubric and material, or find themselves downloading worksheets from random online websites purporting to make things easy for teachers. In the short time I have future teachers in my classroom as a captive audience, I guide them through readings, discussions, exercises, and assignments that will help in their preparation and positioning. I try to impart that this critical work will set them up to carry out and implement all the wonderful teaching strategies they will learn during their time at teachers' college. I encourage them to formulate a teaching philosophy and craft a personal constitution that makes it clear what kind of teacher they are going to be. Without this important work, the theory they encounter means nothing. It is like planting seeds in stony places or topsoil where there is not enough depth to take root.

What Is Warm Demander Pedagogy?

Warm demander pedagogy is situated within the larger framework of Culturally Relevant Pedagogy (CRP) (Ladson-Billings, 1995; Gay, 2000). In describing the role of warm demanders, Lisa Delpit (2012) points out that "nothing makes more of a difference in a child's school experience than a teacher" (2012, p. 71). She describes research participants who credited their success to teachers who "pushed" and "demanded" greatness from them. She invoked Gloria Ladson-Billings' insistence that "school dependent" children (Delpit, 2012, p. 72), such as those who come from low-income and culturally diverse neighborhoods, need the warm demander type of teachers to be successful. Unlike their counterparts from wealthy neighborhoods who have resources outside school and can therefore be successful even in the face of poor teaching, poor children need their teachers to be rich in skill and knowledge.

> Initially coined by Judith Kleinfeld in 1975, James Vasquez used *warm demander* to describe teachers who were successful at teaching students of color (Ellerbrock 2014). Jacqueline Jordan Irvine expanded on Vasquez's work, starting with his definition of Warm Demanders as teachers who provide a tough-minded, no-nonsense, structured, and disciplined classroom environment for kids whom society has psychologically and physically abandoned. Strongly identifying with their students and determined to give them a future, these teachers believe that culturally diverse children not only *can* learn but *must* learn. (Irvine, 1998).

Voice from the Field

Racism will always be a taught behavior, a social construct that must be constantly questioned and addressed. I was teaching physical education to young aspiring Kindergarten children when I was presented with a question from an inquisitive young boy. "Mr. Hunter, why are you black?" Initially I was surprised by the question, but I decided to ask him a question. "What are you?" He said, "I'm white." I directed his attention to the gym walls. "These walls are white." His response after realizing his complexion was definitely not the color of the gym walls was, "I'm yellow white." The identity we accept can be challenged or reinforced. At a very early age, children need to be challenged to evaluate their taught perception of difference, even when it comes to race.
— Nigel Hunter, Elementary teacher

Nigel Hunter's passion for the arts has brought him success in stage and TV productions, including Soul, a Vision TV drama series.

At its core, Warm Demander Pedagogy emerged out of what I like to describe as Firm Black Mother Pedagogy. Many of those who grew up in a Black home will recognize that phrasing. The sheer ability of the Black mother to stop or prevent misbehavior from across the room with her eyes is phenomenal. It is also How Black Mothers Say I Love You (the title of a 2018 play by Trey Anthony). I always interpreted the look from my mother as, "I'm going to whup your behind if you don't stop what you're doing." However, as an adult, I now know the look also says, "I see you," "You need to behave," "Be careful." It is really how Black mothers say I love you. Most recently, I have begun to think about how this might have been informed during slavery. Black mothers had to be able to command and direct their children and other loved ones with their eyes, without saying a word, because it was too dangerous to speak. Black women carry these mothering practices into the classroom. I now realize that I use this same practice on a regular basis.

Making that kind of connection with students is directly linked to my early education in a one-room schoolhouse with one teacher, who everyone called Miss Joyce. Any assistance Miss Joyce received came from people in the village like my grandmother. At the end of the school day, Miss Joyce passed by the homes of her students as she made her way up to her house in the hills. Along the journey, she would stop to talk with parents and grandparents about the weather, view the ackee tree that was blooming, and let them know of the progress being made by their children.

While working as a youth minister some years ago, a chance encounter at a community meeting put me in contact with a Youth Justice Program worker whose job it was to find placements for youth needing to fulfill their court-ordered community service. My first assignment was a young man who was assigned to volunteer at our summer camp. The intake went well, and he seemed ready to participate, but he failed to show up for camp and I could not reach him by phone. When the court worker offered no satisfactory solutions, other than for the placement to be cancelled, I decided to go straight to this young man's neighborhood to try to find him. I remember his startled look when he came to the door. It struck me as possible that no one in his life had ever made such a brash move in a bid to help him succeed. He showed up the next day, proved to be an excellent addition to the camp, and completed his placement without incident. That experience, among others, laid the groundwork for a teaching career that would require me at times to fight for my students, while firmly commanding their best effort.

Voice from the Field: An Interview with Craig Christie

Craig Christie teaches Business at Etobicoke Collegiate Institute. He was born in Jamaica and immigrated to Canada as a child. Bloordale Baseball League honored him with a Community Recognition Award in 2025 for his longtime work as a coach.

Q: Teaching is a second career for you, what brought you to it?
A: I was working in the corporate world, for a bank, actually. An opportunity came up to volunteer with Junior Achievement where you get to spend a day in the classroom with students. While raising a family of my own, I also got involved with local sports team. Teaching was just a natural transition for me.
Q: You are the only Black teacher in this school. You are also the staff sponsor for the Black Student Alliance. How do you navigate being the only one in the building and the expectations that might come with that?
A: I do not see it as an obligation. I was also a newcomer to this country, so I am aware of the challenges that some of our Black students face. If I can be that positive image or role model that they need to see, it's not even a thought for me.
Q: What does "disrupting from within" mean to you?
A: It's not some big superfluous idea. It's the tangible reality of being a well-rounded teacher. It's doing great work in the classroom while being willing to go beyond the walls of the classroom.
Q: Tell me of a time when you disrupted the system:
A: I will share two examples. I had a student who needed a 95 to get a scholarship to a program. His grade was at 93. Am I going to stand in the way of someone's future over two percent? He might have been the first person in his family to be accepted, let alone attend university. I made sure he got the grade he needed to pursue his dream. I had another student who came to class in distress because there was a hole in the ceiling of their public housing unit, and no one was doing anything to help. I contacted her mother and went to the home. It was a really big hole, leaking, with drywall coming from the upstairs. Someone could have fallen through it. I ended up contacting the housing manager, city councillor, anyone I could find, until it was fixed. None of this is in my job description. I could just show up, teach and go home. But I'm here, present for these students at 7:30 every morning, academically, emotionally, socially. That is disrupting!

Michelle Muir has been teaching for more 35 years. She is also a writer, spoken-word artist, professional storyteller, and workshop facilitator. In 2009 she published an anthology of poems titled *Nuff Said*.

Voice from Field

The names. The names that young people call each other in anger would make a lot of adults cringe. Negative comments about race hurt at any age, but in elementary school, knowing how to navigate that and come out of that situation feeling empowered is a lot to ask of anyone. Being right where I need to be, in my elementary school setting, available and ready when a Black student from any grade needs to find a teacher who looks like them. The connection is immediate… it shows in their eyes as they pass me in the halls. Whether it be head nods, high fives, or hugs (the young ones are prone to give impulsive hugs when they are walking in a line); it is a beautiful unspoken understanding of "I got you," "You are my kin and my kind," "Wakanda Forever," and "Ubuntu."
— Michelle Muir, Elementary teacher

Always set out to be the best I could possibly be
Thinking that was the me the students would naturally see.

Surprised I was to find
That many of them were afraid of my kind
Curiously afraid
Quietly afraid
Stereotypically afraid
Passive aggressively afraid
Dangerously afraid
And it makes me afraid on the inside
And being afraid on the inside weighs on me…oh so heavily.
You see
The me they see
Is what Tik Tok and that whole media block and especially TV
Has told them what to think, feel, hear and see when they see all that is me.

And there it is…
Persistently
Consistently
Inexplicable in its inexplicability
Is the fear some students have of me.
— Michelle Muir, Elementary teacher

Being a Warm Demander for Your Students

Michelle Muir's heartfelt prose reminds us that, as teachers, we often labor in very precarious environments. Her words remind us that we cannot allow this important work to be impeded. One of the ways we can ensure our work continues is by equipping ourselves with great tools and resources. This section provides tangible tools for empowering students to become disrupters themselves.

"Remember that curriculum is 'everything that happens' at school. Your response or lack of response is just as much of a lesson as the morning math activity." — Rita Tenorio (2010, p. 93).

STORY FROM THE CLASSROOM

When the "N-word" tries to make a comeback

Lynn-Anne is a first-year math teacher in her early twenties. Her hometown was 95% white, and everyone in her class was white, up until high school when a number of students from the nearby Six Nations reserve, newcomer South Asian communities, and two Black students who had been adopted from Malawi by a Christian family also attended. Choosing to attend university in the city of Toronto made her the first in her tight-knit Christian Reform family to do so. Even more alarming to her family was her decision to not return to the community and teach but to accept a position with the Toronto District School Board. During her first week on the job, she noticed an alarming trend among her Grade 10 students. Black students wantonly threw around the "N-word" as part of regular discourse and mostly as a means of describing other students. She felt unsure what to do about Black students using the word amongst themselves while in class. She was aware that some members of the Black community, including those in the hip-hop community, considered their usage of the word as a way of taking the historical power away from the word.

She was still contemplating whether and how to address the issue, when a student from the South Asian community used the word. No one in the class reacted or said anything; the Black students engaged in conversation with this student did not seem to mind. Lynn-Anne felt strongly that the incident warranted attention but was unsure what to do. As a white teacher she did not want to appear to be stepping out of bounds. She did not want her Black students feeling disrespected. She had also observed one instance in her practicum where the teacher in the classroom completely ignored the students as they had ongoing conversations casually using the word. She decided to consult a colleague.

Lynn-Anne's older and more experienced colleague was also white and had also grown up in a small-town community. He was resolute in his response. "Oh, that one's easy," he told her, "Just refer to the Codes of Conduct. The Ministry of Education, the school board, and our union are all very clear on words that are not allowed. Don't get into it with them, don't make it about your views, just quote the school policy."

That following afternoon, Lynne-Anne spent the first five minutes of class reminding students of words that are deemed inappropriate. In addition to the "N-word," she shared how other derogatory words used to describe various historically oppressed groups are still harmful today. She declared that these words were a violation of school policy and should not be used by anyone at any time within the learning community.

- What would you add to the advice given by Lynn-Anne's colleague?
- What additional actions might Lynn-Anne have taken to address this issue?
- How might this case study apply to your own practice? Have you had racialized experiences in your classroom where you felt unprepared or inadequate to address the situation?
- How did this story shape your thinking about working with students from communities you do not directly belong to?

Expert Tips on Addressing Racist Language

- **Everything that happens in the classroom is curriculum**: In advising teachers about what to do when students make a sexist or racist remark, veteran educator Rita Tenorio maintains that, when incidents happen in our classroom, they also serve as a lesson. Why? Because students are watching to see how the teacher will handle a situation. In Lynn-Anne's case, remaining silent would have sent a clear message that using the derogatory word was okay. It might have also given license to other students who are not Black to use the word. Furthermore, there might have been students who, though silent, were greatly offended by the use of the word. All students were harmed in some way by the use of the word. The harm would have been even more extensive if it had gone unchallenged.
- **Never miss a teachable moment**: In addition to addressing the issue forthrightly, this was an amazing opportunity to educate students on the history of the word. Using a reading or film, or a combination of both, followed by a questionnaire and discussion goes even further than invoking school policy. Students will go away with a valuable lesson and an answer to the proverbial young person question, "But why?" Why is the word bad? Why can't we use it? Why do rappers get to use it, and we don't?
- **A picture tells a thousand words**: Integrate the contributions of African Canadians, Indigenous people, and people of color in your lessons. Display positive images of racially diverse contributors around your classroom. Create a space that conveys a message of inclusion and respect for people of all backgrounds.
- **Establish classroom culture early on**: Warm demanders establish the atmosphere in their classroom and eventually shape the culture. Jacqueline Jordan Irvine tells the story of a teacher calling her student to task when the work he presented did not meet expectations. "That's enough of your nonsense, Darius. Your story does not make sense. I told you time and time again that you must stick to the theme I gave you. Now sit down" (Irvine, 1998). Irvine acknowledges that this tone does not appear to fit the model teacher we all ascribe to be. However, she points out that, in this particular teacher's classroom, this type of admonishment is fitting because the teacher has already established an atmosphere that fosters constructive and frank critique. She has also built relationships with these students, and they understand that the feedback is meant to build, not to destroy. This means that students understand very early on what behavior will and will not be tolerated. They also know what is expected of them and are motivated to meet their teacher's expectations.

Activity: Head, Heart, and Feet

Head, Heart, and Feet can be a very short debrief activity or a more extensive reflection activity.

I was first introduced to Head, Heart, and Feet as a debriefing tool through my work in community development. It is a tool created to help participants debrief a workshop, activity, event, or lesson. One of the greatest attributes of this tool is that it can be easily adapted for any age group or setting. I have used it with preteens, teens, young adults, and older professional adults. I have used it in education settings, faith-based settings, and corporate settings. With younger students, I get them working in groups and employ flip charts and colorful markers so that they can actually draw a character with a head, heart, and feet. They then write their feedback on the respective body part. Older youth have just as much fun with the group artistic endeavor, but I have also used individual worksheets, which often foster more in-depth responses. This tool can be used as a way to either frame a discussion on the topic of harmful words or debrief a presentation or lesson on the topic.

Components of Head, Heart, and Feet	
Body Part	Description
Head	What you observed, learned; what stood out
Heart	How you feel about what you observed or learned
Feet/Hands	What you will do with this information and/or what next steps you will take

1. After an activity, event, or lesson, describe the purpose of Head, Heart, and Feet responses and make it very clear what students are providing feedback on.
2. Instruct groups (if applicable) to pick a spokesperson and a scribe, or determine if everyone will be doing parts of the writing.
3. Ask participants to draw a character with a head, heart, and feet as visible body parts, or provide them with a printed worksheet.
4. Instruct participants to write on the head what they observed (saw/heard) or learned.
5. Instruct participants to write on the heart how they feel about what they observed or learned.
6. Instruct participants to write on the feet what they are going to do with this information, how might it change their behavior, what action will they take, and what the next steps will be.
7. Take ten minutes to allow each group spokesperson to give a two-minute summary of what their group came up with.

Make sure to summarize the feedback in your own words and share this with the students. Congratulate them on their intentional thinking and celebrate their fun and creative drawings by pinning them on the walls around the classroom.

Final Thoughts

Until we are ready to build our own schools from the ground up (not really a novel idea, for it is how many private schools were born), I want to encourage teachers to warmly demand their way to the kind of individual action that ultimately contributes to collective gains. Throughout this chapter, I have sought to give teachers tangible ideas they can implement when putting a match to the building is not an option. I have shared how my positionality naturally led me to embrace Warm Demander Pedagogy, which I have situated as a viable option for disrupting racism from within. I have shared the stories of three teachers of successful students who, in their own right, find ways to positively affect the lives of their students. If, in fact, the carceral education system strives to defeat children of color, particularly Black children, and prevent their success, then every child a teacher can successfully guide through the system is a disruption of that system. It is also the best way to navigate what James Baldwin called "the paradox of education" (1970). While undertaking this very practical and sensical approach to disrupting racism from within, I share Baldwin's words to teachers:

> To any citizen of this country who figures himself as responsible—and particularly those of you who deal with the minds and hearts of young people—must be prepared to "go for broke." Or to put it another way, you must understand that in the attempt to correct so many generations of bad faith and cruelty, when it is operating not only in the classroom but in society, you will meet the most fantastic, the most brutal, and the most determined resistance.

Baldwin lays out what we are up against if we decide to color outside the lines or change the palette. He cautions us to be aware of the resistance we will meet when we demand the best from and for our students, even if we do so warmly. We might even have moments like the scene in the movie *Coach Carter* when the parents show up angry that the coach would dare stop their children from playing basketball in a bid to get higher grades. I once had a coworker tell me, "You don't have to overdo it." Every year I hear from student teachers who tell me of the bare-minimum atmosphere in the schools where they are placed.

But I am buoyed and encouraged by the excellent teachers many student teachers encounter during practicum. I can speak directly to the love and passion manifested in classrooms and the sheer and undeniable expertise many students get to experience every day. I have had some of the finest teachers as guest speakers in my own classrooms. These teachers go over and above; they innovate and seek out the best learning experiences for their students. One of the teachers I had in my classroom this year sought funding so that exceptional learners in his class who could not go on co-op like their peers could have access to an onsite creator studio, equipped with maker machines, graphic design material, and software programs. Then he brought in a professional graphic artist to work with them. The outcome was a graphic novel based on popular figures. This exceptional teacher of exceptional learners is a disrupter, and he is doing it, not with the empty-barrel postulation of the theorists shouting from the ivory tower, but as a teacher, in the field, on the ground, humbly and lovingly serving his students.

7

Being Intentional about Diversity, Equity, and Inclusion

Shelita Walker

Shelita Walker (she/her) is a Canadian educator with almost 30 years of experience in education. Currently the System Principal for Human Rights, Equity & Inclusive Education at the Halton District School Board, she is a passionate advocate for social justice. Influenced by the strong women in her life, Shelita integrates grace, compassion, and self-care into her leadership. A skilled facilitator, she creates brave, inclusive spaces for deep learning on equity, identity, and systemic oppression, working with educators, leaders, and corporate staff to inspire meaningful change.

A special thanks to the many educators who gave me permission to share wonderful activities and student work to help highlight what being intentional about equity, diversity, and inclusion in a classroom could look like and how it affects student learning, engagement, and sense of belonging.

At the start of the 2024–2025 school year, I was filled with a familiar buzz of hope and possibility, as I ferociously consumed all media coverage of the United States presidential race. I was confident that a talented, accomplished racialized woman was destined to make history. I laughed at the absurdity that anyone, besides the blatantly and overtly bigoted and ignorant, could vote for her opponent. She had Beyoncé on her side, for goodness sake! But as the votes rolled in, I realized my own ignorance. I had believed people would simply do the right thing. Over the ensuing months, I watched in disbelief as years of social justice gains were swiftly dismantled.

Canada has its own history of racism and discrimination and, in this nation neighbor to the US, I listened to much of the same hate-filled rhetoric, not just in social media, but in the hallways and classrooms of schools. As a central principal for human rights and equity, I noticed an increased resistance to work that once had been embraced, a growing sense of fatigue and frustration, and constant murmuring complaints: "When are we going to be able to just focus on learning and achievement?" How did we shift so fast from global solidarity movements during the pandemic to dismantling DEI programs and roles? How could I ask educators—many under attack themselves—to stay committed to equity and inclusion?

The truth is, no single event brought us here. Injustice has always existed, and so have those fighting against it—then and now. As educators committed to social justice, we walk the paths of education advocates and activists like bell hooks, Audre Lorde, Gloria Ladson-Billings, Gholdy Muhammad, Bettina Love, and many others. In this chapter, we explore the idea of being intentional in equity work to honor the diversity of student identity and create inclusive spaces for them.

Diversity, equity, and inclusion (DEI) is central to preparing students to be meaningful contributors to a global society. Sustaining ourselves in this work demands clarity of purpose, and is rooted in actions that shape our pedagogical approach and outcomes for students. Academic scholar and black feminist bell

hooks (1994) reminds us that teaching is "not merely to share information, but to share in the intellectual and spiritual growth of our students." Over years of equity advocacy, I have found three key anchors for social justice educators:
- Know Your *Why*
- Create Community
- Centre Joy

In this chapter we will explore these themes, offering opportunities for deep reflection through journaling, practical applicable steps to enhance your practice, and inspiration from Voices from the Field of fellow educators engaged in equity work to guide and support your own equity journey.

Know Your *Why*

Every educator can recall the reason they entered the teaching profession. For most, it was to make a difference in the lives of the students they serve. Deciding to be an educator who wants to create equitable and inclusive learning environments and experiences means that one must also reflect on this call to do equity work, to know why you want to make a difference in the lives of students, specifically those who are marginalized by the education system.

When I first entered the teaching profession, my *why* was based on my own childhood experiences of anti-Black racism, sexism, misogynoir, and financial and food insecurity. I worked in communities in the less-than-attractive teaching areas of Toronto. Overwhelmingly, these communities were made up of subsidized housing complexes, recently arrived newcomers, multilingual families, refugees, and predominately Black and Brown children. As a first-generation Black Canadian, I saw aspects of my own experience in the students and the challenges they were navigating. My *why* was shaped by a commitment to hold the same high hopes and expectations their families had for them that my mother had for me; to create spaces that celebrated their brilliance and affirmed their importance in shaping our world; and to make sure they always knew—without doubt—that their dreams were possible. My role was to give them the tools, support, and belief to turn those dreams into reality.

Knowing your *why* must include knowing yourself—your personal identity, how your identity has shaped your understanding of race and racism, and the personal biases you hold about others whose identities are different (and similar) to your own. Dr. Yolanda Sealy-Ruiz's work on the Archaeology of Self encourages educators to explore this concept by engaging in an "archaeological dig" to identify where and how issues of race and racism live within us and influence our pedagogical practices. This intentional practice helps educators understand how our beliefs about students and their communities shape how we reach and teach them. It is what determines an asset-based or deficit-based approach to the students we serve.

> **Journal Reflection Activity**
> - Think back to the moment you decided to become an educator and ask yourself *What hopes, dreams, or beliefs brought me into this work? How does my reason for engaging in equity work inform the way I teach, build relationships, and create spaces where all students feel seen, heard, valued, and affirmed?*

- Write a teaching philosophy statement that captures who you are as an educator dedicated to fostering equity, inclusion, and belonging.
- Take a moment to reflect on your personal identity: *How well do I understand myself in terms of race, my experiences with racism, my core ideologies, and the positionalities I hold in different spaces? How has my identity shaped my worldview, my interactions with others who do not share my identity, and my role as an educator committed to equity?*
- Write a reflection that considers how deepening your self-awareness strengthens your teaching approach for justice and inclusion.

Voice from the Field

Being intentional about equity, diversity, and inclusion means being intentional with your *why*. Your *why* must be rooted in a purpose, a common goal to change the outcomes of students marginalized by the educational system, which is represented in the disproportionate data of learning and achievement, special education needs, suspensions, expulsions, early leavers, etc. Educators committed to diversity, equity, and inclusion understand that DEI is both a state of being *and* a state of doing. It is an approach that requires intentional and deliberate actions in order to shift and change the outcomes of students' experiences in school. It asks educators to be intentional in how they see their students, design their instruction, and engage with parents, caregivers, and the community at large. It is action-oriented. It is a symbiotic relationship between seeking knowledge and understanding, then actionizing the learning. Without this alignment, DEI work risks becoming performative—well-meaning actions that lack the transformative impact students deserve.

My *why* is rooted in a deep sense of responsibility to the students and families who walk through our doors carrying more than just backpacks—and to those who continue to show up despite being overlooked or misunderstood. I'm especially committed to communities impacted by food insecurity and trauma, where needs are great and voices often go unheard.

— Beth, Special education teacher

Journal Reflection Activity

- Reflect and respond to the following: *Do my teaching practices reflect a belief in all students' abilities? Are the goals I set for my students rooted in high expectations and authentic understanding of their lived experiences? How do I see my students, and is the language I use to describe them asset-based or deficit based?*
- Consider your students and your current teaching practice: *How do I make time to observe students in a variety of contexts? How do I integrate their strengths and interests into my daily planning and teaching?*

Students are diverse in the way in which they learn. Like Beth, understanding the profiles of your students can help you design a learning environment and teaching approaches that support their success. Here are a few practical suggestions:

- Flexible Seating and Choice Boards: Offer seating options and multiple ways to show learning (e.g., draw, write, speak, act, etc.).
- Calm Corner: A quiet classroom space with sensory tools and reflection prompts provides opportunities for self-regulation.
- Universal Design for Learning (UDL): Lessons that incorporate visual, auditory, kinesthetic, and tactile elements accommodate diverse learning preferences.

Create Community

In her book *Belonging: A Culture of Place* (2009), bell hooks expresses the importance of mutual respect, critical consciousness, and active participation in building inclusive communities. She sees educators as community makers who play an active and critical role in fostering learning environments where diversity is celebrated and where every individual feels a sense of belonging.

Creating safe, welcoming, and inclusive communities is critical for student learning, engagement, and well-being. Building and fostering community with and among students means getting to know who they are as people: their hopes, dreams, and aspirations; their gifts and talents. Community-building is intentional work. Whether you're an occasional teacher working in different classrooms or a permanent teacher with a consistent group of students, fostering a strong classroom community is essential. A common misstep is front-loading community-building at the start of the year, only to let it fade as the months progress. While establishing community early on is important, sustaining it throughout the year is what truly makes it meaningful.

Voice from the Field

Each year, Meena uses a range of activities to get to know her students, and for them to get to know each other.

I start the year with a student survey. I let them know the questions are optional, but the more they share, the better we can get to know them. I ask about their names, pronouns, whether they want their birthdays recognized and how. Some choose a birthday sticker, others a desk flag, a note on the calendar, or none at all.

I use some of their responses to create a Who In Our Class… activity. For example: *Who in our class won gold at a recent figure-skating competition?* Students make guesses, and then the classmate reveals themselves and shares more. It's a fun, low-pressure way for them to learn about one another and build connections.

I keep the student surveys and refer to them throughout the year. Students even ask to update them as their preferences change, which I see as a sign of trust and comfort in sharing who they are with me.

— Meena, Intermediate teacher

Establishing a Student-Focused Morning Routine

How students enter the classroom each morning matters. A consistent, student-centred routine provides a soft entry into the day, setting a positive tone for learning and supporting student success. It also offers a valuable opportunity to check in—both with individual students and with the class as a whole. This daily "pulse check" helps you respond in the moment and fosters strong, sustained relationships.

Try This: Greeting Slides

Greeting Slides seek to engage students in a way that helps ease them into the start of their day. A slide could spotlight a quote, a song and artist, a mindfulness exercise, a short video, or any combination thereof. A list is curated based on students' recommended quotes, songs, mindfulness videos, etc.; students are encouraged to include recommendations based in their first/home/heritage language. If there is something happening in the world or in the local community, it can be used as an opener for conversation.

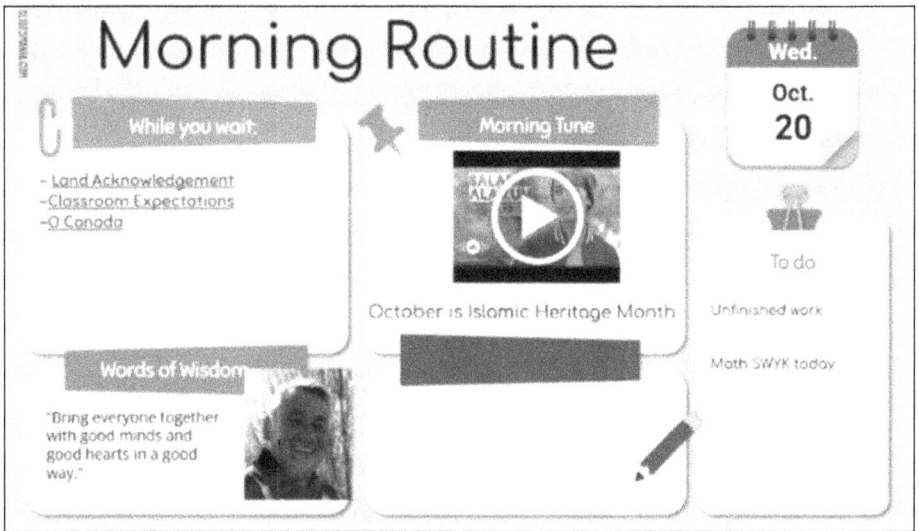

Celebrating Multilingualism

Multilingual language learners can often feel excluded from the class community, with language as a barrier to belonging. Intentionally incorporating students' home language(s) into everyday learning helps to establish an inclusive learning environment.

Try This

- Multilingual Word Wall: Students contribute key terms in both English and their first language. Words rotate weekly based on themes (e.g., family, emotions, science, etc.).
- Language Expert of the Week: A student teaches the class a simple phrase or greeting in their home language. (Can be in incorporated into your morning routines.)
- Bilingual Book Projects: Students create picture books or comics using both languages (English and their home language) and share them in community circles.
- Cross-Curricular Integration: Students use home language resources to support learning in subjects like Science or Social Studies.

Fostering Trust and Open Communication

Inclusive communities are built on trust, and trust must be intentionally cultivated. This means giving students regular opportunities to practice emotional literacy, attentive listening, and communication. By modelling and guiding the development of these skills, educators support students in collaborating effectively and resolving conflicts as they arise.

Try This: Community Circles
Whether students are seated in a physical circle or simply gathered in a space for open sharing, well-facilitated community circles help build trusting classroom communities. Start by co-creating norms that support respectful sharing around topics that matter to students. Explicitly teach attentive listening skills: being fully present, using verbal and nonverbal cues to show interest, and reflecting back to ensure understanding. Tools like a talking piece can help ensure that every student has a turn to speak. Use community circles to address classroom issues, explore student ideas, or collectively solve problems as they arise. Begin with low-stakes prompts (e.g., *What's your favorite movie, color, or season?*) to give students a chance to build confidence and practice the skills before moving into deeper conversations.

Voice from the Field

Empowering students through student-led clubs is one way I nurture voice and leadership. When a student brings me an idea—regardless of their age—I support them in drafting a proposal to present to the principal. It's a meaningful way to ensure they feel seen, heard, and valued as contributors to our school community. Despite the weight they may carry, students light up when their voices are centred. Their energy shifts from being viewed through a deficit lens to being recognized for their talents and gifts. This year alone, several student-led clubs have launched: a skill-building soccer club, crochet and art clubs, a bike safety group, and LEGO and robotics clubs—each initiated by students and supported by teachers. Clubs and extracurriculars aren't extra; they're deeply connected to student learning. They offer authentic spaces for developing competencies like collaboration, communication, critical thinking, and leadership in real-world contexts.

When educators observe students in different settings, we gain insight into their strengths and passions, insight that can shape our daily teaching. When we intentionally connect these experiences to our broader educational vision, we foster belonging, deepen engagement, and create inclusive spaces where every learner can thrive. By valuing what happens beyond the classroom, we strengthen what happens within it.
— Beth, Special education teacher

Centre Joy in Teaching

In equity work, it is often easy to become entrenched in the narratives of suffering. We are exposed to students' horrifying experiences of racism and discrimination, communities immobilized by poverty, individuals carrying the weight of trauma, the scars left by war, and/or the displacements that have reshaped entire populations. This focus on harm can be overwhelming, and you may wonder:

How can I possibly centre joy in the midst of such deep, present suffering? Does focusing on joy somehow diminish the urgency to address the biases and deficit-ideology that exist about (certain) students? Does it not risk distracting us from the critical work of dismantling systems of oppression and supporting those most affected?

In *Unearthing Joy* (2022), Gholdy Muhammad introduces us to the idea that joy is not a luxury but a necessary component of resistance and survival. She argues that in order to engage in equity work meaningfully, we must not ignore the need for joy—especially for those students who have historically been, and are currently, denied it. Muhammad frames joy as a form of resistance to oppressive forces, a way to reclaim agency and humanity. This idea of joy is not about ignoring suffering, but rather about recognizing that joy and struggle work in tandem.

Let's explore how one educator centres joy as a catalyst for his work with students:

Voice from the Field

In my history classroom, students often find both curiosity and joy for topics that they can connect to personally. The simplest facts embedded in more complex and nuanced stories can build bridges between the past and present, and across many identities. I situate the story of The Persons' Case (1929) around the "pink teas" of suffragettes from the Famous 5. And so we reflect on what can be discussed and accomplished over tea, which so many of us can connect to (including me having tea with my Aunties). This act crosses many cultures. But we also reflect on what is lost when we consider those who weren't invited to the Famous 5's kitchen table. Members of the Famous 5 were known eugenicists, openly anti-Indigenous and racist. We connect to their humanity through tea, and reflect on their history from our own perspectives and identities today.
— Ian, Secondary school teacher

> Ian, reflecting on his queerness, knows from personal experience how much more joyful learning is when your identity is affirmed.

Affirming Identity

Choose texts, lessons, and activities that affirm students' identities; replace deficit narratives with narratives that provide a more expansive portrayal of their history, resistance, perseverance, contributions, and brilliance.

Try This

- A Human Library: Students explore a variety of content creators from diverse identities, highlighting specific topics of focus. Curate a variety of TikTok or Instagram clips from these content creators following specific curriculum connections, themes, etc. (e.g., culturally responsive mental health, heroes and heroines of WWI, environmental student activism, etc.). Create QR Codes for each clip. Students have the opportunity for self-directed learning and for exploring independently.
- Affinity Groups: Become a staff rep for your school's affinity space and/or support students interested in starting their own. In many places, school boards are required to have Gender and Sexuality Alliances (GSA). These are student-led clubs aim to create a safe, welcoming, and accepting environment for all students, regardless of their sexual orientation or gender identity. Other affinity groups, such as Black Student Alliances (BSA) or Muslim

Student Alliances (MSA), seek to affirm Black and Muslim identities. As an educator, volunteering to be a staff representative for such spaces allows you to witness the power of student leadership, while contributing, with intentionality, to supporting spaces that are diverse and inclusive.

Building In Joy

- Embed opportunities for critical inquiry that link intellectual development with a sense of hope, purpose, and possibility.
- Foster Creativity: Make space for artistic expression, storytelling, and student-led projects that ignite imagination and allow students to express themselves authentically.
- Celebrate Success: Build a culture of recognition by celebrating learning milestones and everyday victories.
- Model and Share Joy: Bring your own passions, curiosity, and optimism into the classroom to inspire students to do the same.

Putting It All Together

We have explored what being intentional about diversity, equity, and inclusion looks like when we are intentional about our *why*, when we create and sustain inclusive communities, and when we centre joy. But these do not need to be distinct and separate from each other. Let's take a look at the holistic nature of intentionality about DEI in action.

> **STORY FROM THE CLASSROOM**
>
> ### The *Why*
>
> Tanesha is a primary teacher whose why is centred in the belief that affirming identity is foundational to well-being and academic engagement. Her students came from linguistically and culturally diverse backgrounds. As the year began, she observed that some students hesitated to say their names confidently or would anglicize them. She wondered if it was perhaps out of discomfort or habit. Her observation and her belief in affirming student identity prompted her to design a unit that sought to restore the confidence and power of students in their names. Aligned with the Grade 3 curriculum expectations around oral communication, community, and understanding of self and others, her Our Names, Our Stories unit became an avenue for community-building, student affirmation, and joy.
> - What signals in your classroom tell you a student might feel invisible or unsure about sharing who they are?
> - How do you intentionally make space for every student's identity to be affirmed?
>
> ### The Community
>
> Tanesha began with a read-aloud of *Your Name Is a Song* by Jamilah Thompkins-Bigelow. The book sparked a rich discussion about how names carry history, meaning, and culture. Over the week, students engaged in the following activities:

- Interviewed family members about the origins or stories behind their names.
- Practiced saying each other's names correctly and respectfully.
- Created art pieces that visually represented their names using colors, textures, or symbols that reflected their culture or personality.
- Wrote short I Am From poems inspired by their names and identities.

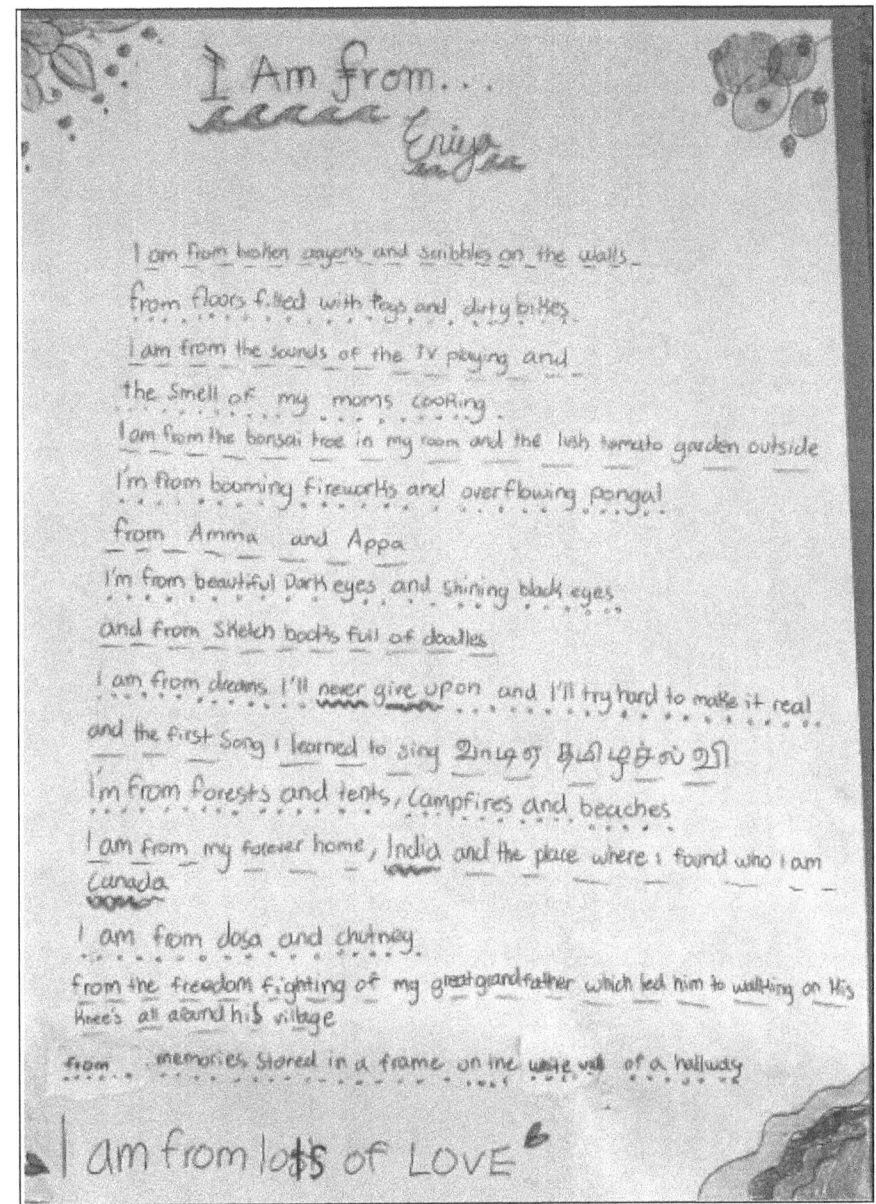

The classroom was transformed into a gallery called The Name Wall, where families were invited to see their children's work during a community celebration. The poems were also compiled and published creating a personal class book, with the students being the authors.

- How do you involve families in your classroom community?
- In what ways can students take ownership of their learning and lead?

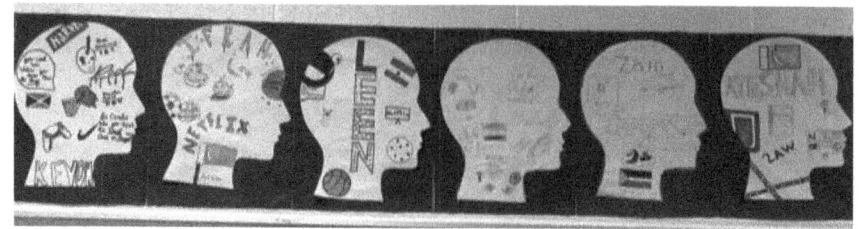

The Joy

Students glowed with pride as they shared their name stories. A student named Mahad said, "I used to think my name was hard, but now I think it's powerful." Other students noticed that their peers were more careful about pronouncing names correctly, making the classroom feel safer. Parents expressed gratitude, noting how their children came home more confident and curious about their heritage. Honoring each student's name led to stronger relationships, deeper learning, and a joyful celebration of who they are.

- When have you seen students light up with pride or confidence in your class?
- How can celebration and creativity be part of how you approach DEI work?

Try This

- Choose a book that centres on diverse identities (e.g., *The Name Jar; Big Ideas for Little Philosophers: Identity; I Am Enough; The Day You Begin*).
- Co-create classroom agreements/expectations about respect and curiosity around differences.
- Launch a small project (e.g., identity poems, family interviews, etc.) where students can lead and teach.
- Create a reflective space: journals, gallery walls, or video interviews that make student voices visible and lasting.

STORY FROM THE CLASSROOM

The *Why*

Erin, an intermediate classroom teacher, reflects on her why and how she used community gardens to fuel student (experiential) learning, well-being, and community building:

> For myself, this experience was rooted in ideologies and movements that live in the intersections of human rights, equity, community, stewardship, sustainability, and food sovereignty.

Erin engaged her Grade 7 students in an experiential learning project that found itself expanding beyond her classroom, as it included every student and engaged community (i.e., parents/guardians, caregivers, community resources and organizations).

- How might projects like this be used to address or challenge systemic inequities (e.g., food sovereignty)?
- How do you invite students from all identities to contribute meaningfully?

The Community

This experiential learning project was cross-curricular and drew on the Grade 7 Mathematics curriculum expectation, particularly Data Management and Probability and Measurement. Because the math was relevant to and connected to the garden—measurement, calculating and ordering volume of soil needed for the beds, etc.—there was a direct positive impact on math engagement and achievement through the program for all students.

In the beginning, students
- Designed their ideal garden space, used measuring tools to determine the area of the garden, and decided to conduct a school-wide survey to solicit what the garden should grow.
- Collected the data from the younger students they would survey, interpreted the data collection, and displayed their results.
- Attended after-school math support (for students who could benefit).

When it came time to build the garden beds, the class drew on the support of the community and gathered on a Saturday to build garden beds. Communication to families went out in different languages, and boxes varied in height to ensure accessibility. The support of interpreters was enlisted to access the wealth of knowledge across cultures and countries. Students and families were engaged to establish a summer watering schedule, and because students from other classes were included in various ways, students were invested in supporting the summer water schedule. Older students worked with younger students to transplant seedlings and care for the garden. Gardens were labelled in multiple languages, reflecting the languages spoken among students.

- How do you reflect and affirm the diverse cultural and ecological knowledge of your school community?
- How do you make space for interdependence, rather than individual achievement, in how students work and learn together?

The Joy

As the garden moved into the harvest season, students were able to make connections and celebrate successes. They captured their learning in traditional ways (school activities and lessons) and exciting ways (being featured in the community newspaper). Students worked with a sustainability chef to learn how to make food products from the harvest (e.g., sauces and jams), and celebrated the harvest by selling the homemade jams and ketchup.

- How are students given room to express themselves creatively (e.g., art, storytelling, food, music)?
- What moments of joy do you observe from your lessons that affirm student identity?

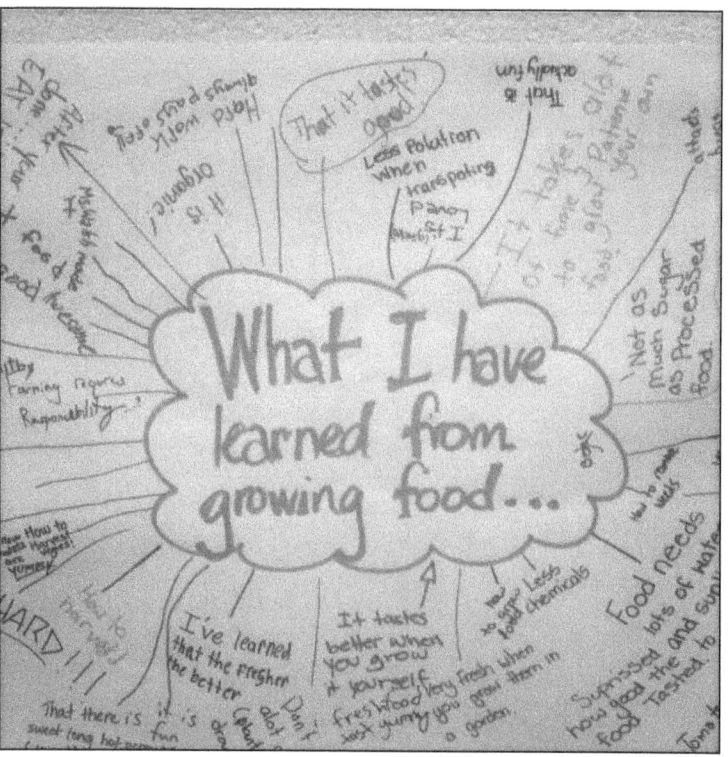

Try This

- Choose a project that is meaningful to students, and connects land, community, and identity. Examples: food insecurity, global citizenship, sustainability, etc.
- Solicit the skills, talents, and gifts of parents/guardians. Invite them to learn alongside their child(ren). Avoid making assumptions of what skills parents possess because of the community you are in or the work that they do.
- Document and celebrate throughout the journey. Capture students' experiences.

Final Thoughts

As educators committed to justice and equity, our work must be rooted in intentionality—purposefully centring diversity, equity, and inclusion in all aspects of our practice. This begins with knowing your *why*: understanding the deep motivations and values that ground your work. Clarifying your *why* keeps the focus on the students and communities you serve, guiding the design of lessons and interactions that truly reflect and honor their identities, experiences, and needs. It helps prevent teaching from becoming a checklist of strategies and, instead, shapes it as a deliberate act of care and justice.

The second vital component is to create community—to build and sustain trusting, affirming spaces where every student feels seen, heard, valued, and respected. Community-building is more than social connection; it is the foundation of belonging that allows students to bring their full selves into the classroom. When students experience genuine relationships and feel safe to share their identities and stories, they develop the confidence to engage deeply and collaboratively in learning.

Finally, we must centre joy in our teaching practice. Before there was struggle or hardship, there was joy, and joy is a powerful force for healing, growth, and strength. Designing lessons that invite students to experience joy—from discovery, creativity, connection, and self-expression—does more than energize their learning; it cultivates and expands the unique gifts and talents each student brings. When joy is at the heart of education, students move beyond surviving to thriving, and classrooms become vibrant, inclusive spaces where equity and diversity are not just goals but lived realities.

By weaving together these three pillars—knowing our *why*, creating community, and centring joy—we engage in equity work that is purposeful, relational, and life-giving, nurturing not only academic growth but the whole learner.

8

Cultivating, Sustaining, Protecting, and Celebrating Joy in Our Classrooms

Tanitiã Munroe

Tanitiã Munroe is a Black Queer scholar whose research focuses on the educational experiences of African, Afro-Caribbean, and Black youth in Canada. She holds a PhD from OISE, University of Toronto, and works as a Senior Research Coordinator with the Toronto District School Board (TDSB) and adjunct professor at Toronto Metroplitan University (TMU). In 2023, she received the Viola Desmond Award.

See Campbell (2022)

Let's be honest—when students walk into your classroom, you want them to feel it: this is a place where they're safe, where they matter, and where learning can actually feel joyful. That joy isn't just something extra. It's essential. It helps students take academic risks, build confidence, and connect meaningfully with what they're learning—and with each other.

For Black students, joy in school carries even deeper meaning. It's not only about engagement or enjoyment. It's about healing, being seen, and resisting the harmful messages they too often receive in and out of school. Dr. Kamshia Childs calls this "cultivating an environment of Black J.O.Y."—Jubilantly creating Opportunities for You. It's a framework that speaks directly to what it means to uplift students by affirming who they are, where they come from, and what they bring.

At the same time, joy isn't just for some students. Every child—whether Black, Indigenous, racialized, 2SLGBTQIAP+, neurodivergent, living with disabilities, or navigating multiple identities—deserves to feel joy in their learning. Our job as educators is to create spaces where that joy is possible for all.

That's what this chapter is about. Grounded in research and lived experience, it offers four key pillars for building and sustaining joyful classrooms that centre identity, belonging, and student voice:

- Cultivating: Laying the foundation by building trust, celebrating students' strengths, and designing learning that reflects who they are.
- Sustaining: Embedding joy into daily routines—even in times of stress—through affirming practices, rich storytelling, and meaningful engagement.
- Protecting: Actively safeguarding joy from bias, harm, and exclusion by creating a classroom culture that prioritizes care and healing.
- Celebrating: Honoring growth, excellence, and identity through rituals, creative expression, and community connection.

You'll notice that many examples in this chapter focus on Black students and cultural experiences. That's intentional. Uplifting Black joy in school is part of the work of equity. But the strategies you'll find here are meant to inspire joy for every learner. By centring students' lived realities and valuing the full diversity of their identities, you create a classroom where all students—especially those historically pushed to the margins—can flourish.

This isn't about perfection or adding more to your plate. It's about shifting the way we see teaching and learning. When we centre joy—not just as a feeling but as a practice—we transform school into a place where students aren't just surviving. They're thriving.

Cultivating JOY: Foundations of Inclusive Practice

Joyful classrooms don't just happen—they're grown. They're planted in trust, rooted in relationship, and nurtured through daily choices that reflect who your students are, what they value, and how they learn best. For Black students—and for many others navigating race, identity, or systemic barriers—school hasn't always felt like a place of joy. But we know that when students see themselves reflected, when they feel emotionally safe, and when their strengths are recognized, everything shifts. Joy becomes possible.

While all students benefit from joyful, affirming learning environments, we must also recognize that for many students, joy in school has been rare—not because they don't carry joy within them, but because the system too often suppresses or overlooks it. Our job is to change that. Educators like Gloria Ladson-Billings and Geneva Gay remind us that when we validate students' cultural knowledge, we don't just include them—we empower them. Carl James encourages us to look closely at how school systems affect racialized students and challenges us to build classrooms that affirm rather than erase. bell hooks calls this work "education as the practice of freedom"—teaching in a way that invites students to show up fully. And more recently, Dr. Kamshia Childs has emphasized how joy itself can be a powerful force for equity, healing, and hope.

So, what does cultivating joy really look like in practice? It starts with creating environments where students feel safe to be themselves—and where their identities, cultures, and lived experiences are welcomed, not silenced.

Creating a Welcoming and Inclusive Environment

Classroom climate sets the tone for everything. When students walk into your room and feel emotionally safe, seen, and respected, they're more open to learning. And when the classroom reflects their identities—visually, emotionally, and intellectually—that's where joy starts to grow. Here are a few ways to make that happen:
- Set up your space intentionally. Include student work, multicultural art, family photos (with permission), and identity walls. These send a clear message: *You belong here.*
- Build community agreements together. Instead of setting rules, co-create shared values and expectations. Invite students to define what kindness, care, and respect look like in your space.
- Include joy in the rhythm of your day. Start class with a gratitude moment. End the week with a celebration circle. Create rituals that make students feel seen and appreciated—especially those who might not always feel that way at school.

- Research (Fredrickson, 2001; Pianta & Hamre, 2009) shows that joy, pride, and curiosity don't just make students feel good—they actually help them think better, connect deeper, and bounce back stronger. Even quick micro-moments like a class cheer, a dance break, or a student shout-out can build an emotional tone that invites learning and reduces anxiety.

Teaching with Intention and Joy

Joy doesn't mean letting go of rigor. It means helping students love the process—even when it's hard. That comes from choice, creativity, and connection. You might try
- Project-based learning with a personal lens. Let students explore issues that matter to them or their communities.
- Arts-infused approaches. Use music, drama, storytelling, or visual art to deepen understanding. These offer students new ways to express themselves, especially those who might not connect with traditional formats.
- Celebrating mistakes. Make room for what bell hooks calls "engaged pedagogy"—teaching that's relational, not transactional. Share your own learning curves and invite students to see setbacks as part of the journey.

When you let students co-create, choose topics, and share their work in ways that reflect who they are, you're not just teaching content—you're building confidence, voice, and joy.

STORY FROM THE CLASSROOM

Memory Monday

In Ms. Reid's Grade 5 class, Mondays became the best day of the week. Every Monday, students were invited to share a family story, tradition, or object that brought them joy. For the first Memory Monday, Ms. Reid's grandmother brought in a hand-stitched quilt from Trinidad, full of color, history, and celebration. She shared stories of Carnival, music, and meals under the palm trees. One quiet student raised her hand to ask a question. Another started sketching a float from memory. By the end of the day, students had created podcasts, drawings, and short plays inspired by the quilt's imagery and the stories behind it. What started as a fabric square became a day of identity, learning, and connection.
- How can you bring family voices or community artifacts into your teaching?
- What projects might let students explore their identities and cultures in creative ways?
- What regular routines—big or small—could help you centre joy each week?
- How does your physical classroom reflect the diversity of the students who learn in it?

When we commit to cultivating joy in our classrooms, we do more than create a positive environment—we build a foundation for students to feel valued, connected, and capable. For students whose experiences have too often been shaped by deficit thinking or invisibility, joy becomes a powerful form of affirmation.

It says: you are not only seen—you are celebrated. Cultivating joy isn't for only some students. Every learner—regardless of background, identity, or ability—deserves to feel that their presence matters and their contributions count. Joy shows up when students can share their stories, take risks without fear, and find themselves reflected in what they learn.

The Memory Monday story reminds us that one intentional moment—one quilt, one story, one invitation to share—can open up space for deep engagement, connection, and belonging. These aren't add-ons to our teaching. They're essential practices that shape how students experience school—and how they see themselves within it. To cultivate joy is to create a classroom where students can laugh, wonder, explore, and take pride in who they are and what they know. It's an everyday commitment to building learning spaces where joy isn't rare—it's expected.

Sustaining JOY: Ongoing Practices for Joyful Learning

Sustaining joy in the classroom is not about one-off celebrations or feel-good moments. It's a daily, intentional practice. When joy is consistently woven into routines, relationships, and instruction, students feel seen, supported, and motivated. For Black students in particular, joy can be a powerful counter to the daily microaggressions, deficit narratives, and structural inequities they face. Yet cultivating joy should never be exclusive. Every student—regardless of their background, learning style, or lived experience—deserves a classroom that supports emotional safety, meaningful engagement, and a deep sense of belonging. When joy is made visible and sustainable, school becomes a space where identity, excellence, and connection thrive together.

As an educator, you have the opportunity to make joy a consistent part of your classroom culture—not just for some students, but for every learner who walks through your door.

Scholars, such as bell hooks (1994), Gholdy Muhammad (2020), and Mary Tichavakunda (2022), emphasize that sustained joy is not separate from academic success—it drives it. Joy reinforces critical thinking, nurtures resilience, and fosters deep, authentic engagement. When we build routines that honor students' cultures, uplift their voices, and value their presence, we are creating the conditions for long-term learning and well-being.

Embedding Joy into Daily Routines

Routines are powerful. They shape the classroom climate and send clear signals about what—and who—is valued. When joy is part of the daily rhythm, it shifts how students show up. Here are four simple, flexible routines that invite joy into your day:

Quick tip: Keep these under five minutes—they're small in time, big in impact.

Ritual or Routine	**Core Practice**	**Purpose**
Joyful Shares	Weekly student-led presentations of a cultural artifact, song, or family story linked to current lessons.	Validates identity, builds public speaking skills, and connects learning to life.

Affirmation Circles	A five-minute morning round in which peers celebrate nongrade-based achievements.	Normalizes public praise, fosters empathy, and builds community.
Joy Anchors	Start the day or class with a story, poem, or song reflecting student culture.	Sets a joyful tone and centres cultural pride.
Mindful Gratitude Pauses	Post-recess breathing exercise followed by a class Gratitude Spark posted on a communal board.	Regulates stress and centres communal appreciation.

When these routines reflect the diverse identities, cultures, and strengths of your students, they send a powerful message: your joy is essential here.

Continuous Professional Growth

Sustaining joy for students means sustaining it among educators, too. When teachers have space to reflect, grow, and collaborate, joy becomes a shared practice, not an individual effort.

> **STORY FROM THE CLASSROOM**
>
> At Ubuntu Elementary, Principal Ayanna Taylor launched quarterly Joy Clinics, where staff explored culturally responsive pedagogy, co-designed identity-affirming lessons, and shared joyful moments from their classrooms. Monthly Joy Walks encouraged teachers to visit one another's classrooms, looking for *joy cues* like laughter, curiosity, and connection. These brief, focused observations led to simple but meaningful adjustments—like opening math with a song or using humor to ease student anxiety. The school's digital Joy Journal, originally a shared Google Doc, became a hub of inspiration. Teachers posted gratitude shout-outs, student poetry clips, and joyful classroom hacks. Each entry celebrated not only the students' growth, but the educators' shared commitment to making joy an everyday occurrence.
>
> The results spoke volumes: absenteeism dropped, engagement rose, and staff retention improved. One student said it best: "We don't want to miss school because joy lives here."
> - How do you currently work with other educators—at your school and beyond?
> - What practices might be put in place to collaborate with your peers in sustaining joyful learning for students and teachers alike?

Feedback and Adaptive Strategies

Sustaining joy requires listening. Students and families are essential sources of feedback about what's working and what's not. Here are a few low-effort, high-impact strategies:

- Student Pulse Checks: One-minute exit slips asking students what lifted their mood, what felt frustrating, and what they'd like more of.
- Family Voice Notes: Invite caregivers to send short voice memos or notes about what their child has enjoyed or struggled with.
- Joy Data Wall: Create a simple visual tracker for students to mark their emotional energy or engagement, giving insight into patterns and needed shifts.

These tools help you adapt routines to meet the evolving needs of your learners. When students and families see their input shaping the classroom, trust deepens—and joy becomes more sustainable.

Long-Term Impact on Learning and Well-Being

Research and real-world practice show that sustained joy drives powerful outcomes:

- Improved Attendance: Students are more likely to show up when joy is part of their school experience.
- Academic Gains: Joyful engagement fuels deeper comprehension, creativity, and critical thinking.
- Greater Resilience: Students exposed to affirming routines and culturally relevant content report stronger coping skills and self-worth.
- Staff Well-Being: When joy is shared, teachers feel more connected, more motivated, and less isolated.

The ripple effects of joy are real. They're visible, not just in data points, but also in hallway smiles, confident presentations, and students who begin to see school as a place of possibility, not pressure.

Sustaining joy in the classroom is about more than maintaining good energy—it's about nurturing a learning culture rooted in care, curiosity, and connection. For students navigating systemic barriers, daily joy is a radical invitation to feel safe, affirmed, and powerful. But ultimately, joy benefits everyone. It transforms school from a place students have to be into a place they want to be. By embedding joyful routines, listening closely to students and families, and investing in educator growth, we ensure that joy isn't a one-time experience—it's a way of being. As educators, you are not just facilitators of learning; you are cultivators of joy, and that work shapes futures. And when joy is sustained, learning is too.

Protecting JOY: Addressing Systemic Challenges

Protecting joy in your classroom means doing more than celebrating students during special months or reacting to harm when it happens. It means taking intentional, ongoing action to create conditions where all students feel safe, valued, and supported every day. For too many, school has been a place of correction rather than connection, of compliance instead of care. As educators, we have the power to change that.

To protect joy, we must first acknowledge the systems that often stand in its way. Dr. Bettina Love (2019) calls on us to adopt an abolitionist lens—treating joy not as a reward but as a right that must be defended through both daily routines and school-wide policies. Dr. Shawn Ginwright (2018) challenges us to go beyond trauma-informed practices toward healing-centred engagement, where collective well-being and cultural affirmation are built into the foundation of our classrooms. And scholars like Ladson-Billings, Paris and Alim, and Baker-Bell remind us that curriculum, language, and pedagogy all play critical roles in either sustaining or suppressing student joy.

So what does protecting joy look like in practice? It starts by asking bold questions: *Whose stories are we telling? Whose voices are welcomed? Who feels safe to take risks, speak up, and be themselves in our spaces?* It continues through deliberate actions: from how we respond to conflict to how we design assignments, from how we use language to how we evaluate success.

Expanded Protective Strategies

The following strategies are rooted in affirming Black student joy, but they can be adapted to foster safety and belonging for all students in your classroom.

Strategy	Core Action	Why It Matters
Restorative Justice Circles	Use dialogue to repair harm and restore relationships.	Centres dignity over punishment; models accountability.
Healing-Centred Engagement	Incorporate breathing, music, and storytelling that reflect students' cultures.	Moves beyond *what's wrong?* to *what's possible?*; positions joy as healing.
Healing Check-Ins	Create space for students to share emotions or reflections.	Normalizes mental-health discourse; builds empathy and connection.
Afrocentric Curriculum Audits	Review content for accurate, affirming Black representation.	Counters erasure; ensures students see themselves reflected.
Linguistic Justice Practices	Honor Black/African Language in writing, discussion, and assessment.	Validates and affirms identity; challenges linguistic bias.
Culturally Sustaining/ Reality Pedagogies	Design learning that draws on students' lived experiences.	Connects learning to life; honors student culture as knowledge.

Mentorship Networks	Link students with educators and role models from their communities.	Builds identity, confidence, and connection.
Bias-Interruption Interventions	Train staff to recognize and address implicit bias in discipline.	Reduces exclusionary practices; strengthens belonging.
Policy Advocacy	Examine and revise school policies that disproportionately affect Black students.	Creates systemic conditions where joy can thrive.

STORY FROM THE CLASSROOM

Circle of Care in Practice

On a rainy Friday afternoon, Ms. Thompson gathered her Grade 10 students in a circle on bright cushions under murals of Black heroes. Holding a river stone talking piece, students took turns sharing—some about recent conflicts, others about sources of joy. Malik voiced frustration over a misunderstanding; Simone offered a sincere apology. What began as tension turned into trust. Over time, the Circle of Care became a regular space for healing, affirmation, and laughter. Participation went up. Referrals went down. And joy took root in new ways.

- How might restorative practices strengthen your classroom community?
- What rituals could help students process conflict and celebrate growth?
- How do your curriculum choices reflect and affirm the students in your classroom?

Joy is not fragile, but it can be neglected if we're not vigilant. Protecting joy is a collective responsibility. It means treating it like any other key indicator of student success. We track engagement. We respond to data. We adjust when something isn't working. Joy deserves the same level of intention.

Start by embedding joy into your school's daily fabric. Use student voice surveys and family check-ins to monitor emotional well-being. Train your staff to recognize and address bias. Build rituals and routines that reinforce healing, trust, and cultural celebration—not just when something goes wrong, but every day.

Leaders play a key role here, too. When principals prioritize joy in staff meetings, when district plans include joy as a strategic goal, and when professional learning time is devoted to healing practices, it signals that joy isn't extra, it's essential.

Finally, protecting joy goes beyond the walls of any single classroom. Partner with families, community leaders, and local organizations. Invite students to see themselves not only in the curriculum but in the leadership of their learning spaces. When young people hear consistent messages—from teachers, parents, and elders—that their voices matter and their stories belong, joy becomes not just possible, but powerful. To echo Bettina Love's words: When we ask, "How are the children?" let the answer be this: "They feel safe. They feel seen. And they feel free to dream."

Celebrating JOY: Amplifying Success and Identity

Celebrating joy in schools is not a one-off event; it's a transformative approach to teaching rooted in relationships, cultural affirmation, and collective empowerment. While this section centres Black joy, the practices outlined here are powerful for all students, particularly those who have been marginalized or left unseen in traditional classrooms. When you celebrate students not just for performance but for who they are, joy becomes a source of motivation, pride, and connection. Grounded in culturally relevant and responsive pedagogy, you are invited to become a "gardener of joy," tending to your students' emotional soil so their intellectual and cultural strengths can flourish. Rita Pierson's famous words, "No significant learning can occur without a significant relationship," remind us that celebrating joy starts with connection.

Cultivate Through Connection

To celebrate your students, start by getting to know them deeply. Build genuine relationships rooted in trust and mutual respect.
- Joyful Circles: Begin or end your week with short gatherings where students share strengths, family stories, or creative sparks. These moments build connection and offer space for affirmation.
- Relationship-Building Routines: Use student surveys, I Am From poems, or casual check-ins to better understand your students' experiences and interests.
- Playful Engagement: Bring joy into learning through routines like Wonder Wednesdays or quick games that allow students to take risks, laugh, and learn.

Sustain With Cultural Wealth

Make celebration part of your curriculum, not just your classroom culture.
- Cultural Traditions in Content: Use quilting to teach geometry or explore local community leaders in social studies. Show students how their communities are sources of wisdom.
- Student-Designed Projects: Invite students to co-create assignments that reflect their identities using frameworks like Identity, Skills, Intellectualism, and Criticality.

Protect Through Restorative Practice and Championing

Celebrating joy also means shielding it from policies and practices that undermine student dignity.
- Restorative Covenants: Work with your students to co-create classroom agreements that centre care, accountability, and healing.
- Champion Logs: Keep a running list of each student's successes, big and small. Share encouragement regularly through notes, one-on-one conversations, or small gestures of recognition.

Celebrate as Curriculum and Ritual

Let joy take centre stage through meaningful, visible celebrations that affirm identity and achievement.

- Student-Led Showcases: Host monthly exhibitions where students present on innovators or change-makers from their communities.
- Creative Exhibitions: Display student art, writing, or performances through hallway galleries, classroom stages, or online platforms.
- Cultural Heritage Events: Celebrate days or months that reflect your students' diverse backgrounds; e.g., Emancipation Day, Caribbean Heritage Month, African Heritage Month.
- Reflective Portfolios: Encourage students to document their growth through portfolios that combine academic achievements with identity reflections.
- Community Connections: Invite families and local artists to participate in classroom life through storytelling, performances, or collaborative projects.
- Digital Affirmation: Use classroom hashtags or digital displays to highlight joyful moments and affirm students' collective power.

Questions for Reflection

- How will you "garden" relationships before content, ensuring every student feels celebrated?
- In what ways can you co-construct covenants that protect joy through restorative care?
- Which routines or rituals will you use to weave cultivation, protection, and celebration into your teaching?
- How might you leverage your students' cultural wealth to sustain a curriculum of joyful rigor?
- What practices—like peer observations or reflective journals—will help you refine your joy-centred teaching over time?

While this work centres Black joy as a starting point, it offers a broader blueprint for inclusive teaching that lifts up all students.

When you embed joy into the fabric of school life, your classroom becomes more than a site of instruction—it becomes a space of equity, healing, and possibility. By cultivating trust, sustaining students' cultural wealth, protecting joy through restorative care, and celebrating through intentional rituals, you affirm the full humanity of every learner. Your role as a "gardener of joy" and a champion of identity holds the potential to transform not just academic outcomes, but also lives. In schools where joy is nurtured, students are not only known and valued—they are empowered to flourish.

Voices from the Field: Practicing Joy Daily

When we began our first Joy Clinic, I told my staff: "This isn't another initiative—it's a commitment to how we show up for our students every day." Joy became our through line. Now, when I walk through the halls, I don't just hear lessons—I hear laughter, curiosity, and care. That's what tells me we're doing something right.
— Ayanna Taylor, Principal, Ubuntu Elementary School

I used to feel like joy was something that had to wait until after the real learning. Now I build it into everything—our math games, our morning messages, our class

playlists. It's made a huge difference. My students trust each other more. They take more risks. They show up with energy.
— Ms. Isabel Lopez, Grade 4 Teacher

We start each week with a Joyful Share—students bring in music, poetry, or stories that matter to them. At first, I thought only a few would participate. Now they're lining up to present. One student said, "It's the only time I feel like school is about me." That stuck with me. Joy is personal. And it's powerful.
— Mr. Jamal Brooks, Grade 7 Teacher

Student Voices: Joy in Their Own Words

> **My Joy Walks With Me**
> by a Grade 12 student
>
> My joy walks with me in the morning light,
> Braids tight, kicks clean, head held right.
> It's in the beat I hum on the bus,
> A tune my grandma taught to just us.
> It's in the hallway high-fives I get,
> The "You got this!" from my teacher's desk set.
> It's when I see myself in a hero's name,
> And the book doesn't treat my life like a shame.
> My joy's not loud, but it fills the air—
> A laugh, a look, a loc in my hair.
> You might miss it if you don't know the signs,
> But my joy's in the pauses, in the poems, in the lines.

> **This Classroom Feels Like Home**
> by a Grade 11 student
>
> We don't start class with silence,
> We start with sound—
> A beat, a bounce,
> Voices wrapping round the room
> Like arms.
> Our teacher asks real questions.
> Not just the "right answer" kind,
> But the kind that need my story.
> The kind that see my mind.
> We sit in circles,
> Not rows.
> We build something,
> Not just know it.
> And when I laugh too loud,
> Nobody flinches.
> They smile.
> This classroom feels like home.
> That's what joy does.

When you embed joy into the fabric of school life, your classroom becomes more than a site of instruction; it becomes a space of equity, healing, and possibility. By cultivating trust, sustaining students' cultural wealth, protecting joy through restorative care, and celebrating through intentional rituals, you affirm the full humanity of every learner.

In schools where joy is nurtured, students are not only known and valued—they are empowered to flourish. As scholars, such as bell hooks, Gholdy Muhammad, Bettina Love, Geneva Gay, and Gloria Ladson-Billings, teach us, joy in the classroom is not just emotional—it is educational, relational, and revolutionary. It is rooted in identity, sustained by culture, and protected by justice. When we cultivate joy intentionally, we honor our students' full humanity, including students whose identities intersect race, gender, disability, migration, language, and beyond. In doing so, we move closer to the promise of truly liberatory education.

Final Thoughts: Joy as Pedagogy, Practice, and Promise

> Centring Black joy in particular is not about exclusion; it is about redress. It is about ensuring that the histories, cultures, and contributions of Black students are not just included but also honored, not just acknowledged but also amplified. And in doing so, we create conditions where all students benefit—where the classroom becomes a site of shared humanity and collective uplift.

Joy is not a reward at the end of hard work. It is the work. It is the pulse of a liberated classroom, the heartbeat of belonging, and the anchor that holds students through challenge, growth, and transformation. When we teach with joy as our compass, we affirm that every child—especially those too often pushed to the margins—deserves to feel safe, seen, and celebrated in the learning space. Throughout this chapter, we've explored joy as more than an emotion. It is a foundation to be cultivated, a practice to be sustained, a right to be protected, and a brilliance to be celebrated. We've seen how joy supports academic achievement, nurtures identity, and fuels connection. We've learned from students, educators, and scholars who show us that joyful teaching is not soft or shallow; it is rigorous, reflective, and rooted in love.

> This is your invitation:
> To teach in a way that not only informs but transforms.
> To create classrooms where joy is not rare, but routine.
> To celebrate your students for who they are—not just what they produce.
> To treat joy as curriculum, as culture, and as a form of care.

You are not just an educator. You are a cultivator of joy. In your hands is the power to shape futures where students thrive, not in spite of who they are, but because every part of them is valued. Let joy guide you. Let it sustain you. Let it be the promise you keep every day you teach.

9

Creating and Sustaining Spaces of Belonging in Our Schools

Nancy Cargioli and Jaclynn Deveaux

Nancy Cargioli has been a teacher for 16 years. Grounded forever in the experiences collected through her years of working with students, she is committed to the goal of reimagining educational spaces that centre tenets of social justice through dismantling systemic barriers that place students at the margins.

Jaclynn Deveaux is a lifelong learner who began her career as an adult literacy and numeracy instructor working with vulnerable communities, before becoming an Ontario Certified Teacher. At the centre of her practice is a dedication to education as a space of love, truth, justice, and joy, where all students can thrive.

Feeling a sense of belonging is intrinsically tied to student success. Belonging can be defined as

> a component of agency in which students feel deeply connected to their school, classroom(s), peers, and teachers and can say, "I see myself, and I am seen and loved here." (Safir and Dugan, 2021, p. 229)

When students do not feel a sense of belonging, it affects their ability to thrive. Dr. Bettina Love notes that, when students feel welcomed and valued by teachers who genuinely listen to them, take up their concerns in their teaching, and make sure each voice in the classroom is heard, it sets the conditions for flourishing.

In order to create belonging, guiding principles centring students and their feelings of belonging must be embedded in your practice. Guiding principles set the conditions for the ways in which you teach, plan your lessons, and care for the students who are in front of you. Belonging in classrooms is much more than physical displays, such as posters that signal perceived inclusion. It is the ways in which teachers plan learning engagements that centre student voice and display vulnerability that make a real difference.

In Dr. Andrew B. Campbell's work on Fostering and Sustaining Intentional Spaces of Belonging, he identifies seven key elements of belonging:
- Connections
- Trust
- Inclusion
- Relationships
- Identity
- Safety
- Membership

From Andrew B. Campbell (2022, March 1)

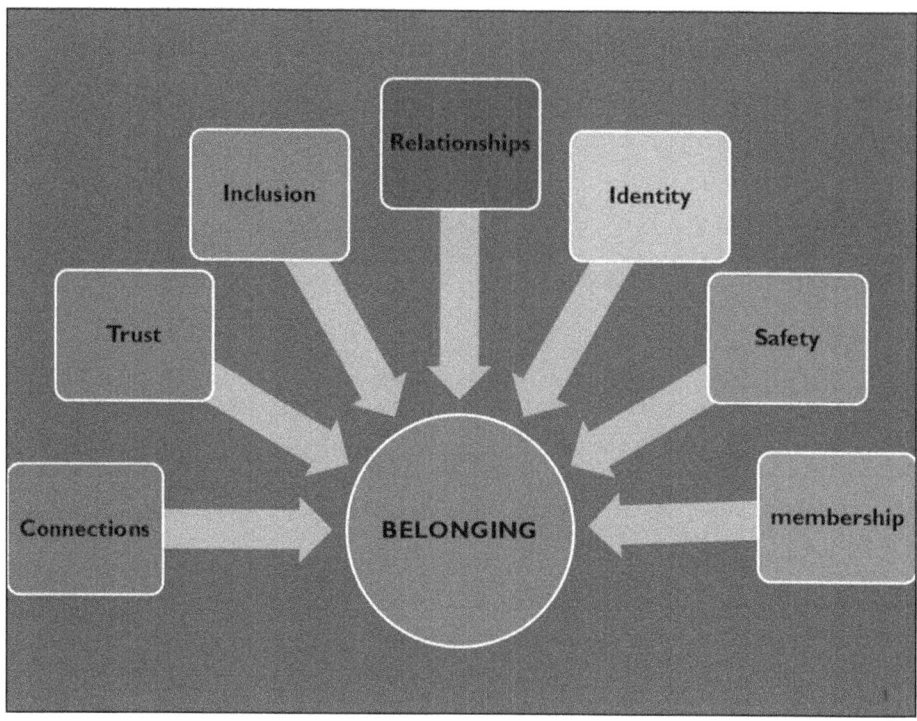

Caring adults who cultivate spaces of belonging empower students to resist the structures that push them to the margins; they hold space for students to reclaim space in classrooms, hallways, and programs; they offer opportunities for them to revitalize their sense of agency, and renew their sense of wonder, curiosity, and potential, so that they can truly flourish. As you reflect on your understanding of cultivating spaces of belonging, consider the following:

- What are the stories and traditions that your students bring?
- In what ways can you leverage the genius that each student brings with them into the classroom?
- How are the stories of your students' pasts and their ancestors accurately and authentically depicted and celebrated? In what ways do you make space to celebrate these stories with joy?
- In what ways do your classroom norms respond to student needs authentically?
- How do your students know that they are necessary contributors within your classroom space?

Cultivating and sustaining belonging requires acts of reimagining, reclamation, resistance, and revitalizing. We invite you to reimagine educational spaces rooted in principles of equity and anti-oppression, as places where all students can thrive, reclaim narratives surrounding the standards of identity, resist traditional Eurocentric models of education, and revitalize curriculum, assessment, teaching, and learning in ways that value varied ways of knowing and being.

> True spaces of belonging are a departure from traditional models of education. From the outside looking in, they could seem "messy" and undisciplined.

STORY FROM THE CLASSROOM

Letting Go of Control
by Nancy Cargioli

Belonging is and always has been paramount for me as an educator. Students need and want to feel a sense of belonging in classrooms that comes through authentic learning engagements that let them know their voice matters and they are collaborative contributors to the overall success of the class.

In my first few years of teaching I felt an incredible pressure to appear as though I had control over my classroom, which was deeply connected to colonial concepts of compliance. It was reinforced over time by the subtle ways colleagues pass judgment. Over time, I realized that control did not have to be compliance; rather, it could be the cultivation and sustaining of student agency. Embracing pedagogical concepts of inquiry-based learning allowed me to consider the ways in which student voice and choice connected to student identity, which ultimately supported and cultivated student agency.

Centring the voices of students in learning disrupts understandings of the traditional role of the teacher. Inquiry-based learning requires that teachers situate themselves as a co-learner among their students. This connects to Dr. Gloria Ladson-Billings' framework of Culturally Responsive and Relevant Pedagogy (CRRP) that asks teachers to leverage the cultural competence of students. Students bring invaluable understandings and perspectives that add to the richness of the learning environment.

This subtle but impactful shift of power dynamics, helped my students trust and feel more comfortable sharing and contributing to classroom discussions, and I immediately felt a sense of relief from the pressure to know it all. This approach is crucial when entering difficult conversations surrounding equity and inclusion.

There was no shortage of critical questions in my Grade 8 classroom. Regardless of my being determined to stick to curriculum, my students would find ways to bring conversations of equity and social justice into the classroom, because it was what they were interested in and what they were experiencing. Tenets of inquiry-based learning and CRRP provided a supportive approach to tackling these difficult but brave conversations.

- What has informed your understandings of classroom management?
- Reflect on control. What does this look like in the classroom? How does this affect students?
- How can cultivating a sense of agency in students shift power dynamics that affect classroom management?
- How can you cultivate agency in your classroom to enable every student to feel like a contributing member?

Identity and Inclusion

Caring for students requires valuing student identity that goes beyond surface level, valuing all aspects of each student's intersectional identities. Classrooms must be ready to receive students as they are, in their fullness. As you plan student learning engagements, in what ways have you considered the identities of students who experience barriers to inclusion?

Historically, educational spaces have not been sites of belonging for students at the margins, as a result of legacies of colonization that have helped determine what the standards of identity are. These standards tend to uphold principles of white supremacy, Eurocentricity, ableism, and patriarchy working together to form a dominant culture. When these standards are reinforced through curricula, resources, and policies; it can create and perpetuate conditions where students and families at the margins do not see themselves reflected and welcomed into education in authentic ways that respond to their lived realities.

When students hold aspects of their identity that do not fit into the dominant culture, they experience barriers to achievement and inclusion. As a caring teacher working to cultivate spaces of belonging, understanding which identities have not been centred in education is foundational. These include Indigenous, Black, and 2SLGBTQIA+ identities; those who are neurodiverse and differently abled; and those who experience socio-economic barriers. It takes courage to reimagine classrooms as spaces of belonging where students who have been pushed to the margins are brought to the centre through acts of radical love. Reimagining, however, doesn't have to be difficult. You are probably already doing this. When you centre student identities by bringing in a mentor text that offers a counternarrative, you are leaning into brave conversations. Consider using these mentor texts with your students:

Téo's Tutu by Maryann Jacob Macias

Not Quite Narwhal by Jessie Sima

Neither by Airlie Anderson

I Am Perfectly Designed by Karamo Brown

These are just some examples of the many mentor texts that teach students that they do not have to conform to societal standards. These books open up spaces for brave conversations that set the conditions for belonging in classrooms in age-appropriate ways.

Learning Engagement: What Makes You You?

As a follow-up to reading mentor texts centred in belonging, facilitate classroom discussions through posing the following reflective questions to build critical consciousness among students.

- *What are some of the things that make up your identity (who you are)? What do you love about you?*
- The many different parts of our identity make each of us unique. This is called *diversity. Why is diversity important?*
- Certain parts of our identity are perceived as having value and holding power. Society has determined that some identities hold more power than others, and these are granted *privilege. Why is this problematic? What power do we have to change that?*
- *In what aspects of your identity do you experience privilege?*
- *In what aspects of your identity do you experience barriers? What power do we have to change that?*
- *Why is it important to live in a world in which we all feel like we belong?*

Classroom Cultures that Cultivate Relationships

Aspects of belonging, such as feeling welcomed and valued, are not conditions that naturally occur. Creating these conditions takes time and effort. Making learning environments welcoming can begin with the physical setup of the classroom, such as creating welcoming bulletin boards, or the ways in which you interact with students, such as knowing and displaying student names, greeting students at the door, or even a special morning greeting or handshake as they enter. However, we need to go further and consider relationships as a key element of belonging and reflecting: *How are relationships cultivated and sustained beyond performative "box checking"?*

Social media have been effective in selling the story of what a welcoming classroom should look like, but does very little to illustrate welcoming conditions that go beyond superficial displays. While these visible examples are an important first step in fostering a sense of belonging, the real work takes place in the ways you take the time to know your students' stories, their histories, and their families. It lives in the opportunities you provide for them to showcase their gifts and talents. This work goes far deeper, and is often unnoticed at an initial glance, but its impact is authentic and is felt by students and their families.

Creating a sense of belonging includes knowing your students deeply through understanding their behavior and through recognizing and responding to subtle changes in action and engagement. This means validating all the ways in which your students communicate with you, including ways that have been traditionally labelled as "behavior." Noticing the varied manners in which students communicate with us can work as a compass, providing valuable information on ways to support students. This requires "rigorous attention to systemic racism, school and classroom cultures, and the micro-interactions that characterize a student's passage through the school day" (Safir and Dugan, 2021, p. 104).

STORY FROM THE CLASSROOM

Coat-Rack Conversations

by Jaclynn Deveaux

The first time I taught Grade 1, I deeply felt the pressure to ensure that students learned the routines and expectations associated with transitioning from full-day Kindergarten into a Grade 1 classroom. It took confidence and commitment to soften the dialogue—both from external sources and in my own head—that was telling me my students should sit still and quietly, all in one space. I knew that authentic learning didn't look like students sitting quietly in rows, or "crisscross applesauce" on the carpet, nor was this standard of behavior that would work for the little bodies that needed to move and wiggle, talk and laugh. The biggest learning for me that year wasn't how to be an outstanding teacher of Grade 1 content. It was that my meticulous classroom set-up, carefully curated classroom decor, and perceived notions of the need for students to conform to a standard set of student-like behaviors did little to foster belonging and community. I learned that I needed to move away from what I saw as standards of behavior in order to create a sense of safety that would allow students to be curious and take risks in their learning so that they could flourish.

> At the beginning of the school year, there was a student who would often arrive late, as the class was settling into our morning routine. This student's first act in my classroom was to hide under the coat-rack. Staff passing my classroom would ask if I needed help, and students were quick to point out that this student wasn't following the expectations.
>
> Instead of forcing this student into classroom routines, I gave them space while I started an activity with the rest of my students. When I had a moment, I'd sit under the coat-rack with this student and welcome them to class, ask how their morning was, tell them how happy I was to see them, let them know what the class was doing and that they could join us when they were ready. Initially, this student wouldn't say much but eventually they opened up.
>
> As many of us do, this student didn't feel good about arriving late to school, and often the first thing they heard upon entering the building was, "Late AGAIN? Tell your mom to leave earlier tomorrow." This interaction was regularly followed by similar comments from other staff or students as they navigated the hallways to class. By the time this six-year-old made it to my classroom, they felt ashamed to walk in and face their peers. Not only did I need to take measures to ensure that this student felt seen and welcomed each day within my classroom space, I also needed to lean into brave conversations with staff to ask that this student be greeted each day in a welcoming manner, no matter what time they arrived at school.
>
> With time and patience, the soft entry and gentle morning conversations had this student entering with confidence, a smile, and a loud "Bonjour!" that was returned enthusiastically by their peers. This student became confident in entering the room, knowing that they were valued, welcomed, loved, important, and supported, no matter what time they made it to school.
> - How do you define behavior?
> - In what ways might redefining behavior as communication shift inherent power imbalances and enable teachers to see students through an asset-based lens?
> - In what ways do you foster relationship and create a classroom culture that encourages communication in different ways?

Classrooms Centred in Safety

A critical step in cultivating spaces of belonging is having an understanding of the systemic issues within education that impose barriers on a student's ability to thrive. Historically, educational spaces were designed through a white-dominant patriarchal lens. Any identity outside these standards has been pushed to the margins. When you intentionally foster spaces of belonging for students at the margins, you are actively addressing systemic barriers inherent within education that continue to negatively affect students. These barriers exist and show up in policies, dress codes, bias and "curriculum violence" (Ighodaro, E., 2009). The evidence of systemic barriers is illustrated in data that demonstrates lower rates of positive well-being, higher push-out rates, disproportionalities in streaming and program access, and higher suspension rates for students at the margins (Ontario Human Rights Commission, 2024).

When you take time, as a caring educator, to understand the history of the system in which you work, it allows you to see the ways in which educational spaces have not been designed with every identity in mind and the harm experienced by students at the margins. Dr. Andrew Campbell identifies this impact as the element of safety. Students must feel a sense of safety in order to feel an authentic sense of belonging. Only when students feel safe can you enter into difficult but brave dialogue with them.

As you work toward cultivating and sustaining spaces of belonging that centre safety, it is important to prepare yourself to engage in conversations that unpack systemic issues. These are conversations that students might not have ever engaged in, but are necessary. As you reflect on your understanding of cultivating spaces of belonging, consider the following:

- It is important to provide students with historical truths and current realities of systemic inequities that exist, while also celebrating joy, beauty, and happiness within communities at the margins. In what ways can you share information on historical truths to build critical understanding, while also centring stories of joy to show the full spectrum of humanity from communities at the margins?
- Have you familiarized yourself with the protected grounds as identified by the Ontario Human Rights Commission?
- What understanding of social action, social justice, and activism do students have? Be aware that conversations at home or information presented in the media can lead to a deficit lens of activism (e.g., words such as *riot* and *futile*, concepts such as *what-about-ism*, etc.).
- Are there oppressions that educators are hesitant to confront within classrooms? What is the impact on students when educators avoid discussing certain world events, identities, or oppressions?
- Are you aware of what social change students would like to see in the classroom, in the world, and in humanity?

When planning learning engagements for students that open up brave conversations surrounding systemic inequities, consider the following texts:

This Book is Anti-Racist: 20 Lessons on How to Wake Up, Take Action, and Do The Work by Tiffany Jewell

When We Were Alone by David A. Robertson

Our Skin: A First Conversation About Race by Jessica Ralli and Megan Madison

The Boy with Flowers in His Hair by Jarvis

Learning Engagement: Understanding Barriers in Society

As a follow-up to reading mentor texts centred in belonging, facilitate classroom discussions by posing the following reflective questions to build critical consciousness among students.

- Long ago, the untrue story of race and gender created a hierarchy of humans that placed the race and gender of the dominant culture at the top, and any race or gender outside the dominant culture at the bottom. The impact of this is still experienced today. *Why is it important to learn this untrue story of race and gender?*
- *Why is it important to ensure our learning spaces are free of discriminatory, racist, homophobic, and ableist language?*

- Words and images have a strong influence on our emotions, thoughts, and actions. Words have power. Words have impact. Words can be used to uplift, or they can be used to dehumanize. The history of discriminatory words is tied to oppression. *What is the impact of hearing dehumanizing words? What is the impact of hearing affirming words? What are some words of affirmation we can use with our classmates?*

Sustaining Spaces of Belonging

In his keynote, Creating, Fostering and Sustaining Intentional Spaces of Belonging, Dr. Campbell asks us to consider *Who determines who belongs?* and, more importantly, *Who gets to determine that learning environments espouse belonging?* Would school trustees, system leaders, school administrators, and classroom teachers and support staff be best positioned to make this determination? Or would we ask students and their families? Leaning into student voice and responding in effective ways "gives us a ground-level view of the ways in which children are included, excluded, marginalized, or just plain invisible in their learning environments" (Safir and Dugan, 2021, p. 104).

Belonging is a feeling. It is an experience, and so the answer can come only from those directly affected. When you ask students and their families about their experience in schooling, you foster connection and inclusion, key elements in sustaining belonging. In what ways are you including student and family voice to inform your instruction?

We can't say that everyone belongs when some don't. Purposefully cultivating spaces of belonging that centre impact on Indigenous, Black, 2SLGBTQIA+, neurodiverse, and differently abled students, and those who are the most affected by systemic barriers, is paramount in sustaining spaces of belonging. Exclusionary practices have been entrenched in the culture of schools, imposing barriers, both intentionally and unintentionally, on students. Classroom and school spaces designed without accessible ramps, automatic door openers, and accessible elevators impose clear barriers to accessing educational spaces. The physical design of schools in many ways is a clear indication of who belongs and who does not. But what about the intangible barriers? School board policies such as dress codes and codes of conduct continue to erode belonging through exclusionary practices. Restrictive dress codes reinforce gender stereotypes and limit cultural and religious expression. It is important that you continue to consider what other policies and practices impose restrictions and barriers that are invisible to the larger, dominant culture.

As an educator, what is within your sphere of influence? The Universal Design for Learning is a pedagogical approach developed by researchers Dr. David Rose and Dr. Anne Meyer as a way to centre belonging through a lens of equity. When you teach in a manner that centres the most marginalized identity in your classroom, every student will benefit by default. This offers the case for equity. When you centre the student or students experiencing the harshest barriers and work to remove these barriers, you are fostering inclusion.

Pedagogical approaches within education, such as the Universal Design for Learning (UDL), Culturally Responsive and Relevant Pedagogy (CRRP), and inquiry-based learning, increase student engagement and sustain spaces of belonging. Teachers can do this work within classrooms through the following practices:

> Sustaining spaces of belonging is predicated on knowing the identities of the students within your space and responding to the factors that impact their sense of belonging.

Critical Examination of Resources
- Which identities appear most often in resources that support the curriculum? More importantly, which identities are under-represented or missing completely?
- In what ways are these identities reflected? Do they centre contributions, joy, and accomplishment while also telling historical truths? Or do they perpetuate a deficit perspective or singular story centred in trauma or challenge?

Culture of Classrooms
- In what ways are students encouraged to leverage the genius of their cultural and individual expression, gifts, and talents?
- Are oral, artistic, and kinesthetic expressions of knowledge, skills, and understandings valued to the same degree as written composition?

Critical Examination of Hallways, Displays, and Decor
- Which identities appear in school hallways, displays, and decor?
- What messages are reinforced in subtle or overt ways through the images that appear?

The work of sustaining equity requires many entry points, it is a *both, and* rather than an *either, or* approach. While we give some examples that illuminate the ways in which teachers can shift their practice, it must be paired with knowing where the work is supported in legislation, policy, and curriculum, in order to advocate for and sustain spaces of belonging.

Reimagining Educational Spaces Centred in Love

Sustaining spaces of belonging centred in love calls upon educators to reimagine educational spaces where students can flourish as their authentic selves. The erasure and misrepresentation associated with curricular violence and dominant narratives traditionally present in education form a *hidden curriculum* that serves to dehumanize the identities of students at the margins. Single stories that have been told have led to a narrow understanding that fails to recognize the fullness of humanity within these communities. Thus, spaces of belonging must be centred in pedagogies that humanize. Historically educational spaces have been sites of harm and trauma for students at the margins, chipping away at their dignity. When you reimagine educational spaces centred in belonging, restoring dignity is paramount. You engage in this when you reflect upon past lessons, learning engagements, and classroom culture, looking for areas that can be revisited with student impact in mind. This is good pedagogy. Continually reflecting on your practice with the goal of improving the conditions for belonging is a critical component of anti-oppressive education. It allows every student in your classroom to feel that they are intrinsically connected, building a sense of membership in the classroom community.

Membership is a critical component of belonging. When every student feels like they are a true member of the classroom, it sets the context for authentic inclusion. This can be done in simple ways. When students are empowered to take on responsibilities and roles in the classroom, this provides them with agency. This approach breaks down inherent power structures, allowing students to feel like they are valuable contributors and fostering civic engagement. When

"If we are not centering children's humanity through love, there is no strategy, no professional book or instructional method in the world that can prepare the teacher to elevate the child." — Gholdy Muhammad

students are included as active participants in the decision-making process within your classroom, you might notice higher levels of engagement, increased initiative, and improved self-regulation, all results of holding high expectations for students (a tenet of CRRP). Consider the example of the student whose job it is to write the date on the board. In our experience, this given responsibility became a point of pride for this student, who did not want to miss a day of school so that they could show up for this role. This is one of many ways you can foster membership and allow students to reclaim space within the classroom.

It is not a mistake that many words associated with anti-oppression begin with the prefix *re-*. which invites us into an understanding of a return. To be clear, this is not a return to traditional models of education; rather, it is a reimagining of education with an understanding of what was missing. We invite you to consider the meaning of these words: *reclaim, revitalize, restore, resist,* and *rejoice*. What implications do they have within the context of reimagining education centred in love? We invite you to critically examine your practices by asking the following questions, tied to Dr. Campbell's elements of belonging:

- How have you worked to build connections with students and families?
- Was trust built? How and with whom? Which families and communities have good reason to mistrust a system designed to exclude them? In what ways can trust with these communities be built in authentic ways that centre impact?
- Did learning engagements centre inclusion, considering the UDL approach?
- In what ways have you fostered relationship-building with and among students?
- How have you centred student identities in learning engagements?
- How is student safety prioritized? Do all students navigate safety in the same ways?
- What does authentic membership within your classroom community look like? Do all students know that they belong and are valuable contributors? Have you asked them?

Practical Suggestions for Cultivating Belonging with Families

- Consider sharing a parent/caregiver survey that includes asking how their children learn best, the goals they have for their children, and what interests their children have, in order to teach in ways that are relevant and responsive.
- Ask what parents/caregivers expect from you as their child's educator. This not only demonstrates that you respect parents and caregivers, but also provides feedback that can guide you in building strong relationships based on trust and integrity.
- Where parents/caregivers have an identified expertise, invite them to share. For example:

    Our class has been learning about sound in Science.
    I understand that your family makes steel-pan drums.
    Would you consider talking to our class about that?

    We are talking about our favorite stories. Do you have a
    favorite book that you might be able to share with the class?

- When a student does something wonderful, let parents know. A simple note in the agenda or a quick phone call would work: e.g., *We have been working on multiplication in class and your child shared a great strategy today! I'm so proud of their progress!*

Humanizing Frameworks

With an understanding of what has been missing in education, reimagining educational spaces that centre belonging requires that we address what has been missing. We need to work to restore this through centring pedagogical practices that rehumanize students with identities at the margins.

Anti-oppressive pedagogies from Indigenous, Black, and racialized thought leaders respond to curricular violence and are one of the many ways you can foster belonging. Within centring frameworks that humanize, it is crucial to unpack challenging conversations in age-appropriate ways with students. Where else will students be able to engage in this dialogue if not in the classroom? A good picture book paired with purposefully crafted critical questions invites students into understandings of difficult concepts, and encourages them to explore perspectives while offering historical and present day truths. Even the youngest students are able to explore big concepts that set the foundation for brave conversations. Our youngest students show evidence of critical thinking and can come up with creative solutions to real world problems. As caring educators, we need to continue to foster criticality and engage in brave conversations.

Voices from the Field

After reading a mentor text *Perfectly Designed* by Karamo Brown, students were asked *What happens when someone feels like they are not perfectly designed?*

If people feel like they are not perfectly designed then they will fell left out and like nobody likes you. — Grade 3 student

People might not feel like they were perfectly designed because they are not the same as others. — Grade 5 student

Students were introduced to anti-oppressive concepts, such as *power* and *agency*, and were asked a follow-up question to lean into brave conversations: *What power to you have to change that?*

We have power to change when someone dose not feel perfectly designed by using our voice. — Grade 5 student

I can tell someone that those words are rude and I can be an upstander. — Grade 3 student

Final Thoughts

Students need opportunities to enter into brave conversations. Often, students are more ready for these questions and conversations than we think they are. Students are curious. They are constantly learning about the world around them through daily interactions. This reality produces a unique experience that leaves students with questions and understandings that can include misinformation or a series of unexamined ideas. As caring educators, we respond to the wonderings our students hold and teach them about the world around them and their place within it. When misinformation is uninterrupted, it affects both the individual and society, leading to long-term impact. In order to be ready for these conversations, preparation is key. These questions can guide this preparation:

- What resources have you used to prepare to enter into classroom conversations surrounding race, gender, and/or ableism?
- How can you prepare your class to enter into conversations about oppression?
- How have race and/or gender, as societal constructs, led to inequities in society? How do you plan to use this information to facilitate conversations surrounding power and privilege?
- How will these brave conversations about societal constructs challenge stereotypes and lead students into action?

As teachers, we lean into these difficult but brave conversations because our students need us to. These conversations set conditions for belonging and centre student safety, building a sense of trust within our classrooms. As a component of belonging, trust forms the foundation of relationship-building. In a system where trust has been broken with communities at the margins, restoring a sense of trust is imperative.

Voices from the Field

In Professional Development, teachers were asked to use humanizing pedagogical frameworks, and reflected on the ways they cultivated a sense of belonging for students.

It created a huge sense of community and showed how well they knew and loved each other even if they don't always say it. It also showed students what they loved and found unique about themselves.
— Elementary school teacher

Students said they felt heard, had space to contribute and were valued for their ideas.
— Elementary school teacher.

These discussions are important to allow students an opportunity to be heard and know their voice matters. Teaching from a [humanizing] framework encourages us to learn from and with multiple communities, and gain new perspectives.
— Elementary school teacher

Reimagining educational spaces that centre love and embody Dr. Campbell's elements of inclusion have the potential to transform education. Earlier in this chapter, we asked you to consider whose voices should be centred when determining if educational spaces espouse belonging. Students and their families have always been, and continue to be, the best source for this answer.

Voices from the Field

Students in Grades 9 to 12 were asked what an affinity space with a caring adult means to them.

Safe space — Grade 9 student

Freedom — Grade 9 student

Non-judgmental space — Grade 10 student

It's an important space where we aren't judged, where we can share our experiences. — Grade 9 student

Just knowing that the space exists changes the landscape. — Grade 12 student

Affinity spaces can be spaces for allyship and diversity, as solidarity and collective liberation is important. — Grade 12 student

A space to share experiences — Grade 11 student

Love — Grade 10 student

Transforming educational spaces requires a *both, and* approach. While we need to look at systemic changes, such as policies, procedures, curricula, and resources, what is equally important is paying close attention to the ways in which your everyday interactions with students create lasting impact. When you engage in this work, students will never have to change or hide aspects of who they are when they enter school learning environments; rather, your learning spaces and you as an educator will be ready to receive them in the true fullness of their intersectional identities.

The dominant culture, societal norms and values, and systemic factors affect the ways in which students navigate safety and well-being, and pose barriers to their ability to thrive. It is within your sphere of influence to change the trajectory of a student's experience. You have the potential to offer a counterexperience and a counterspace for every child who sits before you.

As you continue to engage in this challenging but necessary work, rest, resist, reclaim, restore, and renew your own commitment. The students need you. Know that your work has impact and makes a lasting difference.

10

Fostering Intellectual Curiosity in Marginalized Students

Karen Murray and Rasulan Q. Hoppie

Karen Murray is the System Superintendent for Equity, Anti-Racism, Anti-Oppression and the Centre of Excellence for Black Student Achievement in the Toronto District School Board. Karen has held portfolios including Early Years and New Teacher Induction Program, and was seconded to the Ministry of Education. Karen is an international speaker and author, and was named one of the 100 Accomplished Black Canadian Women (2020).

Rasulan Q. Hoppie is a Superintendent of Education in the Peel District School Board. Prior to this, he was Superintendent of Curriculum, Instruction and Assessment, and of Continuing and Adult Education. He is currently pursuing his PhD in Education at York University. In 2018, Rasulan was honored for Public Service/Education/Diversity/Social Justice by the National Ethnic Press and Media Council of Canada.

Malcolm sits at his desk, intensely listening to his Grade 8 teacher and his peers as they discuss issues about sustainability. The teacher puts on the screen the web page of the Canadian Government's *Active long-term drinking water advisories*, which highlighted the fact that across Canada in First Nations communities there are 37 advisories, and 26 of these are in Ontario. Malcolm puts up his hand in frustration. "Since we have the technology, why do some communities still not have access to clean water?" he asks. The room grows silent. His question isn't one the teacher has prepared for, but it is a powerful question that deserves a truthful response and a critical conversation on climate justice.

These are the moments that are unplanned but essential for teaching and learning—moments that encourage students to interrogate the world around them, ask questions, and identify solutions for a better future. Malcolm's curiosity extends the lesson by inviting his peers and teachers to critically examine systems affecting their communities. As society constantly changes, it is critical for our students to develop the skills to navigate complex issues. Intellectual curiosity connects academic content with real-world challenges, fueling deep learning that moves beyond the pursuit for the "right" answer. This is what we want for our students.

Fostering intellectual curiosity moves students beyond rote-learning and memorization of facts. Nurturing intellectual curiosity requires from teachers a reimagining of our learning environments to one where we are consistently co-creating spaces, developing learning experiences where students can ask questions, inquire, explore, and challenge themselves to take ownership of their learning while eagerly investigating topics of their interest. It requires teachers to change our assessment practices to capture the rich conversations and students' ongoing inquiries.

Intellectual curiosity is inherently tied to culturally relevant pedagogy (Ladson-Billings, 1995), as nurturing intellectual curiosity cannot be separated from academic achievement, cultural competence, and critical consciousness. In other words, curiosity is cultivated when students see themselves, their histories, and their communities reflected in the curriculum and the learning environment. It affirms students' identities, provides opportunities for others to see different perspectives, and empowers students to make connections. Intellectual curiosity is simultaneously an academic skill and a catalyst for positive identity development and critical thinking.

This chapter introduces a new framework to guide teachers in fostering intellectual curiosity. It starts with the critical first step, a reflective process of understanding who we are as educators and the students we serve. It presents strategies for designing learning environments for curiosity—creating, engaging, inquiry-driven classrooms to develop future-ready students. Specifically, these strategies encompass the following four areas:

- Educators' Critical Reflection
- Classroom Climate and Conditions
- Identity Affirmation
- Setting High Expectations

The chapter concludes with key takeaways and recommendations.

These strategies work together to ensure that intellectual curiosity is fostered in every school and every classroom.

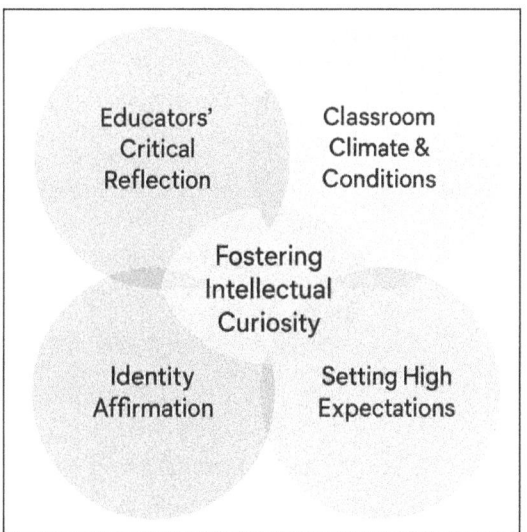

Educators' Critical Reflection

Every day, students enter classrooms from Kindergarten to Grade 12 with diverse ways of knowing, with knowledge and understanding from their families and communities that are intersectional in nature and based on their social, cultural, and racial identities. Teachers enter classrooms the very same way. They are diverse in thinking with a wide range of beliefs, values, and practices.

The first step for teachers in fostering intellectual curiosity in students is for them to engage in their own internal critical reflections. These critical reflections are important, as teachers are socialized in the same type of classrooms and school environments as their students, educational spaces where opportunities to develop their own awareness of themselves are not often encouraged. But we know that understanding one's beliefs, ideologies, and values influences teaching and learning in classrooms. Research has shown that, when teachers engage in critical reflection focusing on their own biases, stereotypes, and assumptions, they develop a deeper understanding of themselves, and are then able to have a deeper understanding of what they teach and who they are teaching (Cole, Chelsea & Hinchcliff, Elizabeth & Carling, Rylee, 2022). Teachers' beliefs and expectations of their students shape students' willingness to feel brave enough to question and explore their curiosity.

Critical reflection also requires a re-examination of classroom practices. For example, Gillan Parekh (2018) found a correlation between teachers' perceptions around student learning and demographic and institutional factors. She identified how teachers' assessments of learning skills were tied to their implicit bias and personal perception. Implicit biases, she found, lead to disproportionate outcomes for, specifically, Black, Indigenous, racialized, and historically marginalized students, denying access to academic success for these students more than others in their classrooms.

Therefore, engaging in a critical reflection invites teachers to consider the impact of their practices on student learning. It also challenges teachers to ask themselves: *Why am I teaching this way? How am I selecting my resources? What conditions are driving my sense of (dis)comfort?* Through this reflection, teachers can understand how their decisions, both intentional and unintentional, influence the curriculum and foster or compromise curiosity-centred classrooms.

Voice from the Field

It is important to review your own knowledge, collaborate with others, and be prepared for difficult and challenging conversations that foster ongoing growth and reflection.
— Teacher engaging in critical reflection

Looking Inward: Reflecting on Teaching for Curiosity

It is important to explore and ask oneself authentic and open-ended questions. Reflect on the following questions, considering how you foster intellectual curiosity in students.

Self
- What are the strengths and limitations in my teaching practices? How can these insights inform my professional learning and growth?
- Do any of my expectations or teaching practices discourage student inquiry? How do I respond when students ask questions that challenge the curriculum or dominant narratives?

Practice
- How am I intentionally designing learning opportunities for students to connect academic curriculum to their identities, communities, and lived experiences?
- How do I select and teach with texts and resources that promote a positive self-concept for diverse student populations (e.g., a positive identity for racialized students)?
- What opportunities do I create for students to pursue their own inquiries?
- How have I made these opportunities accessible to all students?

A Strong Classroom Climate

The classroom environment plays a critical role in shaping learners' educational experiences and concept attainment. Classrooms are spaces where learners feel affirmed, respected, and capable, with their cultural identities recognized as assets. A strong classroom climate, built on mutual respect, high expectations, and community, creates a safe and empowering space for students. These classroom spaces encourage students to bravely explore their curiosities and wonders.

Through curiosity, students achieve academic success, develop cultural competence, and build critical consciousness. These goals are critical for optimal learning conditions, where students ask questions to challenge societal inequities and explore real world issues. For both elementary and secondary classrooms, co-creating and setting clear expectations with students, establishing norms, and posting routines and revisiting them collaboratively throughout the year are instrumental in shaping what optimal conditions look like. These are classroom spaces where students feel comfortable in taking risks to ask questions about issues that matter to them. Maintaining inclusive displays of students' work, utilizing culturally responsive materials, and providing ongoing affirmations when students ask critical questions of inquiry are also key elements that shape positive classrooms. In addition, an organized and welcoming physical environment that supports various learning styles is essential. This could take the form of intentional seating arrangements for collaboration, where students are encouraged to ask each other questions, develop inquiries, and problem-solve together.

You can foster intellectual curiosity by creating inclusive, supportive spaces where all students can thrive academically, socially, and emotionally. You are invited to intentionally design both the physical and relational aspects of the classroom through the following steps:

Step 1: Co-Create Clear Expectations/Norms Together with Students

- Invite your students to co-develop classroom norms. Ask questions like, "What helps us learn best?" and "How can we be respectful to each other?"
- Develop shared expectations. Have students sign them and post them (physically in the classroom as well as in the virtual learning environment) where everyone can see.
- Revisit and refresh these expectations/norms with students throughout the year or as needed.

Helpful tip: These expectations should also be shared with their parents/caregivers.

Step 2: Design an Inclusive, Flexible Space

- Take a walk through your classroom. Does it feel welcoming? Is it organized? Encourage students to share their feelings about the classroom space.
- Consider collaborative seating for group work, quiet nooks for solo thinking, and open areas for movement. Encourage students to use these spaces as they need.
- Include easy access to learning materials and resources (e.g., books, technology, manipulatives).
- Check in with students on an ongoing basis in the collaboration of the classroom design to ensure the space meets their ever-changing and evolving needs.

Helpful tip: Work with your school's teacher-librarian if possible.

Step 3: Reflect Student Identity in the Room

- Display student work proudly and intentionally. Encourage students to choose what they would like to display.
- Use culturally responsive materials, posters, audios, and visuals that affirm the diverse identities in the curriculum.
- Post affirmations or quotes that reflect belonging, strength, and possibility.

Helpful tip: Use student-created resources in classroom displays.

Step 4: Foster a Culture of Dialogue and Encouragement

- Model the kind of respectful, curious conversations you want to hear. Use inclusive language and a positive tone.
- Encourage students to ask questions, respectfully challenge ideas, and support each other's thinking.
- Give specific, strengths-based feedback that acknowledges effort and nudges thinking forward.

Step 5: Set the Emotional Tone

- Be a calm, consistent presence. Your emotions help students feel secure. Model how you would like the classroom to engage with each other.
- Use language that uplifts and guides, especially when managing conflict or redirecting behavior.
- Create space for students to express how they're feeling and to regulate themselves when needed.

Helpful tip: Develop classroom-ready strategies to support discussions that might be difficult and to facilitate open conversations with your students.

Step 6: Cultivate a Sense of Belonging and Curiosity

- Learn students' names quickly—and pronounce them correctly.
- Encourage students to ask questions about the learning or topic. Consider the materials being used and provide guidance or suggestions on resources (e.g., community partners) that could enhance the learning process.
- Acknowledge everyone's contributions. Use inclusive participation strategies so all voices are heard.
- Celebrate challenges or errors as part of learning.

Helpful tips:
Ask students to help you develop a strategy to learn how to pronounce and spell their names.
Help students see that taking risks can be safe and is encouraged in your classroom.

Step 7: Maintain It with Intention

- Revisit classroom norms and routines regularly, especially after breaks or when the energy shifts.
- Reflect on successes (what's working) and challenges (what might need tweaking).

Helpful tip: Stay responsive to the evolving needs of your students and your space.

Voice from the Field

Being in a classroom environment that encourages dialogue allows me as a student to engage with the content in a more meaningful way, as open discussion invites me to share my thoughts and reflect on my perspective and understanding. I feel safe expressing my curiosity by asking questions and challenging presented ideas.
— Grade 11 student

Intentionally setting the conditions for learning is essential for creating classrooms where learners thrive. A strong classroom climate affirms learners' identities, builds mutual respect, and nurtures high expectations and community. When the right look, sound, and feel are in place, learners feel safe, valued, and capable of achieving academic success. Investing in classroom climate is ultimately an investment in student potential, empowerment, and achievement. By doing this, you will foster intellectual curiosity, as the climate and learning environment will be optimal for students to thrive academically, socially, and emotionally. They will feel confident in engaging in the inquiries that matter to their learning.

Affirming Identity and Developing a Love for Learning

Curiosity and wonder are essential drivers of students' growth and development. When students are encouraged to ask questions and explore ideas, they deepen understanding, strengthen critical thinking skills, and develop a foundation for lifelong learning. Fostering curiosity is not only about academic growth—it also plays a crucial role in affirming learners' identities and promoting a strong sense of self. When students see their experiences, cultures, and perspectives valued, they feel empowered to engage more fully. By nurturing curiosity alongside identity affirmation, teachers cultivate confident, engaged students who view themselves as capable contributors to their own learning and to the broader world.

Curiosity is essential to student growth because it drives inquiry, exploration, and meaningful engagement with ideas. When students are curious, they are motivated to ask questions, seek solutions, and connect new knowledge to their own experiences. Wonder sparks authentic engagement, pushing learners beyond passive reception of information toward active participation in their learning. When you use direct instruction to teach the skills students need, you set them up to succeed in exploring their own questions and interests. Classrooms that nurture curiosity often use strategies like inquiry-driven discussions and *I Wonder…* boards. These visual classroom spaces allow learners to post questions driven by their wonderings, encouraging inquiry-based learning, and foster a culture of exploration and critical thinking, all of which help students pursue their interests and deepen their understanding.

These practices honor the natural human instinct to question and explore, rather than trying to control or suppress it. When curiosity is nurtured, students develop a stronger sense of ownership over their learning and are more likely to retain knowledge and apply it in meaningful ways. Creating spaces that celebrate curiosity ultimately leads to more motivated, creative, and independent students.

You can create a classroom environment where curiosity and identity affirmation go hand-in-hand and build joyful, engaged, and inclusive learning spaces through the following steps:

Step 1: Make Curiosity Visible

Set up an *I Wonder…* board where students can post questions any time. Keep it active—refer to it, add your own questions, and let it guide classroom inquiry. Use open-ended prompts and inquiry-based learning to let curiosity lead the way.

Step 2: Celebrate Questions

Model curiosity yourself—wonder out loud, ask thoughtful what-if questions, and show students that not knowing is part of learning. When students ask questions, pause and make space for discussion. Avoid rushing to answers.

Step 3: Affirm Student Identity

Make sure students see themselves reflected in your classroom. Use diverse texts, resources, examples, and perspectives. Invite students to share their experiences and cultures. Make content relevant by connecting it to their lives and diverse communities.

Step 4: Create Emotionally Safe Spaces

Build trust. Encourage respectful dialogue, celebrate mistakes as learning opportunities, and show empathy. Students need to feel seen and safe to take academic risks.

Step 5: Give Voice and Choice

Offer choice in projects and topics. Let students explore areas they care about. When students direct their learning, they invest more deeply.

Step 6: Build Inquiry into Your Routine

Use inquiry-based discussions regularly—tailor them to your students' age and interests. Let them ask the questions and co-lead conversations. It builds confidence and critical thinking.

Step 7: Combine Rigor with Relevance

Don't think of identity-affirming content as separate from academic expectations. Use real-world identity-affirming content to drive literacy, analysis, and synthesis, through direct instruction and the scaffolding of skills. Real-world, identity-connected topics can deliver both rigor and relevance, while allowing students to connect their curiosity with their lived experience.

Step 8: Reflect and Evolve

Invite feedback. Ask students what helps them feel curious, safe, and seen—and adjust accordingly. Growth-minded classrooms adapt with the students they serve. Always be an active listener.

By following these steps, you'll foster a learning space where curiosity is celebrated, identity is affirmed, and every student feels empowered to explore, question, and grow. Curiosity and wonder are vital ingredients for profound, joyful learning, and it is crucial that teachers not only foster these qualities in their students, but also model them. When teachers demonstrate genuine curiosity, they inspire students to ask questions, explore, and engage deeply with the material. By honoring students' identities, teachers create the emotional safety needed for curiosity to thrive. Ultimately, by nurturing curiosity and affirming identity, teachers empower students to not only understand the world, but also discover their own valued place within it.

Voice from the Field

I think it's important to lead inquiry-based discussions with my students to model the power of asking questions. Children naturally ask questions about everything, but they need help formulating questions about what they are seeing. I encourage them to ask questions based on the things they are curious about in their everyday lives. I encourage them to ask questions about all the things they encounter at school and at home. I then provide them with a space to share those questions and lead conversations about their curiosities in the classroom. This leads to deeper and more complex questions and inquiries over time.

— Primary teacher

Setting High Expectations

In today's rapidly evolving education landscape, you, as a K–12 teacher, play a central role in fostering innovation and driving growth. You must create classroom conditions that not only spark curiosity, but also set high expectations, and encourage students to think critically beyond traditional boundaries. Your responsibility is not only to teach and meet curriculum standards, but also to foster intellectual curiosity by cultivating wonder, modelling inquiry, and building a culture of transformation—one classroom at a time.

To bring about lasting change, you need to set high expectations for your students:

- Have a strong belief that *all* students are competent and capable learners. They are coming with knowledge that brings value to the classroom learning.
- Champion a shared vision for the teaching and learning in the classroom, grounded in equity, innovation, and learner-centred practices. Student voice is key.
- Prioritize trust, respect, collaboration, and openness to new ideas.
- Foster intellectual curiosity: explicitly teach and scaffold the skills learners need to pursue meaningful inquiry and critical questions.
- Create an environment in which students feel that taking academic risks and asking questions are part of the learning environment.
- Align resources—whether it's time, technology, or instructional materials—to ensure you and your colleagues have what you need to make teaching fun but also allow for data-informed decisions.
- Form learning networks within and beyond your school that break down silos, grade levels, and sources of knowledge. Embrace families, caregivers, communities, and community partners as valuable knowledge holders.

Voice from the Field

I was nervous and wasn't sure what to expect. I know I need more time to process information and I wasn't sure if I would be able to grasp all of the content quickly enough. However, by my teachers going step by step, it made things clearer and allowed me to process the information at a pace I could manage—without feeling like I was being left behind. I was able to see how things come together to make the full picture. I could ask important questions about the topic because I understood it, and I understood what was being asked of me. So, when we did assignments, they were easier to complete and I was able to contribute meaningfully by sharing my ideas.

— High-school student on starting Grade 9

High expectations occur when we foster belonging by weaving community narratives, learner storytelling, and local histories into lessons—elements often absent from standard textbooks. When you intentionally design space for identity exploration while meeting curriculum goals, engagement and achievement naturally rise.

Reflective Checklist

See page 142 for a reproducible version of this checklist.

As your review this reflective checklist on high expectations, ask yourself if the key themes of curiosity, equity, collaboration, and learner empowerment are evident in your classroom spaces.

Curiosity and High Expectations
- ☐ Am I creating classroom conditions that spark curiosity and wonder in my learners?
- ☐ Do I set and maintain high expectations while supporting all learners to meet them?
- ☐ How do I model inquiry and exploration in my daily practice?
- ☐ Are learners encouraged to ask questions, challenge ideas, and explore topics that matter to them?

Equity and Identity Affirmation
- ☐ Does my teaching reflect and affirm the identities, cultures, and lived experiences of my learners?
- ☐ Am I intentionally designing lessons that highlight diverse voices, community narratives, and local histories?
- ☐ Am I ensuring my curriculum content is both academically rigorous and culturally relevant?
- ☐ Do all learners see themselves as capable, valued contributors to our classroom and broader society?

Explicit Teaching and Purposeful Change
- ☐ Am I thinking beyond traditional educational boundaries in how I design and deliver learning?
- ☐ Have I embedded innovative practices that support deeper engagement and learner agency?

Collaboration and Shared Vision
- ☐ Am I contributing to a shared vision, grounded in equity, innovation, and student-centred learning?
- ☐ Am I fostering a classroom environment rooted in trust, openness, and collaboration?
- ☐ Do I regularly share ideas and learn from peers to break down silos and grow professionally?

Data-Informed Practice and Resources
- ☐ Am I using data to guide my instructional decisions in an equity-driven way?
- ☐ Are my instructional materials, time, and technology aligned with the goals of curiosity, innovation, and inclusion?

☐ Do I adjust my practices based on feedback and reflection to better serve my learners?

By regularly reflecting on these questions, you can ensure your practice is aligned with the transformative goals of today's education landscape—making your classroom a powerful driver of change.

STORY FROM THE CLASSROOM

Ms. Torres is a Grade 9 de-streamed mathematics teacher in an urban secondary school with a diverse population. Her students represent a spectrum of math learners, from students who love math and are self-identified "math people," to students who question their mathematical abilities due to previous challenges with the content, limited access to resources, or a lack of representation. Ms. Torres is actively committed to creating a classroom environment that fosters engagement, encourages collaboration, and affirms students' diverse identities. She sees all her students as mathematically competent and capable. However, despite her efforts to provide learning opportunities that meet her individual students' needs, she is noting that engagement in class content is uneven. Students who are confident in math are thriving in class discussions, group work, and open-ended content. Other students have effectively shut down, refusing to participate, hesitant to take risks, and driven by their internalized beliefs about their capabilities. This prompts Ms. Torres to engage in critical reflection on her teaching strategies and the classroom environment she has cultivated. She knows she needs to design a classroom that nurtures intellectual curiosity in all her students, a classroom environment driven by student inquiries, invitational to wonder and exploration, and relevant to her students' identities and lived experiences. But how should she begin?

Regardless of the teaching stream, it is not uncommon for teachers to encounter student disengagement within the classroom. Think about a moment when you were tasked with responding to varying levels of student participation, and ask yourself:

- How does my current classroom environment support risk-taking, exploration, and student inquiry? What strategies can I implement to invite curiosity and exploration in classroom materials?
- In what ways do I affirm student identities in the classroom, especially for students who might not see themselves as competent and capable in a particular subject area?
- Do I check in with students on an ongoing basis in the collaboration of the classroom design to ensure the space meets their ever-changing and evolving needs? For example, given diverse learners, do I have collaborative seating for group work or quiet nooks for solo thinking?
- In what ways do I include real-world examples to build the bridge from classroom learning, and to demonstrate how this learning affects the world around my students?
- Do I have high expectations for each student in my class and do I scaffold my lessons to ensure all students can meet those expectations?

Final Thoughts

As superintendents and former administrators and teachers across K–12, we have learned the importance of fostering intellectual curiosity in students. Curious young learners are constantly asking questions, exploring ideas, and engaging deeply when given the opportunity to share in classroom spaces. We listen to the voice of students, and they constantly remind us that they would like to be seen, heard, and affirmed. Students are confident, capable, and curious learners, and are ready to extend and enhance their learning experiences. This is why it is essential for us, as teachers, to nurture their curiosity. This nurturing begins from the time students enter their school experience and extends to when they graduate and leave us for their new pathway. Through inquiry-based learning, hands-on activities, and integrated instruction, students demonstrate that connecting their learning to the real world provides them with the skills necessary as learners. These experiences shape students' attitudes toward learning for years to come.

In many of our middle or secondary classrooms, students become disengaged when their learning feels disconnected or irrelevant. Designing meaningful learning experiences and offering students choice and voice to reignite that sense of wonder makes a difference. Together, we believe that intellectual curiosity doesn't just happen—it must be intentionally cultivated at every stage. We encourage teachers to foster curiosity daily in their students by advocating for system-wide approaches that prioritize creativity, critical thinking, and exploration.

Next Steps and Recommendations

Empowerment and Reflection

Empowering yourself to teach students to foster intellectual curiosity through innovation and trust is foundational. When you give yourself permission to take risks and listen to the voices of your students, you create learner-centred experiences that truly respond to your students' needs. This allows you to see the curriculum as a launchpad for curiosity, as it opens up possibilities for creativity, critical thinking, and real-world problem-solving.

To do this effectively, know who you are as a teacher and reflect on your instructional practices while you pursue your own professional growth. Seek out opportunities to design authentic learning experiences that make the curriculum more relevant and shift assessment practices to capture deeper understanding and learner growth. Everything you do, remember to do in *CO–*; i.e., cooperation and collaboration with others.

Advocating for Curiosity and Joy

You play a vital role in shaping a classroom culture where curiosity and student agency thrive. By embracing your strengths, accepting challenges, and integrating inquiry-based and interdisciplinary approaches, you can design dynamic lessons that connect academic content with learners' lived experiences. When you incorporate culturally relevant practices, you affirm the identities of your students and make learning more engaging and inclusive. It also brings joy to your classroom.

When you prioritize curiosity in your classroom, you contribute to a culture of transformation that ripples beyond your own students. Your actions can spark wonder and position you as a driver of change. By aligning your teaching with a vision of equity, relevance, and high expectations, you foster intellectual curiosity and prepare your students, not only to succeed academically, but also to thrive in an ever-changing world.

Reflective Checklist

Curiosity and High Expectations

☐ Am I creating classroom conditions that spark curiosity and wonder in my learners?
☐ Do I set and maintain high expectations while supporting all learners to meet them?
☐ How do I model inquiry and exploration in my daily practice?
☐ Are learners encouraged to ask questions, challenge ideas, and explore topics that matter to them?

Equity and Identity Affirmation

☐ Does my teaching reflect and affirm the identities, cultures, and lived experiences of my learners?
☐ Am I intentionally designing lessons that highlight diverse voices, community narratives, and local histories?
☐ Am I ensuring my curriculum content is both academically rigorous and culturally relevant?
☐ Do all learners see themselves as capable, valued contributors to our classroom and broader society?

Explicit Teaching and Purposeful Change

☐ Am I thinking beyond traditional educational boundaries in how I design and deliver learning?
☐ Have I embedded innovative practices that support deeper engagement and learner agency?

Collaboration and Shared Vision

☐ Am I contributing to a shared vision, grounded in equity, innovation, and student-centred learning?
☐ Am I fostering a classroom environment rooted in trust, openness, and collaboration?
☐ Do I regularly share ideas and learn from peers to break down silos and grow professionally?

Data-Informed Practice and Resources

☐ Am I using data to guide my instructional decisions in an equity-driven way?
☐ Are my instructional materials, time, and technology aligned with the goals of curiosity, innovation, and inclusion?
☐ Do I adjust my practices based on feedback and reflection to better serve my learners?

11

Strength-Based Approaches to Eliminate Deficit Thinking in Schools

Michael John Daniels

Dr. Michael John Daniels is a dedicated educator specializing in primary and special education, currently serving as an administrator at an elementary school that focuses on autism education and intervention. With a passion for exceptional pedagogy, Michael has developed educational practices to meet the diverse needs of all students. Michael also shares his expertise as a university lecturer, inspiring future educators.

Strength is a combination of power, courage, and resilience. A strength-based approach in education focuses on identifying and nurturing students' existing strengths, talents, and interests, rather than solely addressing deficits. This approach in the everyday classroom represents transformational change when we build on existing assets to fully respond to all students' learning needs (Elder, Rood, & Damiani, 2018). The audacity of teachers who attain this strength can transform adversity into achievement through determination and perseverance. Also known as an asset-based approach, pedagogy that leads with a powerful awareness of the rich diversity of learners can enhance knowledge acquisition.

> Strengths-based approaches are premised on the theory and evidence that having and using strengths is associated with, and predictive of, increased quality of life across a number of quality of life markers, including well-being, self-esteem, self-efficacy, work engagement, and reduced stress.
> (Linley, 2023)

Your role as a teacher is complex and requires an intrinsic process to assess decisions and ensure the best outcomes for learners. The reality is that you are overworked, overwhelmed, and often overcome by classroom expectations, making it challenging to maintain a positive mindset. We have all had days when we have thought about early retirement, but reality sets in and we realize our finances say otherwise. Yet this reality does not solve the issues that lead to deficit thinking in your practice. Harnessing your emotional intelligence is a starting point to help you enhance methods and counteract barriers that put you at risk of deficit thinking. Acknowledging what your practice might be missing is not a weakness, but rather a step toward building a strength-based approach to pedagogy that will enhance your ability and students' learning outcomes. However, a deficit-based approach focuses excessively on the challenges faced by learners. Deficits can manifest in your language, in a lack of cultural awareness, in stereotypes, in behaviors, or in stigmas, all of which can negatively affect the ability of students to learn. Achieving an equity-based mentality requires reframing language, relearning processes, and embracing restorative practices that challenge imperialist views on education. When you gain a heightened awareness of yourself and utilize your agency to execute duties, you can channel this engagement into the functional application of a strength-based approach.

We have to believe that every student possesses unique potential, and it is a teacher's responsibility to cultivate an environment that allows students to grow. My decision to leave public education and work at a private school for students with autism afforded me the flexibility to support exceptional learning needs by addressing the gaps in systems that unfairly affect learning potential. By shifting focus from limitations to capabilities, I found I could cultivate an environment where I recognize and build upon students' strengths, rather than dwelling on perceived shortcomings. I believe in advocacy for strength-based practices that challenge systemic inequities, ensuring that all learners receive the support and opportunities they deserve. My goal in writing this chapter is to provide you with practical advice on applying strength-based approaches to overcome deficit thinking, thereby advancing educational equity. I hope to inspire teachers to adopt a growth-oriented pedagogical perspective that transforms lives and dismantles barriers to success.

Strength-Based Approach

The modern classroom encompasses complex diversity that might extend beyond your experiences and training. For students, deficit thinking can manifest as self-doubt, peer comparisons, internalized stereotypes, or cultural shame, all of which can affect their academic success. A strength-based education program strategizes lesson plans that highlight skills, promote inclusion, ensure equity, and recognize the potential of all learning profiles in a classroom.

Strength-based principles in the classroom combine a heightened awareness of professional judgment and pedagogical processes that focus on nurturing your students and distinguishing how best to leverage the unique capabilities of each individual. They focus on identifying and developing your students' inherent strengths, talents, and abilities rather than solely addressing their weaknesses or deficits. This approach emphasizes positive reinforcement, personalized learning, and the belief that every student has potential. Achieving this requires an inclusive and motivating learning environment that fosters self-confidence, resilience, and a growth mindset. Strength-based teaching encourages your students to take ownership of their learning, engage more deeply with content, and develop skills that align with their natural aptitudes. Ultimately, this approach fosters academic success, emotional well-being, and lifelong learning by helping your students recognize and leverage their strengths in and beyond the classroom. Adopting a strength-based approach to disrupting the history of social psychology, which has often marginalized identities such as culture, race, socio-economic status, or a fixed mindset on disability, can be advantageous for learners who are sidelined and can help reduce inequality (Silverman et al., 2023).

Voice from the Field

I am a leadership coach and wisdom teacher who has worked closely with education principals and superintendents to instill hope back into the education system. I focus on aligning educational leaders to think about education with an understanding that is noncolonial in terms of learning and teaching. I stress the importance of seeing a learner for their uniqueness and identifying the gifts in children, which focuses on helping them grow into the best possible version of themselves. I encourage us to utilize as many tools as possible to grow into our greatness.

We must understand that there are no accidents and everyone was called upon. From an indigenous perspective, I stress the importance of community and that individuals are meant to be who they are through a development process. I think that approval of the child and the promotion of the child are priorities, and that colonial practices need to be dismantled. I say the absence of this practice to challenge colonial establishments is increasing mental health problems, and school systems need to address this absence to recognize children's identity to promote and approve them. We must find spaces in school that honor identity, which is necessary for success in a strength-based teaching.

— Aina-Nia Ayo'dele, Spiritual liberation activist

Comparing Strength-Based and Deficit-Based Approaches

Strength-Based	**Deficit-Based**
• Highlights skills • Inclusive • Promotes equity • Recognizes potential	• Focuses on challenges • Focuses on shortcomings • Focuses on negative stereotypes • Minimizes learning opportunities

Disrupting Deficit Thinking with Powerful Pedagogy

When tailoring instruction to disrupt deficit thinking, start with the essentials of engagement. This includes student profiles, their cultural background, needs, strengths, and required supports. Intentionally understanding diverse backgrounds can help contest a pejorative pedagogical perspective, in that it challenges the status quo and demonstrates a profound sense of care for your professional responsibilities. Campbell (2013) states, "deficit thinking is rooted in victim blaming, suggesting that people are responsible for their predicaments and failing to acknowledge that they live in coercive systems that cause harm without accountability." (p. 56)

Challenge yourself to be a disruptor of deficit thinking and develop powerful pedagogy based on the essentials of engagement:

- Values: standard of professional practice
- Ethics: core responsibilities in practice, demonstrating a commitment to students and learning that includes care, respect, trust, and integrity
- Diversity: embracing differences of profiles in a learning community
- Inclusion: humanizing the identities and experiences of disempowered and oppressed learners to develop safe and effective schools (Waly, S., 2020)
- Culture: addressing systemic marginalization using the approaches of universal strengths, difference-as-strength, and identity-specific strength to address inequality and promote strength-based values (Silverman et al., 2023)

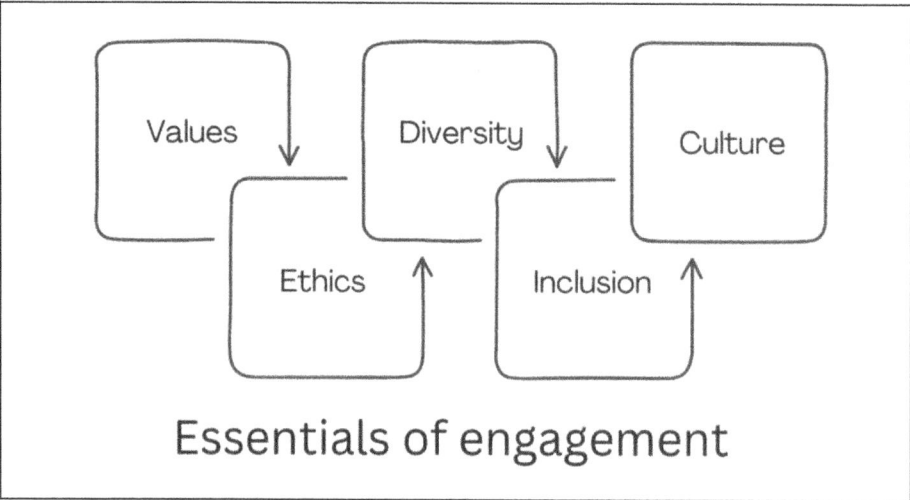

The development of well-structured plans that incorporate culturally responsive pedagogy ensure that inclusive lessons are relevant to diversity and can foster a community of distinct recognition rather than uniformity. Leading with the essentials of engagement promotes deeper learning and academic success for all your students. Approach your classroom with awareness that a philosophy on pedagogy demands finding new insights to improve practice. Dismantling deficit thinking and replacing it with a strength-based approach requires ongoing self-improvement and self-awareness to develop powerful pedagogy that has a positive impact in the classroom.

Questions for Reflection

- Think of a time when a strength-based approach helped you shift focus from weaknesses to strengths.
- How have strength-based practices influenced your mindset when facing challenges?
- What strengths improved collaboration, motivation, or outcomes in your personal or professional life?
- What strategies have you found most effective in your classroom toolkit?
- How have you overcome deficit-thinking to apply strength-based approaches?

Voice from the Field

I co-lead an inner-city school, and I know the experiences and struggles faced by students and educators first-hand. I see children for who they are and their capabilities. My strength-based approach is to honor and celebrate any achievement of children, as long as they try their best. The key to making children feel a sense of worth is to eliminate the word *disability* and remind them that we all learn differently. I am committed to supporting all and engaging with students, staff, and families to build rapport. I think the educators at my school are on the same page, and communication is the key to that success.

I am an Afro-Latina Indigenous woman, and the cultural and racial differences are important for me to acknowledge in my school. I am one of two staff members leading the Black Student Alliance that teaches students about Anti-Black and Anti-Indigenous learning in a secure environment, where kids can share their thoughts safely. Parents know their kids are safe because this is a loving and caring school, and the staff treat the students as they want their children to be treated. I always teach students to speak up for those who cannot speak for themselves and be the voice for those who do not have one.

— Ena Maxam, School administrator

An Enabling Environment

When you build a classroom environment rooted in compassion, you create a safe space where students can thrive. A positive learning environment that addresses emotional well-being and social development provides an inclusive atmosphere that encourages academic success. It can enhance your students' experience by promoting engagement, collaboration, and a sense of belonging. Model respect, collaboration, and open communication to your students, which are necessary for supportive relationships in a thriving culture of learning. Prioritizing mental health awareness ensures emotional well-being, while care-centred classrooms create safe, supportive spaces for learning. Integrating mindfulness can help manage stress and enhance focus, promoting a balanced mindset. Emphasizing health, wellness, nutrition, and diet reinforces physical and cognitive vitality, enabling individuals to perform at their best. By adopting these elements as strength-based approaches, you can shift away from deficit thinking and recognize methods to nurture each student's unique potential.

Creating a Positive Learning Environment

Trust and Emotional Safety	**Inclusivity**
• Morning Check-in	• Diverse Representation
• Active Listening	• Culturally Responsive Teaching
• Safe Space Norms	• Varied Participation
• Teacher Vulnerability	• Pronoun and Name Respect

Collaboration	Inspiring Engagement
• Classroom Agreements • Peer Mentorship • Shared Leadership Roles • Restorative Practices	• Student Choice • Celebrating Success • Breaks and Movement • Mindfulness
Emotional Validation	**Empowering Voice and Agency**
• Affirmation Wall • Emotional Regulation • Quiet Zone • Conferencing	• Modelling • Feedback • Implied Choice • Interest-based Learning

STORY FROM THE CLASSROOM

Ian Labelle-Stackhouse is a veteran elementary school teacher with an engaging and personable demeanor. Trained as a French teacher, Ian has been working at his current school for the past 22 years, most recently serving as a Kindergarten teacher for the last 12 years. He brings both professional and personal experiences that have shaped his strength-based perspective on practice. In his early career, Ian struggled to find a school environment where colleagues shared the ethics of a strength-based approach. More recently, finding himself divorced after a nearly two-decade marriage, Ian has been navigating a new life path to co-parent his now 20-year-old adoptive mixed-race son as he explores a new relationship.

These experiences prepared Ian to lead his classroom as a positive and affirming space, where he seeks to highlight strengths in diversity, whether it be race, gender identity, learning styles, or neurodiversity. He believes that pathologizing differences to measure normalcy is a negative response. Instead, he thinks one should challenge the status quo by adopting a different perspective. Ian finds ways to let children shine, and he models the possibilities that challenge norms. His progressive-minded approach is to acknowledge systemic racism while teaching pro-social, anti-social, pro-equality, and anti-equality in school during friendship blocks. His direct approach involves identifying and recognizing barriers to implementing change.

Ian's school has implemented a Black Student Alliance and an ally group that teaches about micro-aggressions that have caused trauma, and he believes it is necessary for learning to be uncomfortable to make progress. Ian calls out injustices, both to fulfill the social justice mandate of his school and because he does not want to be viewed as complicit if he ignores inequalities he witnesses.

Community is key to a strength-based approach in his classroom, and Ian has introduced musical theatre to his school as a tool for collaboration with students, colleagues, and parents. Celebrating learning is key to developing a sense of pride in his students, and his classroom cheer is one such way he can instill a positive mindset. Despite his wealth of professional experience, Ian acknowledges that he has failed, is flawed, and recognizes the need to remain engaged in reflection of his practice, to listen, and stay committed to improving his practice.

- Describe life experiences that have shaped your strength-based learning.
- What does a strength-based teaching approach look like in your classroom?
- Why do you focus on strengths-based teaching vs. deficit thinking?
- How does the community contribute to your strength-based practice?
- How would you evaluate your overall strength-based approach to overcome deficit thinking?

Individual Structures and Strength Consciousness

Individual Structures
- Personal agency
- Self-awareness
- Growth mindset
- Overcoming cognitive dissonance
- Interpersonal emotional regulation

Individual structures are ideas that arise from personal internal psychology that influence the external experiences of an environment (Major, 2012).

As a Teacher

Maintaining a consciousness of yourself and your environment is essential for successfully applying everyday strength-based approaches to eliminate deficit thinking in the classroom. This process begins when you are self-reflective, self-aware, and willing to self-explore, allowing you to understand your own needs. Daniels (2024) found that individual structures and personality traits were key factors in promoting a commitment to practice and responsibilities that can combat the challenges of classroom demands. Personal agency is essential for overcoming cognitive dissonance and achieving a growth mindset in teaching. You must be transparent about lived experiences that might prevent you from attaining strength-based approaches derived from a positive attitude. Barriers in practice, trauma-informed teaching, emotional labor, burnout, and self-efficacy can all suppress your motivation to challenge obstacles that must be overcome so you can contend with deficit-based thinking and shortcomings within the education structure.

For Students

A heightened consciousness of yourself enables you to systematically identify your strengths, fostering self-awareness that can be transformed into potential practice. By methodically recognizing talents, skills, and past successes, this process shifts focus from perceived shortcomings to existing capabilities, creating a foundation for intentional growth and leading a strength-based approach in the classroom. Modelling and teaching this strength-based mindset to your students can develop habits of optimism that emphasize possibilities and reframe weaknesses as areas for growth. The resulting empowerment encourages resilience, transforming self-doubt into a roadmap for achievement grounded in authenticity and self-trust, which enables you to maintain a strength-based approach in the classroom.

Voice From the Field

As a South Asian woman and a child of immigrants raised in the public school system, deficit thinking was not just something I witnessed; it was something I lived. I grew up navigating a system that often overlooked the strengths, values, and cultural richness of families like mine. That experience shaped my perspective and became the driving force behind my 25-year commitment to education and autism.

Early in my career, I realized that labelling children based on what they couldn't do often stripped them of dignity, identity, and opportunity. I saw how quickly children, especially those from diverse backgrounds, were defined by what they lacked instead of who they were. So I built my practice around a different philosophy. My progressive approach to autism intervention and education aligns with a strength-based teaching approach. It was born from the belief that every child has capacity, every family has value, and every culture holds insight that should guide how we teach and connect.

Diversity isn't an add-on; it is foundational. I teach my teams to meet children where they are, to honor identity, and to embed cultural understanding into every plan. Rather than focusing on limitations, we focus on possibilities. We celebrate unique learning styles, integrate family voices, and adapt programming through a culturally aware lens. That shift alone changed trajectories. We build trust, foster belonging, and create space for children to thrive as their authentic selves. Deficit thinking holds no space when strength leads the way.

— Am Badwall-Brown, Clinical director and founder of Missing Links Autism

Positive Affirmations

Use lessons on Positive Affirmations as an introspective exercise for your students to develop an understanding of their strengths; see Positive Affirmations K–Grade 6 on page 158, and Positive Affirmations Grades 7–12 on page 159. You can also use the results as a guide for your teaching practice to tailor your lessons and help students use their capabilities in their learning.

Positive Affirmations K–Grade 6
- Examples of top strength: Artist, Helper, Builder, etc.
- Use stickers for engagement.

Positive Affirmations Grades 7–12
- Examples of affirmations:

    My imagination helps me solve problems in unique ways.

    I am strong and can overcome challenges.

    My kindness makes a difference in the world.

    I am a lifelong learner full of wonder.

    I contribute value to my team.

    I lead with confidence and care.

    I am capable of managing my tasks.

- Use this tool to guide one-on-one discussions or group workshops.
- Encourage students to share affirmations as a Strengths Wall display.
- Revisit assessments quarterly to monitor progress and growth.

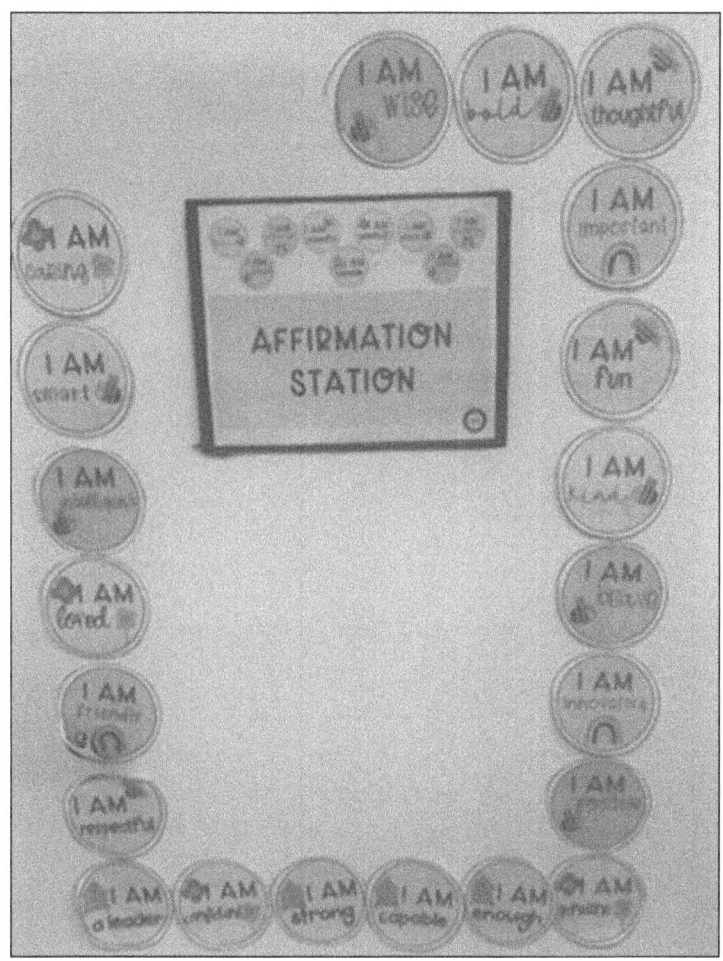

Journal Activities: Strength Spotlight and Strength Mapping

Objective: To help students cultivate equity in their self-perception by recognizing their strengths, reflecting on challenges, and developing a growth mindset through structured writing.

My Superpower and My Growing Seed (K–6)

Materials Needed
- Journal or worksheet with prompts
- Colored pencils/markers
- Stickers or cut-out images for creativity (optional)

Journal Prompts

1. Strength Spotlight
    - What is one thing you did really well this week? (e.g., helped a friend, solved a problem, tried something new)
    - Draw a picture of yourself using this superpower!

2. Challenge Cloud
    - What was something hard for you this week? How did you handle it?
    - Draw a rain cloud, then add a sun because challenges help us grow!

3. Growth Garden
- What is one thing you want to get better at? How can you practice it?
- Draw a seed growing into a flower or tree to show your progress!

Reflection Question
How can you use your superpower to help others?

Strength Mapping and Growth Pathways (7–12)
Materials Needed
- Journal or digital document
- Vision board supplies (magazines, quotes, etc.) (optional)

Journal Prompts
1. Strength Inventory
   - List 3 personal strengths (skills, traits, or values). How have these helped you recently?
   - How can you use these strengths to support equity in your school/community?
2. Challenge Reflection
   - Describe a recent obstacle. How did you respond? What would you do differently next time?
   - How does this challenge connect to fairness or perspective-taking?
3. Growth Pathway
   - Identify one area for improvement (academic, social, emotional).
   - What steps will you take to grow in this area? Who or what resources can help?

Reflection Question
How can a growth mindset help create a more equitable classroom or community?

Facilitation Tips
- K–6: Use storytelling, art, and group sharing to reinforce strengths.
- 7–12: Encourage peer discussions or anonymous strength-sharing to build collective equity.
- For all ages: Revisit entries periodically to track progress and celebrate growth.

Voice from the Field

To reduce deficit thinking, we must prioritize emotional intelligence, encouraging education to emerge intrinsically rather than from external rewards or validation. Unfortunately, much of our system is designed to move kids from A to B rather than create an environment for them to thrive.

Strength-based learning is only possible when a child is connected to their authentic selves and in an environment that celebrates critical thinking, innovation, and creativity over blind obedience.

For there to be less deficit thinking, teachers need to focus on the journey of learning rather than the end result.

— Patricia Selib, Social entrepreneur and Transformational coach

Instructional Innovations

The practical application of strength-based approaches in your classroom underscores the need for instructional innovation that leverages your students' unique abilities. Implementing various strategies can form the foundation of your lessons.

Inquiry-based learning tailors lessons to students' interests, extending beyond the confines of the curriculum to provide a holistic, experiential learning experience. This form of learning also encourages co-constructed knowledge building that develops a partnership in education. Such a process promotes active participation of teachers and students, expanding awareness to move beyond the traditional curriculum, and inspires trust as part of the learning relationship. Moreover, it removes the conventional educator role that expects passive student participation and shifts to building an active and confident learner. Apply scaffolding techniques to build on prior knowledge and guide students toward new understanding, breaking down complex concepts into manageable steps.

Universal Design for Learning (UDL) offers multiple means of representation and expression to ensure diversity in learning. This process builds upon inquiry-based learning and challenges traditional methods that maintain a colonial structure, replacing them with an authentic knowledge-building approach that leverages student strengths. Interrupting conventional learning methods from the early stages of learning prepares the classroom to proactively incorporate strength-based approaches. Pre-emptively planning and organizing, with structured yet flexible rubrics guiding self-assessment and peer feedback, ensures that expectations are void of right or wrong, focusing instead on demonstrating knowledge acquisition. When you consciously and intentionally reflect on student progress through one-on-one meetings, adjusting strategies to reinforce strengths rather than focusing on deficits, the shift to strength-based learning becomes natural.

Instructional Strategies in the Classroom

This…	… Leads to this
Understanding student profiles	Identifying needs/strengths/supports
Developing effective/differentiated plans	Culturally responsive pedagogy
Modelling a growth mindset	Developing a strength-based culture
Inquiry-based learning	Scaffolding new understanding
Learning Environment	Student experience
Assessment and feedback	Ability to reflect and adapt

Voice from the Field

Strength-based learning has been the heart of each role I've held in my 20-year career. A strength-based approach isn't just about the language that appears on a report card. Intentional shifts in both language and mindset are interconnected in the same way that affirmations work to shift beliefs. When we transform our thought patterns toward what students CAN do versus what's missing, students, in turn, start to think and feel differently about their learning.

Building positive, affirming, and lateral learning partnerships with students that celebrate what they know and can do builds agency and challenges traditional, teacher-centred, and transactional colonial hierarchies. When learning is transactional, the amount of work, or "quality" of work is often perceived as a character judgment (lazy, disruptive, etc.) as well as an academic one, and this thinking deeply reinforces existing systemic inequities. From conversations in staff rooms to the phrasing on rubrics and assignment criteria, an emphasis on gaps ultimately perpetuates the white-supremacist, hierarchical, ableist thinking and gatekeeping that has created obstacles for marginalized students, narrowing their success opportunities to colonial ideals of achievement. A strength-based approach is about the possibilities of authentic and individualized learning. It is transformational.

— Johanna Lankin, Educator

Community Care

Building a culture of compassion in your classroom is crucial to creating an environment that adopts strength-based approaches, allowing students to thrive.

As a principal, it is vital that I ensure my school environment adopts a community of care, allowing my staff to have access to social resources, such as mentorship, professional development workshops, and leadership coaching, which can provide them with the tools and emotional support needed to foster inclusive, asset-focused classrooms. New teachers who participate in induction programs can experience a smooth transition into their career by embedding strength-based philosophies from the outset, ensuring support and confidence.

Peer mentoring is part of a collaborative environment where colleagues can lean on one another to share strategies, reflect on their practices, and foster a growth mindset that reinforces a culture of strength. Additionally, collaborative inquiry can inspire you to engage in reflective dialogue, challenge your biases, and collectively develop equitable teaching practices.

Together, these supports create a nurturing professional ecosystem that empowers you to recognize and build on students' strengths, ultimately transforming classroom culture and improving outcomes for all your students. This holistic framework can enhance your classroom dynamics and empower you to cultivate empathy and resilience, ultimately fostering a more inclusive and effective learning community.

Social Resources

Peer Mentoring

Community Support

Induction Programming

Collaborative Inquiry

STORY FROM THE CLASSROOM

Engaged community members and activists Doug Keer, a social worker and human rights activist, and Michael Went, a former LGBT activist, are no strangers to operating with a strength-based perspective to overcome life's challenges. Queer parents of a mixed-race family, they adopted their son, who at two years old was diagnosed with leukemia and received treatment until he started school. Soon after starting school, it was identified that their son had delays in learning, and he needed academic support. Fortunately, the school in their neighborhood offered a customized education opportunity that met the needs of families.

Families were heavily emphasized as a core pillar of leading in this school, which offered a unique approach that prioritized and fostered community. The school celebrated diversity and fostered an affirming, positive environment, reinforced by the collective efforts of its educators. The administrators were allies who offered support and awareness of queer identity and Black history, and provided representation within the school community. Traditions linking the school to the neighborhood established strong community building, representing the student body. Despite the school having a population of only about 120 students, the classes were diverse in terms of differences and racial representation. This city-centred school motivated students and exposed social justice teaching as a regular aspect of the curriculum. Equity was embedded in the entry lottery program to maintain a pool of diverse students, along with strong, diverse leadership. Longevity in practice provided consistency among staff, which in turn built a thriving learning community.

- Could you share your journey and explain how a strength-based outlook was necessary for you?
- What influences have shaped your insights into a strength-based perspective?

- What made your child's elementary school the best choice for their education?
- How has diversity factored into your experience to overcome deficit thinking?
- Explain the role people have in your life have played in your achieving a strength-based attitude.

Final Thoughts

When you adopt strength-based approaches in the classroom, you deliberately shift from a deficit-based perspective to an asset-based one. As I close this chapter, I challenge you to reflect on the content presented and determine how effectively you are leading with strength-based practice in your classroom. If you discover discrepancies, I encourage you to be honest with yourself and use this authenticity to apply the ideas from the stories from me and the other voices in your practice. Be gentle with yourself, but also hold yourself accountable to deliberately explore strength-based principles in the process of integrating powerful pedagogy, to create learning experiences that affirm and amplify students' capabilities.

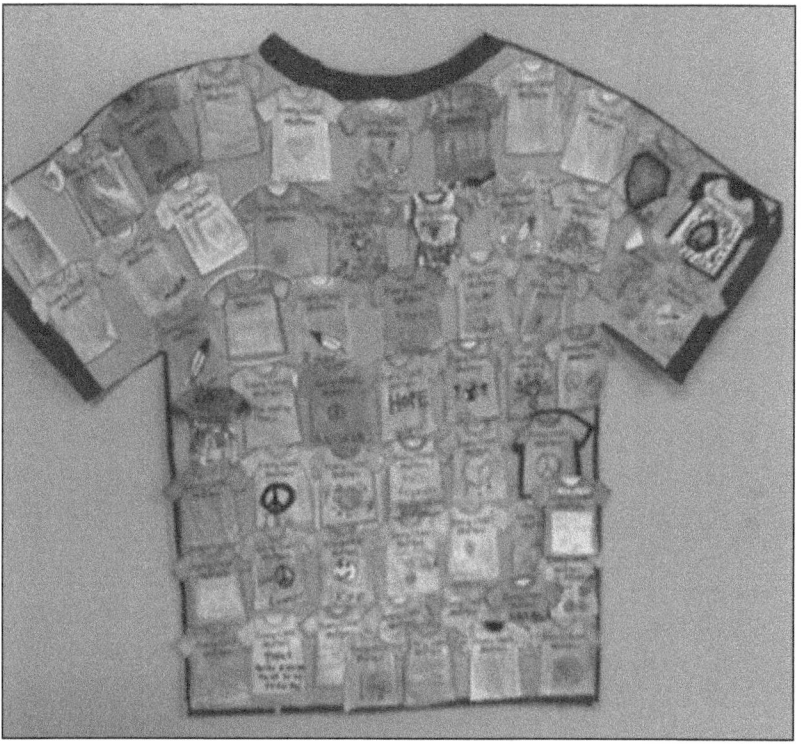

Remember that environmental enablers, such as inclusive and supportive classrooms, along with individual structures like self-awareness and personal agency, can foster resilience in your students. Cultivate a strength consciousness that ensures you recognize and nurture each student's unique potential, while implementing instructional innovations that provide dynamic, student-centred opportunities for growth. Ultimately, when you secure a community of care, it underscores the collective responsibility of colleagues and families to foster a culture of belonging and empowerment. Together, these elements can guide you in transforming your practice, ensuring every student is valued, supported, and inspired to thrive. I hope that this chapter leaves you with a sense of optimism and an awareness of the possibilities that can result from strength-based approaches that eliminate deficit thinking in schools.

Positive Affirmation Tool K–Grade 6

Name: _____

Part 1: My Superpowers

Circle the emoji that matches how you feel about each statement.

☺ = Yes   😐 = Sometimes   ☹ = Not Yet

Strength   **Emoji Self-Check**

Idea Maker: I like to create new things.   ☺   😐   ☹

Problem Solver: I figure things out.   ☺   😐   ☹

Kind Heart: I help others feel happy.   ☺   😐   ☹

Try-Again Champ: I don't give up.   ☺   😐   ☹

Part 2: Draw and Say

My Top Strength

Draw yourself using your favorite strength. Caption: I am a _____.

Daily Affirmation

Trace drawing and repeat: "I am caring. I am smart. I am ME!"
- ☐ Monday
- ☐ Tuesday
- ☐ Wednesday
- ☐ Thursday
- ☐ Friday

Positive Affirmations Tool Grades 7–12

Rate each statement from 1 (Rarely) to 5 (Always).

Creativity: I enjoy coming up with new ideas.	☐ 1 ☐ 2 ☐ 3 ☐ 4 ☐ 5
Resilience: I keep trying even when things are hard.	☐ 1 ☐ 2 ☐ 3 ☐ 4 ☐ 5
Kindness: I help others and show empathy.	☐ 1 ☐ 2 ☐ 3 ☐ 4 ☐ 5
Curiosity: I ask questions and love learning.	☐ 1 ☐ 2 ☐ 3 ☐ 4 ☐ 5
Teamwork: I collaborate well with others.	☐ 1 ☐ 2 ☐ 3 ☐ 4 ☐ 5
Leadership: I guide or inspire others.	☐ 1 ☐ 2 ☐ 3 ☐ 4 ☐ 5
Organization: I plan and stay focused.	☐ 1 ☐ 2 ☐ 3 ☐ 4 ☐ 5

Top Strengths: List 3 strengths you scored highest on.

1. _____

2. _____

3. _____

Affirmation Creation: Write a personal affirmation based on your #1 strength.

I am _____ because I _____.
(Example: *I am resilient because I keep going even when things are tough*.)

Growth Opportunity: Choose one strength to improve and write an affirmation for it.

Every day, I am getting better at _____.

Practice Positive Self-Talk

Challenge: Repeat your affirmations daily for a week.
Morning: Say your affirmation aloud.
Night: Reflect on how you used your strength that day.

12

Working with Parents to Establish Everyday Equity Practices

Matthew Sinclair

As the child of Guyanese immigrants, Matthew has seen how acknowledging the various social locations in our society and taking action to counter oppressive narratives can inspire change. He continues to use his privilege and influence to create positive shifts in the education system. Most importantly, he is a proud Black son, brother, husband, and father of three amazing sons.

"Did you know that a tree has to grow in two directions at the same time? The nature of a tree is both gravitropic and phototropic. Gravitropic means it grows away from light, that's the root system. When the seed is under the ground, it has resistance. Once it breaks through the Earth growing up, it grows towards light and away from ground. That is one of the most beautiful pictures of the way life works. It's the work you do in the dark when it's difficult that makes the work that everybody sees in the light."
— Myron Golden

This quote is a beautiful metaphor for the potential that lives in all of us to grow. Not only do trees grow in both directions, but the complexity of the root system is also the same complexity of the fruit system, which creates symmetry. It can be a challenge to balance the introspective work that is needed in the dark and the tangible work that the world sees, especially when it comes to equity issues. The fruit system, without a foundation of work on ourselves and knowledge-building, can at times land as performative allyship. Conversely, simply reading and learning about oppression without ever applying the learning is not going to effect change. Oppressed groups need to feel the support and advocacy for it to be real.

A culture of inclusion cannot be limited to simply student–teacher interactions. Families and community play an integral role, as they not only inform students' worldview but also are, and will always be, experts on their children. They also carry the culture and heritage that represents the identity of our students, which we want them to feel comfortable representing at school. Educator connections with families and caregivers can completely transform a student's educational experience and the trajectory of their life. We need the families of our students to be aware of why our classroom is a place where differences are celebrated, and recognize that we seek to learn about each other as much as we learn academic material. Regardless of pre-existing biases that caregivers might have, students need to understand why offensive behaviors, expressions, and thoughts will not be tolerated in our classrooms. We also want the classroom community (formed by the educators, students, and their families) to see first-hand how the classroom is genuinely reflective of their identity and the world around them. Social justice is at the centre of how we prepare students to be global citizens by recognizing and having the tools to dismantle oppression.

We want to establish positive relationships with our students' families that will ensure they see you, their child's teacher, as a trustworthy and supportive part of their child's life. Investing in this connection is helpful, as you nurture the student in front of you while also embracing the amazing adult they will grow to be. This means prioritizing relationship-building and connections that go beyond parent–teacher conferences or newsletters. Genuine connection is how we can best navigate the eventual challenges with students or their families that happen throughout the year. These connections are formed by making intentional efforts to learn about the cultural backgrounds, values, and lived experiences of families. Throughout this chapter you will find strategies for this work, including ways in which we can provide families with language and approaches that they can take with their child to help their development. See page 172 for a reproducible letter to parents/caregivers that can be used with families to establish a foundation of equity and social justice.

Equity in Action

We speak often of meeting people where they are at, and this chapter suggests opportunities and various entry points without judgment. Regardless of where you find yourself, there is always work to be done. We are constantly learning, and this chapter is intended to support your journey. The visual below provides tiers that represent various levels of understanding of equity issues.

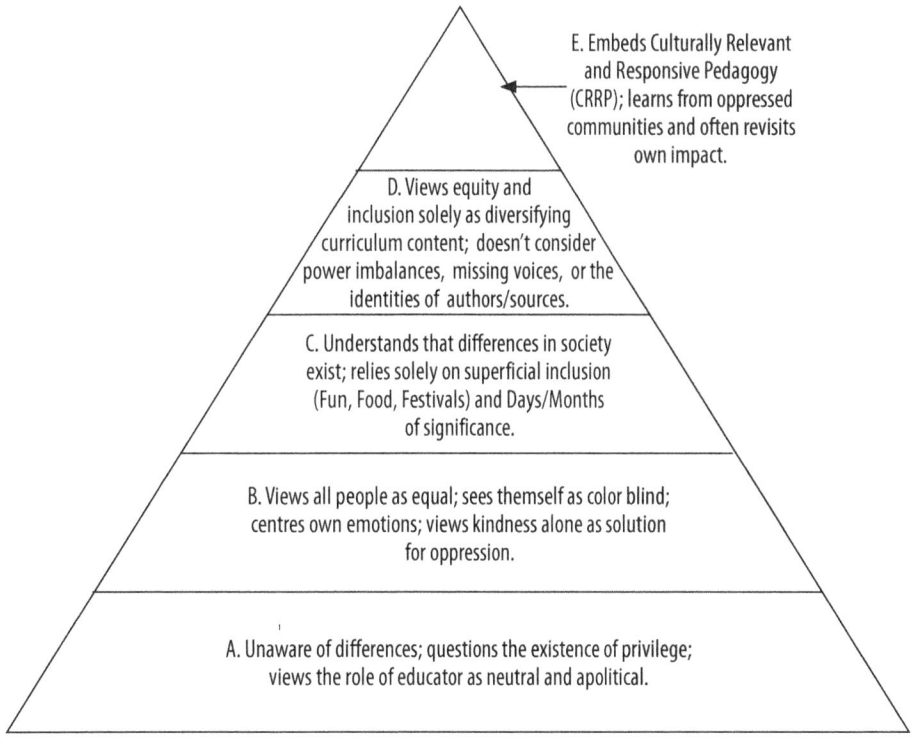

The tiers are based on the realities that many educators and caregivers develop on their equity journeys. This chapter is intentionally layered in the following structure:

- Level of Learning (from the bottom up)
- Root Work: background learning and awareness-building
- Real-World Example: Story from the Classroom/Voice from the Field
- Fruit Work: actions that can be taken

Unlearn: Level A

Root Work

Unaware of differences; questions the existence of privilege; views the role of the educator as neutral and apolitical.

Society normalizes oppressive systems that create privilege for some and often inform us to compartmentalize parts of our lives. Rather than seeing social justice as part of the education system, individuals in this tier attempt to separate these two aspects of their lives. To do so is not a privilege available to everyone, based on their lived experiences. "It is a privilege to learn about oppression instead of experiencing it." We need to proactively approach the relationships we create with students and their families.

Strategies to support this work include
- Using diverse and accessible tools (Google Translate, TalkingPoints app, multilingual newsletters and phone calls, etc.) to reduce barriers and promote inclusive communication
- Contacting students' families via email or, ideally, by phone, with a positive observation and connection that you have made early in the school year.
- Providing opportunities for families to share their needs by proactively asking about the languages spoken at home, their preferred language of communication, translation resources.

For many caregivers and families, we are their introduction to the education system, and the ways we navigate this will leave the strongest impression on families. One of the ways we can counter traditional, privilege-based approaches is providing access. Below are questions and context for you; see page 173 for a reproducible 5Ws and an H handout that can be sent home for parents as a guide to communication with family members for the year.

Where Does Your Community Congregate?

Sometimes it's easier for us to go to the community, rather than have the community come to us. If possible, alleviate transportation or access issues by hosting school events at a community centre rather than the school building if there are issues of accessibility (public transportation, abilities, distance from most families). Technology has made various methods of meeting much more accessible, including speech-to text-transcription, translation, or online meetings.

When Is the Best Time to Contact You?

Many people work overnight shifts, and the more access to information we have from parents, the better. Our workday might not be the same as theirs. Asking parents to share their preferred timing also provides a us with a window into the at home life of the student.

What Are Your Expectations for Your Child this Year? What Are Their Goals for this Year?

Asking this question explicitly makes sure we aren't making assumptions, and it places everyone's priorities together. Importantly, if we ask this question following lessons on goal-setting or procedural writing, it links curriculum with connections at home in a transparent and natural way.

Who Should Be Contacted?

We should not make assumptions about the best person to contact in the student's life. The contact person could vary based on the day of week, as work schedules, custody situations, and other factors might inform these situations. Multigenerational and multilingual families might also have specific communication needs that we should be aware of.

Why I Might Contact You

The year should start with a sunshine message (a positive you've noticed) paired with connection. Use the initial connection to make clear that you are supportive of the student's learning journey. Other reasons to reach out include sharing of good news, inquiring about changes that you notice, and addressing concerns.

How Do I Best Contact You?

Most educators now use a communication app that provides easy access to information and evidence of student learning. A phone call could be an option, but messages or email can also increase accessibility. Families might speak multiple languages home, and written messages could ease translation. Deconstruct privilege and increase access by using an app that offers translation options; e.g., Class Dojo.

STORY FROM THE CLASSROOM

The Impact of Nationality

In a traditionally homogenous school board, several communities have recently experienced a significant shift in demographics, seemingly overnight. Based on its location close to the border, there has been a huge influx of newcomers to Canada. Many of these families are being settled in the community due to escaping conflict in their country of origin and/or are settling in Canada as refugees. Staff and the families in the community who have been at the school for an extended period have rarely had to consider many equity issues and are now forced to deal with a variety of new realities: a large multi-language learner population; a more transient population; and a school board that is not equipped to provide adequate and timely supports. These challenges are leading to issues of miscommunication and frustration that range from outright xenophobia to difficulties from being under-resourced.

- How can these educators find ways to support their new students?
- What connections and supports should they consider to reimagine existing school practices?

Fruit Work

Your ability to show empathy and connect with families will largely influence their perception of their new school and community. This is important on an emotional level and serves as another reminder of how and why teaching is not a neutral or apolitical position. Practical strategies that can support family–educator relationships on this tier include the following:

- Connecting with possible board supports, possible settlement workers, and/or cultural centres will allow you to support students while positioning yourself as a learner.
- Use a trauma-informed approach with all students, but especially those who are newcomers or from marginalized communities.
- Provide opportunities for students to take the lead and, in the process, allow them to teach you about their culture. Positioning yourself as a learner is an act of vulnerability that allows your students to feel more comfortable taking chances in their learning. Display evidence of this diversity in the classroom.
- Consider finding a mentor family or support for new families to the community, especially those are who multi-language learners. This can ease transitions and intentionally build community.

Unlearn: Level B

Root Work

> Views all people as equal; sees themself as color blind; centres own emotions; views kindness alone as a solution for oppression.

People in this tier inflate the effect of kindness to the point of viewing it as a method of liberation. The danger of this approach is that it oversimplifies oppression and operates from a sympathetic, deficit mindset about oppressed communities, where sympathy can easily lead to lowering expectations for marginalized students. Families have high expectations and goals for their children and our role is to support those goals, not impede them. Kindness and charity will not eradicate systemic oppression. As Ralph Nader says, "A world with more justice will need less charity." Actions that provide insights into the root causes of oppression will expand the approach from sympathy to empathy with action. Ways we can make this progress can include learning more about student's home culture, by directly asking the child though projects and doing our own research online.

STORY FROM THE CLASSROOM

The Impact of Class

At a school that is diverse culturally and socio-economically, the parent council is planning Grade 8 graduation activities, which have typically consisted of an overnight trip, the ceremony, and a graduation dinner. The members of the parent council represent the most affluent families. Unaware of their shared class privilege, the council suggests a $100 per student dinner following the ceremony. Including the trip, the cost of graduation would exceed $500 per student.

Staff raises the issue of affordability and possible inequities between families. The parent council feels frustrated at not being able to offer their children the ceremony that they want. The next response is to use their affluence

and kindness to subsidize the costs for other families. They have gone from being unaware of their privilege, to centring themselves and using charity to solve the perceived problem. While the intention behind this thought may be positive, the impact would not. The parent council speaking on behalf of oppressed families and denying them the opportunity to provide for their own children was a problem. The school's administration intervened and told the council that all families could proudly support a more affordable dinner, and that was eventually approved for all students.
- Consider the parents on your school's parent council. Do they reflect the socio-economic diversity of the school community? If not, how could this be corrected by accessing more parent voices?

Fruit Work

The issue of equity can present itself in a variety of ways when it comes to socio-economic class. We should not judge or make assumptions, but we should consider affordability when deciding everything from field trips to indoor shoe policies. This might necessitate a shift in practice, which will require reflection and the acceptance that you will make mistakes. Give yourself the grace of patience and don't be afraid to apologize to your students or their families. Acknowledging mistakes and expressing genuine regret can strengthen relationships, especially with families from marginalized communities.

Annual Checkpoints for Equity Growth

Entering the School Year: New Year #1

How will you
- Provide students and their families a blank slate to show their growth, regardless of previous perception?
- Allow yourself, your students, and their families to build relationships together?
- Reach out proactively to each family in the fall?

Caregiver–Teacher Interview

- Contact families in advance to describe the interview structure. Let them know that you will be providing time, not just for their concerns, but also for them to speak to the goals and expectations they have for the year. Focus on building together, as this could be one of only a few direct interactions with most parents.
- How can you support and ensure alignment between the student's goals and the family's goals for the student?

January: New Year #2

- What have you learned about your students' families so far? Is there evidence of this learning visible in the physical classroom?
- Reflect on how your predictions/assumptions have been altered from August to this point.

This is a great self-reflective tool for you to assess progress throughout the year.

- Some students/families are more demanding/talkative than others. How can you connect with those students/families that you have not had a chance to get to know yet?

    End of the School Year

- What did you learn about your school community this year?
- Has your school community changed in terms of demographics, engagement, and/or equity-minded accomplices on staff?
- What steps can you take to further your individual professional development?

Learn: Level C

Root Work

Understands that differences in society exist; relies solely on superficial inclusion (Fun, Food, Festivals) and Days/Months of significance.

Social justice dates can be referred to throughout the year to highlight cultural, religious, and oppression differences. These days might be mentioned on classroom calendars, on the announcements, or during school assemblies. Historically, there hasn't always been consideration of how we embed culture in the curriculum throughout the school year. This can create a "field trip" effect to equity, where it becomes feast or famine: if a child is absent on the day of significance, they might not see their identity reflected for another year.

Families from ethnic backgrounds might compare how different cultures are recognized. This can feed the "crab in the bucket" mentality, where all oppressed groups are forced to compete for minimal opportunities, rather than working together. We need to be aware of how use our privilege to embed culture meaningfully and to actively tie conversations on oppression back to the liberation of all people.

Voice from the Field: Culture and Race

As a student in Ontario, I have few memories of opportunities where my culture or lived experience was reflected in the classroom. One of the few was as a primary student, when a particularly thoughtful teacher hosted a potluck for my class. Each student had to bring in food from our culture to share with the class. I recall bringing in homemade Guyanese beef patties, while other classmates offered latkes, pakoras, and various treats. It was a fun experience to taste foods from around the world, but there was no tie to classroom work or additional embedding other than that day.
— Winston, Parent

Fruit Work

In the 1990s, the broad approach to multiculturalism was well-intentioned, but now it is crucial that educators find ways to make more meaningful connections with families when embedding culture. Opportunities to celebrate diversity still exist, but consider ways to make deeper, more meaningful connections.

Student Assignment: Family Flag

> This activity, for students to complete with their families, can be scaffolded based on grade level.

We have been learning about symbols and flags in our classroom for countries, provinces, tribes, social justice movements, etc. What are their roots? What do the colors and/or symbols represent? Have they changed over time?

An example of a flag that has evolved over time is the LGBTQ-PRIDE rainbow flag: it has added pink, white, and blue from the trans flag and brown and black to represent black and brown skin.

1. Consider: What symbols and/or flags represent your family?
2. Design your own flag to represent your unique heritage, ethnicity, culture, and identity. Choose two to four symbols and three colors.

Re-Learn: Level D

Root Work

> Views equity and inclusion solely as diversifying curriculum content; doesn't consider power imbalances, missing voices, or the identities of authors/sources.

Educators in this tier have consciously chosen to reflect the diversity of their students in their learning materials. This is a wonderful way to make caregivers and family members feel seen. Not all educators are willing to make the effort or spend the time and money required to keep updated with diverse resources. As a parent, it is extremely reassuring when I see my children's educators making the effort to reflect the identity of the students in their class back to them through books and resources.

Educators should also consider the authors that are telling the stories. That authors have lived experience is an important factor and needs to be part of the process. For example, texts that have a focus on differing abilities or neurodivergence should be written by authors who are speaking from their experiences of oppression. There is nothing like the power of telling one's own story.

STORY FROM THE CLASSROOM

Decentring Self

Ms. Thompson is an educator who attends workshops and participates in equity professional development opportunities. She consistently ensures days of significance or religions celebrations are integrated in her classroom, using books and/or videos. This is appreciated by the community, especially those families that have, in her opinion, "well-behaved" students. When she taught my first child, my wife and I recall feeling positive about her, since our child would routinely come home excited, as a book, flag, or celebration he recognized from home would be shared in the classroom.

When our next son, who does not acclimate as easily to new situations as his brother, was in her class, our experience was very different. Though he had thrived in daycare and all other social situations, he struggled with the transition to this classroom. He did not easily conform, a trauma response from his adoption at two-years-old, which created discomfort that sometimes presented as misbehavior. Ms. Thompson's frustration and rigid approach created a heightened level of tension between her, our son, and our family on a regular basis. It became clear that she viewed her dedication to diverse curriculum as being enough to represent equity, without extending it to understanding and accommodation of individual students. She labelled our son as difficult, often using deficit language. Families who questioned

classroom structure were routinely met with defensiveness. Our son has since returned to thriving in subsequent years, highlighting the negative impact of this approach. The ability to see families as experts on their children was not something Ms. Thompson could adjust to, as she viewed the classroom as solely her domain.
- How can you build in practices that ensure parent and student voice?
- Why is it important to prepare for potential conflict(s) with caregivers?
- Are there school or board supports that can guide a teacher's interactions with students and families?
- How can we balance our ongoing root work with palpable fruit work without reaching a plateau in our equity journey?

Voice from the Field

As a parent, I think back to my son's time in your class. He was different and excited from day one. Teachers have to care. Even though it's been seven years, my child still remembers you as an educator, Mr. Sinclair. He's now twenty-one and what he says stood out is that while other teachers may have cared about him, you were the one who showed and *told* him that you cared. That made the difference.
— Ms. Blake, Parent of former student

Fruit Work

Decolonizing our content is great, but if we are not consciously decolonizing our practice, it will reveal itself in our relationships with families. The best educator–family relationships are reciprocal, and actively display shared power in centring the development of the student.

Here are some strategies for when you must contact a caregiver if there is an issue with a student from a marginalized community:
- Use a trauma-informed approach. Consider how your messaging and approach could be perceived by the caregiver.
- Reflect on the students' previous experiences within the school. What approaches were effective? How can you ensure you don't replicate recent or historical harm?
- Take a curious approach to behavior. Rather than making judgments, ask questions and provide space for the caregiver to share their perspective before and after you share your concern.
- Ensure caregivers know you are continuing to build a partnership with them; that you need their active collaboration in ensuring students meet and exceed both academic and behavioral expectations.

Re-Learn: Level E

Root Work

Embeds Culturally Relevant and Responsive Pedagogy (CRRP); learns from oppressed communities and often revisits own impact.

Educators in this tier understand that, when power is shared with families, student engagement and achievement increases. Students and their families who consistently see their identity and realities reflected in the classroom thrive.

Open-ended assignments and flexibility in how the curriculum is covered create a foundation for a healthy classroom environment. Over time, the school community, itself, will provide opportunities for new and, at times, unanticipated learning opportunities.

When the school embraces this approach, it allows students, educators, and families to consistently grow and evolve. This can also lead to creative extracurricular clubs and opportunities. Communication with parents about classroom norms is balanced with a school culture of understanding and growth, allowing the school community to contribute and learn together. In this tier, the educator explicitly exposes students to various equity issues with the understanding that experiences of oppression make communities more alike than different. Diverse experiences of marginalization are present, but liberation remains our goal.

> **STORY FROM THE CLASSROOM**
>
> ### Challenging Power
>
> I taught a group of intermediate students who had routinely been labelled as difficult. It took some time for them to truly trust me and my teaching partner as their educators. Each time they experienced choice and saw more of their culture reflected, they felt more at ease. Several times throughout the first term, I had to actively position myself as a learner with these students, especially since they had been together for many years and had a strong established culture as a group. As trust built and students understood that social justice was truly embodied in our class, part of this process was students using assignments as opportunities to openly question school practices that replicated oppression within society.
>
> I recall students asking why the girls' sports teams did not have as many games or practices as the boys' teams. Similarly, after a lesson on consent and male privilege, a group of young women challenged the existence of the school dress code. These questions reflected their learning and prompted conversations with the administration about why certain rules were in place.
>
> - How can we provide suitable ways for families and students to question authority?
> - What steps will you take to manage discomfort when families or students question you?
> - What can you do to show empathy and balanced opinions if students/families share opposing views on an issue?

Fruit Work

The actions in this tier reflect challenging tradition and putting ourselves on the same plane as our students and their families. In terms of authority, the teacher is the professional in the room, but also a fellow learner and classroom citizen. Are we able to step back and listen to our students rather than treat them dismissively? If so, can we ensure that we are comfortable with the vulnerability required by letting our students lead?

This approach requires open communication with families. Not every family is going to support the way that some social justice themes are intertwined in the classroom. Some of these families could be marginalized themselves, but might have discomfort with certain topics, especially if they have not been aware of these themes culturally. It's important to be aware of board policy, Ministry information, and any relevant advisories from teaching regulatory bodies that support equitable education. Teachers are not on an island in this work, as people or in terms of policy.

How can we re-imagine our approach to parent and cultural engagement? Many families are not able to engage with a school through the existing and somewhat outdated model of parent councils. Consider how technology and online meetings can provide space for different voices to be a part of the decision-making process. Also consider how and when schools look for diverse voices to come to the table. Too often, equity is an add-on at the end of planning rather than being a part of the process from the beginning. Oppressed communities do not simply want a seat once the table is built, they want to be a part of shaping the size, material, and other planning steps for the table itself.

> An example of a community initiative uses a model that can be replicated at the school and institutional level. The core group of organizers and planners is made up of an academic expert, an educator, and a community member with rich cultural history. These three parties work together and in concert to plan and execute opportunities that can serve the community. One voice is not over another, and they work as a group seeking consensus before moving forward. As a parent, the opportunity to replicate a process like this at the school level would be fantastic, as it would ensure voice, power, and possibilities are all open and shared among all parties.

Voice from the Field

We could just tell how much some teachers wanted to be there and actually work with us. Others just could not be bothered. The ones who seemed happy and enjoyed coming to work made me want to go to school. I never wanted to miss a day in Grade 8. None of us did.
— Steven, Former student, now 23 years old

STORY FROM THE CLASSROOM

My Grade 8 English program focused on social justice, ensuring that we explored various forms of oppression, even if they weren't visibly present in the classroom. One year, after discussing queer racialized heroes like Bayard Rustin, Alok, and Laverne Cox, a quiet student approached me after class. They shared that the discussions on trans identity had resonated deeply with them, and they had researched the topic online. I thanked them for their vulnerability and asked what they needed, both in the moment and moving forward. Importantly, I asked if their parents were aware, which they were.

A week later, the student returned with more articles and insights on gender, and expressed that they were considering new pronouns and a potential name change. I listened, provided space, and assured them they could lean on me, along with their parents. The student eventually felt ready to speak to their parents about it, and the next day this student came in excited to share that the conversation went well. I offered to address the class about using new pronouns and their new name, and most classmates adjusted quickly.

This experience showed me how influential our content choices can be. A few intentional discussions on oppression created a life-changing space for this student, who now studies gender-affirming studies in university.

- How do you use your privilege and/or lived experience to provide connection(s) with your students?
- What can you do to model allyship and privilege with marginalized communities?
- How do you ensure you provide students safety while also allowing them to take the lead in their own learning?
- How would you navigate supporting this student if they had not told their caregivers?
- How would you share this identity and pronoun change with colleagues and classmates to centre this student's safety?

Sample Letter to Parents/Caregivers

Dear Caregiver,

Welcome to our class. I look forward to getting to know you and the students over the course of the next year. Our classroom culture will be grounded in principles of equity that will ensure all students can see their identity reflected, accepted, and celebrated in their work. This approach has many benefits, including, but not limited to, aligning itself with Ministry and school board plans, creating global citizens, ensuring students stay engaged, and providing important opportunities for us to learn from one another.

As their caregiver, you will play a key part in our school year. Students will often be completing assignments where they share their culture and identity, which will require conversations with you. Reflecting the diversity of our school and classroom is an enriching experience that creates deep bonds and allows students to see these spaces as their own.

Students will learn about a variety of cultures and social justice issues. This diversity is part of the beauty of learning and something we celebrate, not simply tolerate or question, in our classroom. You can support your child by

- maintaining openness to new ideas
- ensuring you reflect on your own biases
- setting a good example of respectful communication
- maintaining empathy throughout the school year

Below is a template for a great introductory activity on the difference(s) between equity and equality, which you can complete with your child in your home. Please feel free to use any relevant cultural personal examples when you fill in the circles.

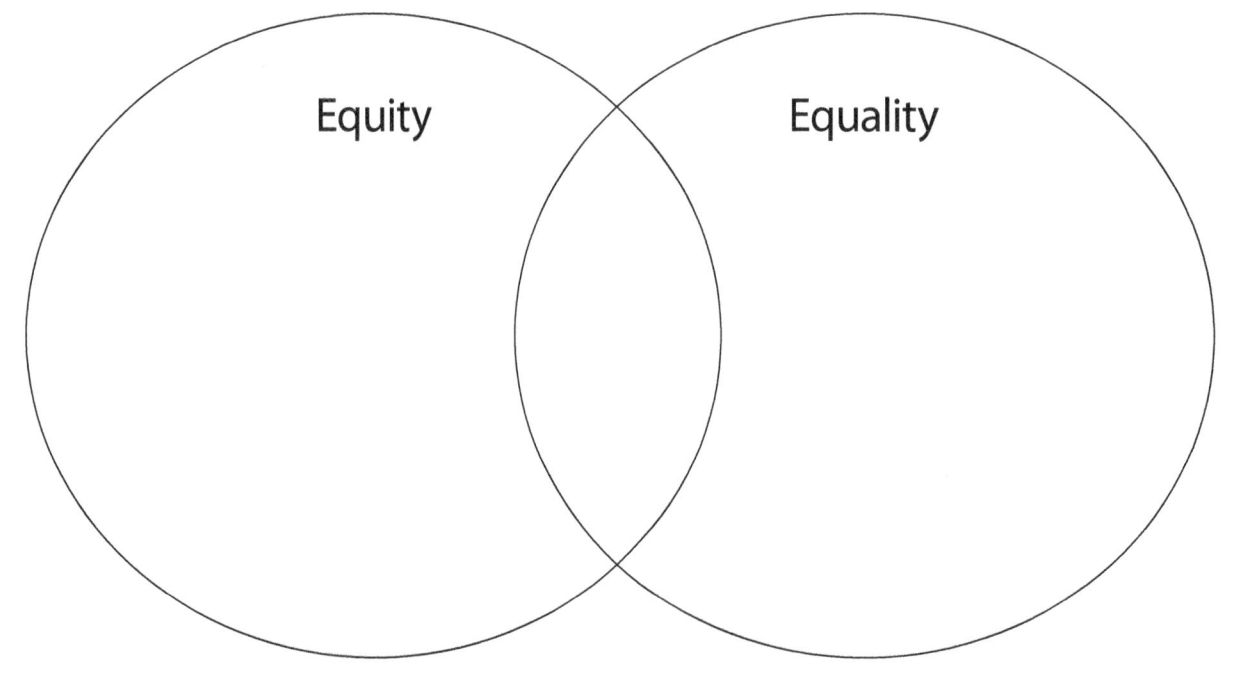

5Ws and an H

5Ws

1. Where Does Your Community Congregate?

_____

_____

2. When Is the Best Time to Contact You?

_____

_____

3. What Are Your Expectations for Your Child this Year? What Are Their Goals for this Year?

_____

_____

4. Who Should be Contacted?

_____

_____

5. Why Should I Contact You? (Additional Reasons for Contact)

_____

_____

An *H*

How Do I Best Contact You?

13

A Seat at the Table

Camille Logan and Shelby A.E. McPhee

Camille Logan is an educational leader with more than 30 years of service in public education. Most recently serving as Associate Director of School Improvement and Equity at the Peel District School Board, Dr. Logan led strategic initiatives to transform curriculum and instruction, dismantle systemic barriers, champion Black student success, and build identity-affirming, inclusive learning environments. Her impact has been recognized through honors that include the National Harmony Award and the Ontario Supervisory Officers' Association Distinguished Leadership Award.

Shelby A. E. McPhee (he/him) is an educator, researcher, and equity practitioner, with years of experience in middle and senior schools, as well as post-secondary education settings, in The Bahamas and across the Greater Toronto Area. Shelby most recently served as Coordinator, Diversity Equity and Inclusion at Branksome Hall. Additionally, he is a PhD Candidate in the Department of Political Science at McMaster University, where his research centres marginalized communities, with a particular focus on race, identity, and belonging.

Getting to the Table

Voices from the Field: Camille and Shelby

More than three decades ago, I entered education with a desire to make a difference. Born and raised in a predominantly white community, my school experiences were marked by my consistently being the "other," as I was often the only Black child in my class, and sometimes in the entire school. My educational experiences were shaped by marginalization, often reinforced by educators, the curriculum, and my peers. Moving through Ontario's public education system, at times I felt the pain of being pushed to the margins, discouraged from reaching my potential, and denied opportunities to thrive (Kumashiro, 2000).

Still, I will never forget my Grade 1 teacher, who truly saw me. She made deliberate efforts to centre my learning, highlight my strengths, and affirm my presence. She constantly corrected students who intentionally mispronounced my name or who told me, "Go back to where you came from," knowing full well that I was born in Ontario. In the 1970s, despite the normalization of anti-Blackness in schools and society, my teacher took leadership of her classroom. Though she may not have called herself an activist, her actions reflected a deep sense of responsibility and active leadership. Her classroom was a space where I felt seen and protected, and felt that I mattered.

When I became a teacher, I carried these early memories with me. I knew the power educators held and understood how a single moment of affirmation could change a child's trajectory. I recognized that transformation doesn't come from policy alone. As a teacher, and later School Administrator, Superintendent, and Associate Director in two of Ontario's largest and most diverse public school districts, I have consistently worked strategically within my sphere of influence. Whether it be at the classroom, division, at school level, or for an entire district, I worked to champion equity, and anti-racist and anti-oppressive pedagogical practices, just as Mohammed Khalifa (2020) has told us "to at all times, contest oppression."

The origins of my leadership were developed while leading in the classroom, which is a vital site where the roots of injustice can be challenged and transformative change begins. My orientation to my practice, regardless of my role, has always been one of contestation, disruption, and dismantling, coupled with the equally critical, and sometimes forgotten, elements of cultivating and nurturing. To lead from the classroom is incredibly significant, as it is a space to disrupt injustice at its roots.
— Camille Logan

I came to education in an untraditional way. Although I spent my childhood playing school with my then neighbor, I never pursued higher education with an idea that I would become an educator. My own teacher education remains fragmented, having been shaped across different contexts and unexpected opportunities. For my first teaching assignment, teaching was to be a short stint, but I ended up remaining longer than expected because of the relationships I formed. From early in my career, I began to understand that the real work of education happens within the connections that we make and the care that we offer. For me, the transformative power of relationships in education kept me grounded, and my own commitment to equity kept me focused.

As a student, navigating questions of his own identity within an anti-Black, deeply religious school context in The Bahamas, I had many teachers who cared, but few who truly took the time to connect with me and offer the support that was needed for me to feel a sense of belonging. As I reflect, one teacher (Mr. D) had a great impact on my life, not only because of his direct and assertive demeanor, but also because he listened, explained, and believed in my potential. He actively championed my well-being and modelled daily what it meant for educators to centre care in their leadership. Years later, when I returned to my alma mater as a teacher, Mr. D was still there, and his mentorship through the years became my blueprint. In my own classroom, I carried on with this intentional relationship-building. I centred radical care. I enacted a pedagogy that was rooted in love. Inspired by bell hooks, I came to understand the classroom as a site of activism. In all of my own teaching settings, I encouraged students to critique systems, question structures, and imagine new possibilities, all while centring radical care.
— Shelby McPhee

It is within this context that we use the table as a metaphoric place that invites us to consider the classroom itself as a site of leadership, activism, and transformation. When you, as the teacher, step into equity-centred leadership and begin to champion the success of your students and colleagues, then classrooms, schools, and education, in their entirety, can begin to change. Regardless of where you are on your journey or who you are, your leadership in schools and your position at the table is important. Once you arrive at the table, your activism, through your teaching, your mentorship, or your equity-centered care, has the potential to change and transform your school.

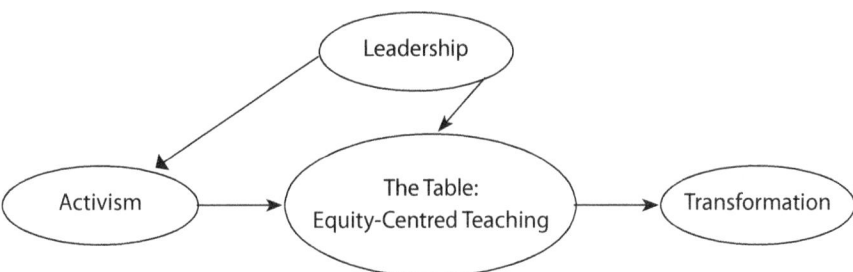

The Table as the Classroom

You Are a Leader

While the concept of leadership might conjure up ideas of formal roles, your seat at the table does not have to be defined by a title. Whether you are leading from your classroom or contributing in broader professional spaces, such as in the role of consultant, you carry both positional power and professional agency. You have the capacity to champion change, disrupt inequities, and shape learning environments that affirm and empower every student in your care. This is your superpower as a teacher!

Educators ready to engage in active and brave conversations are aware that education has a history of built-in oppressive systems that reflect dominant forces embedded within society, including the legacies of colonialism, capitalism, and industrialization. These systems are long-standing and, in reality, are carefully orchestrated to sift and sort students based on social identities, such as race, gender identity, ability, and class. This, in turn, reproduces existing social hierarchies, rather than dismantling them (Dei, 1999; Dei, 2000; Gay, 2000; Ladson-Billings, 2014). Therefore, your role as an educator seated at the table is to not only be conscious of this reality, but also to disrupt it.

> ### Questions for Reflection
>
> - Am I committed to creating a classroom where every student feels seen, valued, and celebrated for who they are?
> - Can I identify patterns of inequity in my school or classroom? Am I willing to explore ways to address them?
> - Am I open to deepening my learning through culturally responsive, anti-oppressive, and equity-centred practices?
> - Do I believe in the power of collaboration and know that meaningful change happens in partnership with others?
> - Am I able to lead with purpose, grounded in my values and guided by a commitment to equity and student success?

You might ask, *Can I be a leader without a formal title?* Yes, you can! Formal titles, such as lead teacher, department head, etc., should be seen as opportunities, not destinies. All you need to be a leader is dedication and commitment. You do not need to wait for a formal position of authority or special permission in order to lead. As a teacher, you've already earned that! You have the opportunity, by virtue of being the facilitator of the learning environment each and every day, to guide, to challenge, and to interrupt dominant thinking, actions, and behaviors that fail to serve students who have been historically marginalized (Poekert et al., 2020). Don't be afraid to "assert your influence beyond the classroom, make decisions, and help frame future actions" (Bixler & Ceballos, 2023). Taking up your seat at the table becomes even more effective when you, as a teacher leader, not only influence the professional community of your colleagues, but also cultivate student leadership within classrooms and schools.

See page 186 for a reproducible chart with questions used by students to support the their critical analysis of the content in the various media sources they chose to explore as part of the unit.

> **STORY FROM THE CLASSROOM**
>
> John was proud of having two years of teaching under her belt. Excited about the upcoming focus of learning for her students on media literacy, she decided to tackle concerning behaviors she was witnessing in her classroom. The students were influenced by the many forms of media they consume each day, and often emulated the inappropriate forms of humor, in and outside of the classroom. This issue was widespread across the school, and corrective measures were being put in place, largely led by the principal.
>
> John decided to create a media literacy unit, where students identified the ways in which commercials, advertisements, newspapers, and approved social media outlets use stereotypes and reinforce them, normalizing them as ways to characterize individuals by gender, race, ability, faith, and other markers of identity. The lesson was designed to develop the critical thinking skills of her students. Not only did students identify and analyze stereotypes, but they were taught to understand the impact of these representations on themselves, peers/friends, families, and the wider community. Through better understanding, her students decided to create a campaign designed to counter stereotypes in the media and to bring greater awareness of this issue to curb the behavior of their peers in the school and classrooms.
> - What issues in your school and/or wider community could benefit from teacher-led action?
> - How can you create space for student voice and agency in your classroom?
> - How are issues raised by students in your classroom being addressed and responded to in ways that reflect their voice?
> - How do you support the development of critical thinking, empathy, activism, or advocacy in your students?

The impact of the unit was profound. Through the learning, students finally understood what the many discussions and lessons from their principal and teachers were attempting to teach them. Through this case study you can see that deep learning was led by a teacher early in her career. She took up the mantle of leadership. She noticed an area of need for her students and the school, and worked to build the capacity of her students, whose learning in turn affected the overall climate of the school. This is the magic of the seat and how you can change not only your students, but the entire school.

When Teachers Stand, Students Rise

Long-standing research has identified that students who are empowered to lead are better positioned to identify and dismantle barriers, champion change among their peers, and contribute to the betterment of the learning environment to support improved outcomes for all. As a teacher leader, you recognize that student leadership is not a peripheral goal of equity work; rather, it is central. You have the power to leverage and amplify student voice, and to cultivate agency and leadership as essential elements of your classroom's transformative potential. bell hooks (1994) reminds us that classrooms are "radical spaces of possibility." Affirming student voice in your practice means more than encouraging participation; it requires you to validate students' lived experiences, identities, and knowledge as critical to the learning process. Geneva Gay (2000) emphasizes that culturally responsive teaching seeks to "unleash the higher learning potentials of ethnically diverse students by simultaneously cultivating their academic and cultural strengths," (p. 36). When you centre student voice, you challenge dominant narratives that often silence or marginalize historically underserved students and, instead, you co-create a space where every learner knows they matter.

When you nurture students as leaders, you can empower them to excel academically, take ownership of their learning environment, contribute meaningfully to decision-making, and be recognized as agents of change within their schools and communities. Just as you must claim your own seat at the table, you also have the opportunity to make room for your students by honoring their voices as essential to transforming their school experience. In classrooms and schools committed to equity, anti-racism, and anti-oppressive practices, student leadership should not be the exception; it should be the expectation and a reflection of the shared power you cultivate in your learning environment.

Voices from the Field

When we learned that students expressed a lack of belonging, and concerns regarding suspension rates confirmed it, we knew something had to shift. With support from our principal, we turned to those most affected, our students. Together with families and community, we co-created a culturally responsive mentorship and leadership initiative for male-identifying students, grounded in *seva* (selfless giving).

The idea was student-born, connecting older students with younger peers within our school and neighboring elementary schools. As teacher leaders, we helped students design and lead mentorship sessions, engage in service projects, and build their own leadership identities. As an outcome of the initiative, families shared that they felt more connected with their children and the school, and students started to see themselves as capable, valued, and impactful.

Through this work, we saw first-hand how teacher leadership is able to amplify student voice. We guided student leaders to facilitate group discussions, select texts reflecting their lived experience, and applied their learning across courses with greater confidence. These moments served to build a culture of collaboration, trust, and purpose throughout the school and school community.

The impact was clear: increased student engagement and sense of belonging, and stronger peer relationships resulted in reduced suspensions, and a renewed sense of pride in our school.

— Phylicia McPherson and Sarah Canton, Teachers

> Thank you for supporting me when no one did. Ever since you have been helping and supporting me, I have been doing better in all aspects of school. Aspects such as staying out of trouble, having better marks and overall am more involved with the school. I have not gotten suspended ever since you have been there for me and my grades are like how I had them in grade 8. Also, I am in many clubs in the school and this is all thanks to your guidance. Your support makes me feel good because I know there is always someone in my corner rooting for me. To conclude, thank you for supporting me when no one did and continue to support me to this day.

> **Questions for Reflection**
> - In what ways can I collaborate with colleagues to address systemic inequities that have been identified in our school?
> - How can I involve/engage and/or collaborate with families and community?

When you meaningfully cultivate student leadership, you empower young people to recognize inequities, speak up for themselves and their peers, and take an active role in creating a more inclusive and just learning environment and community. In your classroom, when you position students as co-constructors of knowledge and community, you nurture their critical consciousness, agency, and leadership skills, which are significant tools needed to challenge injustice and to spark transformative change. When you occupy the seat at the table of advancing equity, your leadership is not just a professional responsibility; it is a moral imperative.

Voices from the Field

Responses from high-school students to participation in the Punjabi Boys' Mentorship Group.

- Thank you for allowing me to join the Punjabi Boys' Mentorship Group class. You gave me the opportunity to demonstrate that I am a responsible student and a leader. I also appreciate the conversation we had before entering the class.
- Thank you for creating this safe space for me. I feel like I am not alone when things get hard. I feel like I can get through anything when I feel stressed, and most importantly, I feel like somebody.
- PBMG helps me develop my leadership skills by mentoring little kids from elementary schools and presenting to families. It also helps me get better marks so I can get into university.
- Before PBMG, I did not feel connected to the school and was focused on the wrong things. Now, I am focused on school and doing better. I enjoyed volunteering in the community and helping other students. My grade 12 year has been the best. Thank you.
- I am grateful for your support and care for me and all your students. I appreciate you taking the time to sit down with me and help me figure out my future plans. It means a lot and has given me a goal to strive towards.
- Thank you for giving me another opportunity and not losing faith in me.
- Through the PBMG, I have learned from my mistakes and am committed to changing myself. I am determined not to disappoint my parents, teachers, or peers.

The Table as the School: Positions of Responsibility

Although teacher leadership doesn't necessarily require a formal title or position to be influential, there are designated/formal roles within schools that educators are appointed or assigned. The scholarship on teacher leadership underscores the significance of these roles in shaping the school learning environment for staff and students. Here, the seat at the table is technically reserved, and is typically filled through an administrative selection process, although some spaces might be open to peer nomination or self-application (Wenner, J. A., & Campbell, T., 2017).

You might be in a formalized leadership role: lead teacher, department head, or instructional coach. These roles often include specific portfolios or responsibilities, such as mentoring colleagues, designing and/or delivering professional development, and/or fostering professional learning communities (PLCs). As you might have experienced and noted in research, your leadership has many benefits, including improving the collaboration in the school. However, there are also challenges that come with formalized roles, which will require skillful navigation (Skinner, B., Leavey, G., & Rothi, D., 2019).

Formalized Teacher Leadership Role Challenges

Changed Dynamics with Colleagues

- Perceptions of alignment with administration over peers
- Shifts in peer relationships, due to increased visibility or influence
- Heightened power dynamics that might affect collaboration
- Erosion of trust or assumptions of bias toward administration
- Resistance from colleagues to leadership action and/or initiatives
- Difficulty maintaining previous peer identity while navigating leadership expectations

Changed Dynamics with School Administration (Principal/Vice Principal)

- Expectations to direct or manage colleagues with no formal authority
- Pressure to deliver difficult administrative messages and/or decisions
- Being positioned as a liaison or intermediary in ways that could negatively affect relationships with peers
- Requests to share information about staff sentiment or peer feedback that breaches confidentiality and/or professional boundaries

While stepping into formal teacher leadership can be powerful, you must also be aware of how your seat at the table might be used by others. If you are the first or only one with a historically marginalized identity, your presence might be tokenized (Wenner & Campbell, 2017) because, sometimes, the seat is more about optics than impact (Ahmed, 2012, 2024). That's why it's essential for you to be critically conscious of your role, to name truths, to advocate for those often unheard, and to hold others accountable, so that policies, practices, and resource decisions truly reflect a commitment to equity and student success.

> ### Reflection Questions
>
> - How am I using my seat to dismantle systemic inequities and disproportionate outcomes in my school?
> - In what ways does my leadership amplify marginalized voices of students, families, and communities?
> - How do I navigate relationships while remaining grounded in work that challenges the status quo?
> - What strategies will I employ to navigate the risks necessary to move equity forward?
> - What difference am I making? For whom? And how do I know?

Despite the tensions and challenges that can arise, your presence in a formal teacher leadership role can truly matter. Although navigating these dynamics requires clarity and courage, it also offers an opportunity to model integrity, build bridges, and influence school culture from within. By staying grounded in your purpose and values, you can take up the seat by leading with authenticity and continuing to create space for more equitable and collaborative approaches to teaching and learning. Your leadership can be a quiet nudging or loud disruption—it's up to you—as long as it makes a difference for students and makes room for others to rise alongside you.

A Seat Beside the Principal

An important element to make note of is the support of your principal. In many ways, this support can either create the conditions for your leadership to thrive or unintentionally limit its potential (Wenner & Campbell, 2017; Sasere & Mathashu, 2024). When your principal actively works to cultivate an environment where you feel well-resourced, affirmed, and trusted, you are more likely to lead with authenticity and impact. This kind of support includes mentorship, along with dedicated time and space for your leadership work. It could look very different in various school and/or board environments and might include meaningful professional learning, designed to build your skills and confidence as a change agent while seated at the table.

It is important to recognize that leadership doesn't always come naturally, and that's okay. As you grow into your role, the support of your principal can make a significant difference in building the skills, confidence, and presence that you need to lead alongside your peers. This is critical for leadership rooted in advancing equity, anti-oppression, anti-racism, and culturally responsive practice. When school leaders invest in your growth, they help create the conditions, for not only you to thrive, but also for those who make up the school community. When you thrive, the impact extends to your colleagues, students, families, and the wider school community in transformative ways.

Voice from the Field

As a principal committed to cultivating a culture of distributed leadership, I intentionally "provide seats at the table" by creating conditions for teacher leadership to flourish. By recognizing the strengths within my staff and inviting them to lead initiatives, mentor students, and contribute to decision-making, I empower educators to be active agents in student success. This approach aligns with our school's vision: *An equitable, inclusive learning environment where everyone feels they belong.*

In response to concerning student behavior and suspension data, I invited teachers to co-design strategies grounded in student voice. Together, we shifted from a disciplinary lens to one focused on empowerment, belonging, and co-ownership of the schooling experience for students. Guided by student and community voice, teachers led mentoring programs, facilitated student-led learning, and helped students see themselves as valued members of the school community.

Informed by the work of Susie Wise and Gholdy Muhammad, I view leadership as more than delegation, but rather about intentionally fostering a culture where equity, voice, and relationships are central. A mural at our school's entrance reads, *"Welcome, You Belong Here,"* reflecting our shared values. But it is through our daily actions and teacher-led initiatives that this message becomes a lived reality in our school.

— Nadine Deerr, Principal

It is important to remember that, as a teacher leader, whether formally appointed or informally initiated, you are a vital change agent in your school. Stepping into leadership requires more than just passion; it calls for support, trust, and the various conditions necessary to grow. When your principal actively fosters a culture of trust and collaboration, you are more likely to lead with confidence and purpose. Without that support, even the most committed leaders can struggle to make a lasting impact. Your leadership deserves to be nurtured, and your voice has the power to shape your classroom and/or school for the better.

Holding the Door: Inviting Others to the Table

Supporting and Mentoring Teachers

Claiming your seat at the table is a powerful action for you to take. It's not only about recognizing your agency and stepping into spaces where decisions are made, but also about holding the door for others to join the table. True occupation at the table is about using your presence to create access for others, especially those who have been historically excluded from leadership and influence. As a teacher leader, your responsibility extends far beyond participation while occupying the seat; it includes making room for others to join, contribute, and eventually take up space alongside you and/or after you leave.

In this work, the South African philosophy of *Ubuntu* provides a meaningful metaphor for leadership. Ubuntu, often translated as "I am because we are," embodies the notion of the collective, that one's success is not achieved in isolation. Ubuntu reminds us all that leadership is not a solitary journey. When multiple voices are welcomed, affirmed, and empowered, equity, inclusion, and the disruption of oppressive practices become embedded within the school culture and are not seen as anomalies, but rather as professional expectations for all staff (Etomes, S. E., 2024). Therefore, your success is deeply connected to the collective. Equity work, then, must be done in solidarity, grounded in shared responsibility, relational trust, and a commitment to building community (Wane, 2008; Wu et al., 2018; Sasere & Mathashu, 2024). As a teacher leader, one way you can engage Ubuntu is by mentoring other teachers to help bring them to the table.

Voices from the Field

Thank you for starting PBMG and Chai with families. It means a lot to me and to our community. It helps parents connect with teachers and creates a better relationship between teachers and their parents.
— Parent

Thanks for creating the Moms' group. This group helps me support my son at home, and the strategies shared are really helpful.
— Parent

My concerns were monumental, but now I am at peace knowing that the teachers are so supportive and provide opportunities for my son to succeed in school and lead other students. Thanks to the leadership of the principal and her team.
— Parent

This initiative helps students feel a sense of belonging in the school. It shows that the school cares about who they are, their culture, and their lived experiences. The community appreciates the work the school is doing to help the students. We love the work the school administration is doing for the students through the many programs and activities.

— Community member

STORY FROM THE CLASSROOM

Ashely, a middle and senior school teacher, recalls their first day in the classroom, when they were wholly unprepared to teach and uncertain of what they had stepped into. The students in that room had recently experienced displacement and moved to a new city with limited resources, so they arrived with a trauma that manifested in behavioral challenges. Standing in front of the class, it was clear to Ashely that traditional tools of classroom management would not suffice. A passing teacher noticed and stepped in with the intention of collaborating with them to assist with managing the students. She first asked permission to intervene, then helped settle the room.

Although she never took on the title of a mentor, this teacher became one, because she affirmed a novice teacher's voice rather than diminish it. While she was a senior teacher with more years in education, she recognized identity and respected the context that her younger colleague brought to the work. She encouraged Ashely to lean into those traits as assets for connections in the classroom. In this way, what emerged was a mentorship grounded, not in hierarchy, but in mutual respect and understanding. It reflected what we believe is a core framework for equitable teacher leadership: one where mentees are supported in recognizing the completeness and powerful nature of their own voice and authentic identity.

- How would you create a mentorship program that centres support rather than hierarchy?
- In what ways have you ever affirmed the experiences, voices, or identity that new teachers bring to the classroom?
- What tools or frameworks do you offer new teachers like Ashley to help them disrupt control over compassion?

As a teacher leader, your mentorship must affirm others, in order to create the necessary conditions where authenticity, critical reflexivity, and transformative action can take place. Ultimately, through your affirmative mentorship, you will equip teachers with the necessary tools to model the same for their students. Through affirming teachers, you will help them find their voice and enact a pedagogy from a place of authenticity. When they find their own voice, teachers are better able to connect with students on deeper levels and create more opportunities for meaningful connections both inside and outside of the classroom.

In this context, affirmation becomes a pedagogical act of defiance. It rejects the idea that teachers who might not have official titles hold a deficit, and it embraces the power of lived experience as a source of cultural wealth. In this equity-centred relationship, affirmations invite teachers to take their rightful seat at the table by amplifying their own voice.

Ways to support new teachers at the table:
- Help them reflect on their *why.*

- Normalize vulnerability and growing from mistakes.
- Access professional development communities.

Supporting and Mentoring Students

As a teacher leader, when you help teachers find their voice, your students benefit, because your new teachers are able to lead with purpose and better equip students with the tools necessary to become advocates for their own well-being. By modelling how to use your own voice to speak up for equitable resources and opportunities in schools, you demonstrate what it looks like to challenge systems and navigate institutional resistance. This kind of modelling doesn't only include demonstration, but it also requires real support for the times students do speak up. Effective teacher leaders guide students through advocacy, helping them understand how to engage with systems and structures of power. It is within this context of mentorship and support that teacher leaders are not just instructors, but also co-conspirators in advocacy.

> **STORY FROM THE CLASSROOM**
>
> A group of students envisioned a Pride assembly that broke from traditional norms of whole-school events. Their plan was to include personal narratives regarding coming out and navigating school life as queer youth. Students were met with strong resistance from administrators, who deemed the proposed assembly format too controversial. It was here that a powerful opportunity for mentorship and support opened up. Ashely, the teacher, acting as both an ally and educator, stepped into a coaching role to help students prepare to advocate and to retain the authenticity of their voice while engaging with institutional boundaries. The aim was not to walk in front of students but rather alongside them, to model advocacy in action, affirm their voices, and offer guidance. Through their own advocacy, supported by Ashely, the students got their assembly, and the teacher mentor agreed to review their script as a facilitator to ensure that institutional demands were met, but also to ensure that students remained at the centre of their own narratives.
>
> This moment reflected a broad truth: helping your own students to lead is a radical pedagogical act and supporting their advocacy affirms that their voice matters, and that they can, and should, demand a seat at the table. Coaching them to revisit the conversation with administration helped equip them with skills in negotiation, determination, and strategic communication —all critical components for leadership. More importantly, it reaffirmed the importance of student voice and teacher empowerment working in tandem in the school context.
> - Do you view yourself as both a learner and a leader, capable of mingling curiosity, care, and courageous action?
> - Do you trust that your voice, experience, and leadership can contribute to a more just and joyful learning environment?

As an educator, you do not need a formal title to be a leader; however, when you do receive one, you must use it to create space for others to come after you. Similarly, in the classroom, as a teacher leader, you have the responsibility to mentor your student leaders in making the classroom and beyond sites of activism. Teachers who know who they are and stay grounded in their core values of equity are able to model what it means to lead and advocate for equity in schools. By walking alongside your students, you show students that they do not need to wait for adulthood or for a formal title to take on leadership for change. Instead, equitable mentorship teaches that leaders must be grown. In supporting student development for leadership, we not only expand what it means to have a seat at the table, but we also pull up more chairs to the table.

Final Thoughts: Pulling Up More Chairs

Throughout this chapter, we have explored the evolving role of the teacher leader as a cultivator of voice, a builder of trust, and an advocate for equity. Cognizant of the fact that all teacher leaders do not hold formal positions, a seat at the table symbolizes the responsibility educators have in disrupting inequality in schools and re-imagining educational spaces. For us, it was never enough to simply have a seat; we must then constantly ask ourselves: *How am I using this seat? How have I been accountable? How have I made space for others?* In taking up space, teacher leaders must hold to their core values, especially in environments where resistance is systemic and we must constantly push for an equity that transforms the table. By taking up space, mentoring other teachers, and supporting students, we are engaging in a radical act of expanding the table, always remembering that the table is never full and that the work of justice is not finished. So keep pulling up more chairs.

Social Media Analysis Chart

Media Type	Title: Overview:	Who is represented? Who is missing?	How are they represented? What characteristics are being emphasized?	Describe the message and/or ideas being conveyed	Identify any concerns with the message(s) and/or representation (are they fair/accurate?)	Identify any stereotypes and/or misrepresentations you wish to discuss in your analysis
Commercial						
Approved Social Media Source						
Television/Streaming Show/Series						
Video Games						
Movies						
Memes and GIFs						
Other:						
Other:						

14

Holding and Supporting High Expectations for Black Students

Veronica Montague, Keisha Evans, Kai Gordon, Sheldon Dixon, and Jason Brissett

Veronica Montague is a Graduation Coach for Black Students within the Toronto District School Board (TDSB). Veronica has worked with children, youth, and families for more than 20 years in both the education and community sectors. Her goal is to support Black youths on their journeys and career pathways—helping them recognize their talents and empowering them to believe in themselves.

Keisha Evans is an educator, social worker, and advocate with more than 25 years of experience supporting children, youth, and families. She specializes in equity, anti-racism, and mental health. As a Graduation Coach for Black Students, Keisha leads programs and workshops that foster student success, dismantle systemic barriers, and create inclusive, trauma-informed spaces where all students can thrive.

Kai Gordon is a Graduation Coach for Black Students at the TDSB with more than 15 years of experience in education and community development. Holding a Master's degree in environmental studies from York University, she specializes in student retention, policy, and partnerships. Kai collaborates with families and communities to support Black youth through inclusive dialogue, empowerment, and academic success.

What Are Graduation Coaches?

A Graduation Coach for Black students is a specialized role within the education system, designed to provide targeted support that promotes the academic success, well-being, and post-secondary pathways for Black students. As Graduation Coaches for Black Students, we are immersed daily in the lives, dreams, and brilliance of Black youth. Our roles are deeply relational and grounded in care. We serve not only as mentors and advocates, but also as facilitators of possibility—co-creating the conditions for Black students to thrive academically, socially, and emotionally. Whether we're supporting students one-on-one in school hallways or coordinating large-scale initiatives through the Centre of Excellence for Black Student Achievement, our work is centred on a singular truth: Black students can and do achieve at high levels when belief—not bias—guides expectations.

Graduation Coaches engage students in tangible, transformative ways. We design and deliver programs that build academic confidence, expand post-secondary awareness, and nurture leadership. From the summer leadership programs to culturally affirming mentorship circles, literacy development, STEM initiatives, and career exploration workshops, we help students navigate secondary pathways while holding on to a strong sense of who they are. Our work also involves building partnerships with families, educators, and community leaders, to ensure that Black students are not navigating these systems alone. We collaborate with teachers and administrators to challenge deficit narratives and advocate for access to rigorous learning opportunities. This often means helping educators reflect on the expectations they set, the messages they

Sheldon Dixon has worked with the TDSB for more than 10 years and currently serves as a Graduation Coach for Black Students. A Bishop, DJ, and youth advocate, he empowers young people through music, mentorship, and his L.O.V.E. model—Leadership, Overcoming, Value, and Example—promoting accountability, purpose, and self-authentication to inspire community impact and success.

Jason Brissett is a Graduation Coach for Black Students, with 19 years at the TDSB. Drawing from his experience as a pastor and immigrant from Jamaica, he supports Black students and families through culturally responsive mentorship. Jason is committed to dismantling systemic racism and creating inclusive pathways for student success across K–12 education.

> send, and the practices they uphold—because too often, Black students are underestimated, overlooked, or implicitly told that excellence is out of reach.

A Grade 11 student once reflected, "When a teacher actually believes in me, it makes me want to prove them right—not because I have to, but because I can." That simple yet powerful sentiment reflects what research has long confirmed: students rise when they are seen, heard, and believed in. Yet for many Black learners, this remains the exception, not the norm.

Black students are overrepresented in non-academic and applied-level courses, streamed out of opportunities for academic advancement, and disproportionately subjected to punitive discipline (James & Turner, 2017). These outcomes are not rooted in a lack of ability, but in systemic barriers, implicit biases, and lowered expectations that often go unexamined in schools. When educators assume that Black students "aren't ready" for advanced work or interpret confidence as defiance, we send a message—intentionally or not—that they are not expected to excel.

To hold and support high expectations through an equity lens means rejecting these deficit-based assumptions. It means shifting our gaze from what students lack to what they bring—cultural knowledge, resilience, creativity, and critical insight. It means designing learning that is both rigorous and relevant, rooted in real-world application and reflective of students' lived realities. It means offering high-challenge tasks alongside high-support scaffolds to create learning environments where all students, particularly Black students, are set up to succeed.

High expectations must also be understood as a form of care. They are not about pushing students for the sake of achievement scores; they are about believing in their capacity and humanity enough to offer meaningful opportunities for growth. Supporting high expectations requires educators to consider not just what is taught, but how and why—examining how policies, practices, and pedagogy can be reimagined to serve, not sort, students.

This chapter offers real-world strategies, classroom activities, and reflections grounded in our experiences as Black educators and Graduation Coaches. It is not about adding more to your plate—it is about reframing what's already there: how lessons are delivered, how feedback is given, how classroom norms are established, and how success is defined.

We offer this work with compassion and joy. The goal is not perfection, but intention—an invitation to affirm Black student excellence, challenge inequities, and reimagine classrooms as spaces of liberation. By holding and supporting high expectations, educators become partners in the transformation Black students are already leading.

Reimagining the Role of the Educator

Teaching with high expectations and cultural responsiveness is not a script—it's a stance. It means believing, deeply and consistently, that Black students are capable of greatness, and then doing the daily work to help them see, name, and live into that greatness. It means resisting the urge to lower the bar, even when the system around us does.

> Every strategy shared in this chapter, every reflection offered, comes from what we've seen and learned while walking alongside Black students in schools and in programs led through the Centre of Excellence for Black Student Achievement. These are not just theories—they are best practices informed by lived experience, relationships, and results.

It also calls us, as educators, to look inward: to unlearn harmful assumptions, to examine how our own identities shape our beliefs, and to stay committed to growth. This isn't always comfortable work—but it is necessary, joyful, and transformational. When we teach with this mindset, we move beyond simply managing classrooms—we begin cultivating spaces of possibility. We shift from hoping Black students succeed to ensuring they are supported, affirmed, and positioned to lead. We become co-conspirators in the pursuit of a more just, equitable, and liberatory education system—one lesson, one moment, one student at a time.

We have seen what happens when Black students are believed in, challenged, and cared for. We've seen what's possible when educators commit to doing better—not perfectly, but intentionally. This chapter is an invitation: to hold and support high expectations not as a burden, but as a gift—one that every Black student deserves, and every educator has the power to give.

Reframing the Deficit Lens

In many classrooms, Black students are still seen through a deficit lens—a mindset that assumes there's something wrong, missing, or lacking in them, their families, or their communities. This way of thinking shows up in subtle and not-so-subtle ways: when students are underestimated, when their behavior is misread, or when they're excluded from opportunities to lead, create, or shine. A deficit lens focuses on what students don't have, instead of recognizing what they bring.

Decades of research has shown that Black students face more barriers in school than their non-Black peers. For example, Dr Carl James and Tana Turner's 2017 report *Towards Race Equity in Education* highlighted the experiences of Black students being streamed into lower academic tracks, suspended more often, and being less likely to be placed in gifted programs—even when they have the potential. These outcomes come from a lack of belief, support, and opportunity. And they reflect a school system that often treats Black students as problems to manage, rather than young people full of brilliance and promise.

We see the impact of these narratives every day. From the books that don't reflect their histories, to the hallway interactions that feel more like surveillance than support—Black students often carry the weight of being misjudged. These experiences shape how they see themselves, and whether they feel like school is a place where they truly belong.

Voice from the Field

I was always told I was a "handful" in class. But no one ever asked *why* I stopped raising my hand. It's not that I didn't care—it's that I got tired of being wrong before I even spoke. Once I had a teacher who actually listened and saw more in me, things changed. I started seeing more in myself.
— Grade 9 student

Stories like this are far too common. The truth is, the way teachers see their students—especially Black students—can either open doors or quietly close them. When educators expect less, offer fewer challenges, or assume students aren't ready, it sends a message that excellence isn't meant for them.

We also know that Black students are disproportionately placed in special education programs and rarely seen in gifted ones. Many times, behaviors like frustration, curiosity, or even confidence are misunderstood as disrespect or defiance, so Black students are over-disciplined and heavily surveilled for showing up as their authentic selves. Black girls, in particular, are often labelled as having "attitudes" when they speak up or express themselves, rather than being seen as leaders or thinkers. As Dr. Venus E. Evans-Winters (2005) reminds us, Black girls are too often treated as problems to fix, rather than people to support.

Add to that the fact that schools often overlook the strengths Black families bring—like cultural wisdom, community care, and advocacy—and you have a system that's more focused on what's perceived as wrong than what's right. Scholars like Diane Reay (1998) and Annette Lareau (2003) have shown that when schools value only one kind of parent involvement—like volunteering or helping with homework—they miss the deep, meaningful ways Black families support their children's learning outside the classroom.

What's most harmful is how these deficit ideas shift attention away from the real problem: the system itself. When we focus only on what students supposedly lack, we ignore the need to change the structures, expectations, and teaching practices that make school harder for them in the first place.

To reframe the educational experience of Black students, we must centre their brilliance, histories, and cultural knowledge. Several scholars and frameworks offer guidance in disrupting deficit thinking and moving toward more humanizing, rigorous, and liberatory pedagogies:

- Dr. Gholdy Muhammad (2020) reminds us that teaching should build students' skills, identities, intellect, and critical thinking—all rooted in their history and culture.
- Zaretta Hammond (2015) teaches us that high expectations and deep learning go hand in hand, especially when students trust their teachers and see themselves in the work.
- Geneva Gay (2010) encourages us to make sure our teaching reflects the lives and cultures of the students in front of us.
- Carl James (2010) pushes us to look closely at how race and identity shape Black students' school experiences right here in Canada—and challenges us to do something about it.

Reframing the deficit lens is about changing how we teach, how we listen, and how we show up. It's creating classrooms where Black students are expected to do well, supported when they struggle, and celebrated when they succeed.

Strategies in Practice: Teaching with High Expectations and Cultural Responsiveness

Creating classrooms where Black students feel both challenged and deeply supported requires intentional strategies that are grounded in high expectations and cultural responsiveness. When we teach with both in mind, we affirm that excellence and equity are not opposites; they are inseparable.

In our work, we've seen that what matters most isn't simply what teachers teach, but *how* they teach, *why* they teach it, and *who* they imagine students to be. Holding high expectations goes beyond academic rigor—it is about belief. These expectations require us to view students, not through a deficit lens, but

---

This section shares classroom-based strategies and real-world examples across three key areas: planning and curriculum, classroom culture, and assessment. These practices centre Black student identity, voice, and excellence, helping educators move from theory to transformative action.

as holders of brilliance, possibility, and power. Drawing on the work of Gloria Ladson-Billings, we understand that culturally relevant pedagogy is essential for affirming student's identities and promoting academic success. Our work in schools is rooted in cultural competence: building relationships, affirming cultural knowledge, and ensuring that our collaboration with educators reflect the lived realities of Black students.

Planning and Curriculum: Centring Identity While Elevating Rigor

One of the most effective ways to support high expectations is by embedding students' lived experiences, cultural knowledge, and histories into the curriculum. For Black students, too often the curriculum either erases their presence or portrays their histories only through trauma or struggle. A culturally responsive and rigorous curriculum disrupts that pattern.

Embed Black Identities and Histories across Content Areas

Teaching with high expectations doesn't mean waiting for February to talk about Black excellence. Whether you're teaching literature, science, art, or math, there are powerful ways to centre Black contributions, critical perspectives, and cultural narratives year-round.

- In English Language Arts, this could mean studying novels by authors like Angie Thomas, Lawrence Hill, Chinua Achebe, Ngũgĩ wa Thiong'o, or Edwidge Danticat, and inviting students to draw connections between the themes in those works and their own culture, identity, or lived experiences.
- In Science, explore innovations by Black scientists, such as Katherine Johnson, Dr. Kizzmekia Corbett, or Juliet Daniel, or examine the impact of environmental racism.
- In History or Civics, teach about local Black change-makers alongside global movements, allowing students to see themselves reflected in both resistance and innovation.

Co-Create Learning Goals with Students

Instead of presenting pre-set goals, invite students to articulate what success looks like for them. This builds ownership and aligns expectations with personal aspirations. A teacher might say, "Here's our curriculum expectation, but how do you want to show me you've mastered this? Let's figure out what success looks like together." This positions students as partners in their learning, rather than passive recipients of knowledge.

Design Rigorous, Meaningful Tasks—Not Rote Learning

High expectations are also about deeper, more engaging work. Give students real-world problems to solve, space for creative expression, and opportunities to lead. Instead of multiple-choice worksheets, consider

- A community-based research project
- A podcast series on a social issue students care about
- A math inquiry exploring income inequality in local neighborhoods

These tasks require critical thinking, collaboration, and reflection—all markers of high cognitive demand.

Classroom Culture: Building Relationships that Challenge and Support

Rigorous learning environments must also be emotionally safe. High expectations without care become pressure. Care without challenge becomes complacency. The balance lies in building a classroom culture where students feel affirmed *and* stretched.

Offer Feedback that Fuels Growth

Culturally responsive educators move beyond vague praise ("Good job!") to specific, actionable feedback that helps students grow:

> "Your paper is strong and clearly communicated. Now push further—can you include one more example that complicates your point of view?"

This kind of feedback shows students they are capable of more and that you believe in their capacity to get there.

Practice Warm Demander Pedagogy

Coined by Lisa Delpit, the term *warm demander* refers to educators who combine high expectations with deep, culturally grounded care.
- They build strong relationships based on respect and accountability.
- They don't lower the bar for students—they *raise* the level of support.
- They address off-task behavior with consistency and connection, not control or shame.

See Chapter 6 for more on Warm Demander Pedagogy.

An educator might say, "I'm holding you to this standard because I care too much about your brilliance to let you hand in something that doesn't reflect it."

Set Clear Expectations and Scaffold Access

Transparency is key. Students must know what is expected and how to reach those goals.
- Break tasks into manageable chunks without diluting the rigor.
- Use models and exemplars that reflect diverse student voices.
- Use sentence starters, graphic organizers, and peer scaffolding strategically—not because students "can't" but because they *can*, with the right tools.

Classroom norms should be co-constructed and revisited often, reinforcing that your classroom is a learning space where excellence is expected, mistakes are part of the process, and every student is capable of meaningful growth.

Voices from the Field: The Impact of Belief and Representation

I see how my daughter has been able to thrive and build her confidence through the programs and opportunities—and the value of educators believing in her.
—Parent of a Grade 10 student

This parent witnessed first-hand how her daughter's confidence and academic engagement grew when educators held high expectations and integrated culturally affirming content. When the student saw herself reflected in the curriculum and classroom conversations, her participation deepened—and so did her sense of belonging.

These reflections remind us that holding and supporting high expectations is about doing better, with purpose, care, and cultural awareness.

Once I started reading books that reflected people like me, I didn't feel like school was just something I had to survive. I felt like I could be smart and Black at the same time.
— Grade 8 student

High expectations don't mean pushing students without support. It means scaffolding with intention, affirming their brilliance, and refusing to lower the bar.
— Secondary teacher

Belief is powerful. When educators look at Black students and expect greatness, students begin to expect it from themselves.
— Hall monitor

Assessment Practices: Redefining Success and Honoring Multiple Ways of Knowing

How we assess student learning reflects what—and *who*—we value. Traditional assessments often fail to capture the full range of Black students' intellectual contributions, creativity, and cultural knowledge.

Incorporate Multiple Ways of Showing Knowledge

Recognize that standardized tests and essay formats are not the only valid demonstrations of learning. Consider offering students other options; for example

- Oral storytelling
- Artistic representation
- Infographics or digital media
- Performance-based assessment (e.g., debates, dramatic monologues, spoken word)

These formats can reflect Black cultural traditions (such as oral narrative) and offer space for students to express their thinking in ways that resonate with them.

De-centre Eurocentric Notions of Success

If success is measured only by how well students conform to dominant norms, grammar, tone, standard English, or abstract logic, we risk mis-recognizing the brilliance that shows up in other forms. A culturally responsive approach to assessment recognizes

- the political nature of language
- the value of emotional intelligence and community wisdom
- the legitimacy of lived experience as evidence

You can design rubrics that value insight, originality, and critical connections—not just technical precision.

STORY FROM THE CLASSROOM

In a Grade 9 classroom, a teacher introduced a Genius Hour project, inviting students to explore a topic of personal passion while incorporating core research and presentation skills. Inspired by conversations during Black History Month, the teacher encouraged students to focus on Black innovators past and present—scientists, artists, entrepreneurs, and change-makers whose contributions are often absent from textbooks.

> One student, Tosin, had rarely participated in classroom discussions. He often kept his head down and rarely turned in assignments. But when given the opportunity to choose his own topic, he selected Gil Scott-Heron, a figure he had learned about from his older cousin's music collection. Instead of writing a traditional report, Tosin asked if he could create a spoken word performance blending Scott-Heron's influence with his own voice. The teacher agreed—and helped him draft, revise, and rehearse his piece.
>
> On presentation day, Tosin stood in front of his peers and delivered a powerful performance that left the room silent. For the first time, he saw himself not just as a student—but as a scholar, an artist, and a leader. This moment didn't happen by chance—it was the result of high expectations paired with meaningful, culturally relevant learning.
> - How can you provide opportunities for student choice that reflect their cultural identities and lived experiences? Consider where in your curriculum students can take creative risks or share personal knowledge.
> - In what ways can you recognize and nurture the different forms of brilliance your students bring to the classroom? Think beyond traditional academic markers—what counts as intelligence or success in your space?
> - Are you offering rigorous tasks that also affirm students' identities? Reflect on how your lessons challenge students while also making space for cultural relevance and voice.
> - How do you respond when students like Tosin show potential in nontraditional ways? Are you flexible in allowing alternative demonstrations of learning (e.g., art, spoken word, storytelling)?
> - How do your expectations and support signal to Black students that they are capable, valued, and seen? Consider how your grading, feedback, and classroom management practices align with this belief.

Addressing Resistance and Re-Imagining Accountability

Holding high expectations for Black students isn't only about what we teach, it's about how we show up. It's about care, commitment, and being honest with ourselves. This work is personal. It's emotional. And, yes, it can be uncomfortable.

Unlearning bias isn't easy. Many of us were trained in systems that didn't teach us how to talk about race—let alone how to disrupt racism. So it's no surprise that resistance shows up. Sometimes it's internal: "I don't see color," or "I treat all my students the same." Sometimes it's fear of saying the wrong thing, or feeling defensive when race comes up. Sometimes it's thinking, "I've worked in these communities—I get it."

And sometimes the resistance comes from outside. School culture doesn't always support deep equity work. There's pressure to move quickly, check the box, post the right message. But lasting change? That takes more than a one-time PD session or a new policy. It takes ongoing, supported, relational work. And let's be honest—some educators are afraid of the pushback from families or colleagues if they name anti-Black racism or challenge biased practices.

But here's the thing: discomfort isn't a sign that you're failing. It's a sign that you're learning. If we truly want to hold high expectations for Black students, we have to look at how we respond to that discomfort: Do we shut down? Get defensive? Or do we lean in and keep going?

This brings us to accountability. In too many schools, we have witnessed that accountability has been reduced to rules, rubrics, and compliance checks. But from a place of practice, real accountability is about relationships. It's about asking: "Am I keeping my promise to my students?" Not just to teach them curriculum, but to see them, hear them, believe in them—and build a space where they can thrive. That kind of accountability doesn't come from the top down. It grows from the inside out. It asks us to reflect on how our choices and expectations, and even our silence, shape students' experiences. And it reminds us that the people we are truly answerable to are the students and families most affected by our work.

Accountability isn't punishment. It's not about blame or shame. It's about committing to get better—for our students, not just ourselves. So what does this look like in practice? It might mean rethinking how you respond when a Black student pushes back. It might mean reviewing how you grade, or how often you're calling home—and why. It could mean listening more to students' experiences, even when what they say is hard to hear.

You won't always get it right. None of us do. But the goal isn't perfection; it's presence. Show up with honesty. Stay open. Keep learning. That's how we move from performative equity to real change. Because when we reframe accountability as care—and back that up with action—we build classrooms where Black students are not just expected to succeed, but supported to soar.

> **Questions for Reflection**
>
> - In what moments have I felt discomfort or defensiveness when discussing race in my practice, and what might that reveal about my own learning and growth?
> - What does it look like to keep a promise to my students—not just academically, but emotionally and culturally?
> - Who holds me accountable in my daily work? How do I listen to them?
> - What messages do my classroom expectations send to Black students about who I believe they are?
> - In what ways have I responded to discomfort in conversations about race, and how might I begin to use that discomfort as a tool for growth rather than a reason to withdraw?

Practical Tools for Everyday Teaching

Supporting Black students through high expectations is about transforming the small, everyday moves we make as educators. These tools and strategies reflect lessons we've learned from walking alongside students, partnering with families, and collaborating with educators across schools. They are grounded in best practices we've seen work—whether in a classroom discussion, a hallway check-in, or a re-imagined assessment. It's in the questions we ask, the materials we choose, how we respond to mistakes, and how we define success. This section offers practical tools you can integrate into your daily routines, tools that foster rigorous, culturally relevant learning environments where Black students feel seen, challenged, and fully supported.

This work matters because we've witnessed what happens when Black students are truly seen, heard, and expected to succeed. We invite you to try these practices not for perfection, but in the spirit of reflection, care, and transformation. Every strategy shared here is part of a larger commitment—to Black student excellence, and to creating classrooms where all students are challenged, supported, and empowered to thrive every single day.

Checklist: Planning Lessons and Selecting Resources

Curriculum and Content

☐ Do the materials reflect the voice, history, and contributions for Black communities (and not only during Black History Month)?
☐ Are Black students invited to co-create and give feedback on what they're learning?
☐ Do I create opportunities for Black students to contribute culturally relevant resources (like books or media) to the learning environment?

Classroom Culture

☐ Are students encouraged to take risks, learn from their mistakes, and not be afraid?
☐ How do I promote student voice in my classroom?
☐ Am I using specific strategies to make Black students feel included within my classroom?

Assessment Practices

☐ Are rubrics co-created or transparent so that students know how to excel?
☐ Is student voice taken into consideration in how they're assessed and what success looks like?
☐ Are students being assessed in ways that speak to their identity, culture, and lived experiences?

Commitment to Growth and Excellence

Many Black students have shared with us that they feel pressure to get things right the first time, fear being judged for asking questions, or hesitate to bring their full selves into classroom spaces where their identities might not always be affirmed. In response, we developed an anchor chart of shared commitments, grounded in what students have told us they need in order to feel safe, motivated, and respected in their learning; see chart on page 197. These statements were not pulled from theory alone—they reflect real conversations, honest reflections, and the daily realities of the students we serve.

We encourage you to co-create this anchor chart with your students early in the school year or semester to anchor students' knowledge and set shared expectations rooted in care, effort, and high standards. Doing so helps anchor students' understanding of classroom norms, expectations, and the mutual responsibility we all share in building an environment rooted in care, high standards, and effort.

Our Commitment to Growth and Excellence	
Student Commitments	**Teacher Commitments**
I will ask questions when I don't understand.	I will honor all questions and support learning.
I will try, even when things feel hard.	I will scaffold challenges without lowering the bar.
I will learn from my mistakes and try again.	I will give feedback that helps you grow. I will believe in every student's potential.
I will bring my full self into this space.	I will create a space where all identities are valued.

Keep this chart visible and refer back to it regularly, especially during moments of struggle or transition.

Lesson: Speaking Truth to Power: Personal Narratives and Social Justice

Grade 8 Language Arts

This lesson reflects a best practice we've seen come to life in classrooms where educators intentionally centre student voice, identity, and social consciousness. As Graduation Coaches, we've supported lessons like this with teachers who are committed to holding high expectations while affirming students' lived experiences. These types of learning experiences allow students to explore critical themes while building literacy skills in meaningful, culturally responsive ways.

Objective
Students will write and perform personal narratives that explore identity, belonging, and justice, drawing connections between their lived experiences and broader social issues.

Key Features
- High Expectation: Students are tasked with crafting compelling, structured narratives that include figurative language, thematic coherence, and oral performance skills.
- Cultural Relevance: Students explore works by Black authors and activists (e.g., Afua Cooper, Lawrence Hill, Kagiso Lesego Molope, Dionne Brand) and discuss how personal experience can shape public impact.
- Student Choice: Students choose the format—spoken word, podcast, or traditional essay—and connect their story to a social issue that matters to them.
- Collaborative Revision: Peers offer feedback through structured protocols focused on clarity, emotion, and purpose.

Why It Works

This lesson balances challenge and support, affirms cultural identity, and pushes students toward excellence while nurturing voice and agency.

Student Tools for Reflection and Goal-Setting

Too often we focus on teacher expectations without creating space for students' aspirations. These tools invite students to reflect on their growth, set realistic goals, and name the supports they need, while centring their voices. These tools are meant to be practical and adaptable, and grounded in real relationships. Students see that we are holding them in high regard; we are not holding anything over them; we are standing beside them, building trust, affirming their potential, and supporting their growth. High expectations for all students are powerful when they are constructed with students and not imposed on them.

Reflection Prompts

Offer these prompts to students weekly or at the conclusion of a unit.
- What is the one thing you are proud of this week and why?
- How can I support you in your learning?
- How are you supporting your peers in the classroom?
- How can you learn to set goals that support how you complete your assignments?

Goal-Setting

Invite students to fill out a goal-setting form monthly or at the beginning of a term. You can review this chart with students during check-ins. It reinforces the message that you are a partner in their learning and success, and that you centre their voices. See page 201 for a blank goal-setting template.

Area of Growth	My Goal	Why this Matters to Me	Support I Need
Academic	Example: Improving my math score this week	So I feel more confident in class and do well on upcoming tests and assignments	Feedback from my teacher, help from a peer mentor or tutor, extra practice time, online learning tools
Personal	Example: To improve my time management skills	So I can stay on top of assignments, reduce stress, and make time for things I enjoy	Family encouragement, check-ins with a caring adult, use of a daily planner or time management app, reminders from peers

Final Thoughts: Teaching as Liberation Work

This work is about showing up with intention, humility, and an unwavering belief in Black students' brilliance. Holding high expectations is not merely an instructional strategy. It is a political and emotional stance. It is an act of love, a declaration of trust, and a commitment to justice.

As Graduation Coaches for Black Students, we are not observers of this work—we are living it daily. We walk alongside students as they navigate systems that have not always seen them fully, and we partner with educators striving to do better. We witness the transformative impact of classrooms where expectations are rooted in care, where curriculum reflects students' lives, and where educators choose courage over comfort. We support, not just students, but also the teachers who are committed to reimagining what success looks like for every learner.

We know this: Black excellence is not an anomaly; it is a constant. It flourishes when educators believe deeply, plan intentionally, and teach with both head and heart. Our job is to help create the conditions where that excellence is recognized, nurtured, and celebrated. We are not just teaching content; we are building futures. Each lesson, each interaction, each choice we make holds the power to affirm or diminish, to open doors or close them. And when we hold high expectations with care, when we centre identity and nurture agency, we are doing more than teaching—we are participating in liberation.

Voice from the Field

I don't want to be a teachers "maybe." I want to be their "yes." I want them to believe in me like it's a fact, not a favor.
— Grade 10 student

Let that be our call to action. Let us teach, lead, and dream alongside our students, not with perfection, but with purpose. Because to hold high expectations is not to demand more from students. It is to give them what they have always deserved.

Checklist: Planning Lessons and Selecting Resources

Curriculum and Content

☐ Do the materials reflect the voice, history, and contributions for Black communities (and not only during Black History Month)?

☐ Are Black students invited to co-create and give feedback on what they're learning?

☐ Do I create opportunities for Black students to contribute culturally relevant resources (like books or media) to the learning environment?

Classroom Culture

☐ Are students encouraged to take risks, learn from their mistakes, and not be afraid?

☐ How do I promote student voice in my classroom?

☐ Am I using specific strategies to make Black students feel included within my classroom?

Assessment Practices

☐ Are rubrics co-created or transparent so that students know how to excel?

☐ Is student voice taken into consideration in how they're assessed and what success looks like?

☐ Are students being assessed in ways that speak to their identity, culture, and lived experiences?

Goal-Setting

Area of Growth	My Goal	Why this Matters to Me	Support I Need
Academic			
Personal			

15

Collective Care While Doing the Work

Michelle Forde

Michelle Forde, M.Ed., OCT, is a principal and a consultant in education policy at Toronto Metropolitan University (TMU), with 15+ years experience in advancing human rights across learning systems. She designs leadership programs for Ontario's Ministry of Education through TMU's Chang School. Michelle also conducts research with TMU-CERC-HECW, supporting evidence-based change across education systems, bridging research, policy, and practice.

"The healing power of mind and heart is always present because we have the capacity to renew our spirits endlessly, to restore the soul."
— bel hooks (1999, p. 210).

Every day in education, we open our hearts to visitors who join us, each bringing gifts of insight, renewal, and a fresh sense of purpose as we welcome their lessons. Students arrive with vitality, colleagues offer insight, and caregivers bring wisdom to deepen our practice. The steady rhythm of human connection is central to our vocation. We hold space for others while also tending to ourselves. Welcoming others into our interior landscape, again and again, requires a balance of capacity and care. Without it, we risk depletion.

The psychological toll of our work is significant, and further compounded at the margins. The constant need to advocate, educate, and defend equity work necessitates an unending wellspring of energy. Racial battle fatigue, microaggressions, and persistent inequities require constant vigilance. The cognitive and spiritual load is borne by all caring educators and staff, to varying degrees. Still, we persist.

At its heart, the practice of collective care affirms and sustains our shared humanity through daily actions, intentional strategies, and mutual support to foster justice in education. Collective care is our conscious practice as a community of educators, calling us into self-awareness, shared cultural wisdom, healthy reciprocal relationships, collective action, and a commitment to collective growth. When we honor our own capacity, we create the necessary conditions to support students, caregivers, and colleagues, while also attending to our own well-being. Collective care creates space for us to speak honestly about the demands of justice in education, and to name the harm when our daily realities as educators are minimized or dismissed. Our conscious practice builds a culture where well-being is recognized as essential to how we teach and lead. Collective care is reflected in how we support one another as a community of educators, and prioritize rest as our shared responsibility in maintaining balance as we lead.

This chapter offers a framework for sustaining collective and individual well-being in justice-centred education. Drawing on daily practices that are both accessible and sustainable, we explore ways to welcome each new insight, whether from a person or a feeling, with attentiveness and openness to learning. These practices were developed in conversation with colleagues across a diversity of roles and lived experiences. Their reflections, offered with honesty and generosity, remind us that the cultivation of well-being is not individual. It is reciprocal. Their willingness to name struggles and speak truths is yet another gift.

This chapter also invites you to engage in reflective journaling. Richard Wagamese, Anishinaabe keeper of stories, whose teachings live eternally, reminds us, "Write spontaneously every day for 15 minutes. Our hands are our interpretive tools. They bring our spirit out in words and language" (Wagamese, 2016). A stream-of-consciousness journaling practice is more than a wellness strategy. Daily reflection nurtures our vision, guiding us as we navigate with integrity. Through this, we deepen our awareness, strengthening connections between ourselves, our community, and the world we are building together.

Collective Care

This visual represents the five interwoven dimensions of collective care. This chapter will offer practical strategies for each dimension to guide our shared practice as a community of educators.

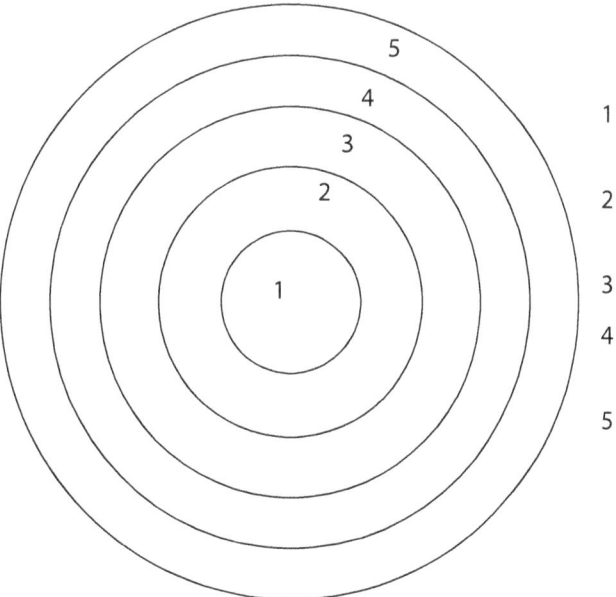

1 Self: awareness and inner practice

2 Culture: story and teachings

3 Relationships: connection

4 Community Practice: interdependence

5 Community Growth: positive social change

Collective Care as Culture

> "To tell. To shape air into sounds of language that lifts, transports those who hear it. We're all storytellers, really. That's what we do. That is our power. Not to tell people how to think, feel, know, but through our stories allow them to discover questions. Turn off your TV, devices, talk. Share stories. Be joined, transformed."
> — Richard Wagamese (2016, p. 172)

Our stories, born from breath, carry the profound ability to transport and transform, opening new realms of understanding for both the storyteller and the listener. As educators, we are storytellers every day, entrusted with the experiences that our students, colleagues, and caregivers share. Our work inherently demands a high degree of care from us, a commitment we embrace whole-heartedly. The challenges to our well-being are systemic and profoundly felt within our bodies. How we feel inside is also shaped by our social world, influencing both our struggles and our healing.

Colonial legacies in our schooling systems continue to affect our communities, including in our classrooms and teaching. Yet, within this challenge lies a powerful opportunity to learn from the wisdom of multiple ways of knowing, including Black and Indigenous ways, and allowing them to pave the way for a more equitable future. Our current climate creates an opening to embrace Black and Indigenous wisdom. Their distinct yet converging histories sustained through centuries of survivance hold essential teachings, not only for the purpose of inclusion, but particularly for the deep practice of unlearning. Drawing from her legal and lived expertise, Métis educator Chelsea Vowel writes:

> Oppressions can overlap, and this is important to understand in the context of settler colonialism. Non-Indigenous peoples can buy into and reinforce settler colonialism by supporting the… exploitation of resources as a method to achieving greater civil and social equality. Reinforcing anti-Black racism or settler colonialism does not undo the marginalization faced in other aspects of life, but the complexity of the relationships between all peoples living [in Canada] is something we cannot lose sight of. (2016, p. 18)

The legacies of colonial harm reverberate through all communities and thus compel us to rebuild together. African-American molecular biologist Dr. Beronda L. Montgomery offers additional critical insights distilled from teachings within our natural environment:

> Leaders would do well to remember the lessons of polyculture, the cultivation of diverse plant species together. The Three Sisters System [of planting] shows us. Humans are [similarly] interdependent in ways we often overlook. Everyone benefits when we cultivate people's diverse talents and promote synergies and collaborations among them. (Montgomery, 2021, p. 144)

Dr. Montgomery explores the Three Sisters teachings from Indigenous scientist Dr. Robin Wall Kimmerer's *Braiding Sweetgrass*, documenting similar polycultural traditions in Africa. Research has revealed that growing plants like plantain and cassava together—as Indigenous peoples grew corn, beans, and squash together—yields far more bountiful harvests. These highly productive and sustainable Black and Indigenous agricultural practices existed long before Western science. As educators, we can draw inspiration from these cultural epistemologies to revitalize current pedagogical practices.

Just as the Three Sisters nurture each other's growth, our efforts in team practice and collaborative professional learning foster collective well-being within our school community. Similar patterns of healthy growth and connection are replicated for our students when they are engaged in dynamic learning groups and peer-to-peer mentorship. Both plant and human life flourish through the fellowship of polyculture, yielding the full extent of our natural potential.

Broad leaf thyme is widely grown in African and Caribbean communities for culinary and healing purposes. The soil and roots ground the image in ancestral wisdom; shared cultural knowledge is the foundation for collective well-being. Plant stalks reflect the many ways our relationships sustain collective growth. The flower symbolizes reciprocity and renewal, as our collective energies produce a beautiful bloom whose seeds sustain future generations. Water flows into the soil, representing healthy environmental conditions as essential elements that enable communities to flourish.

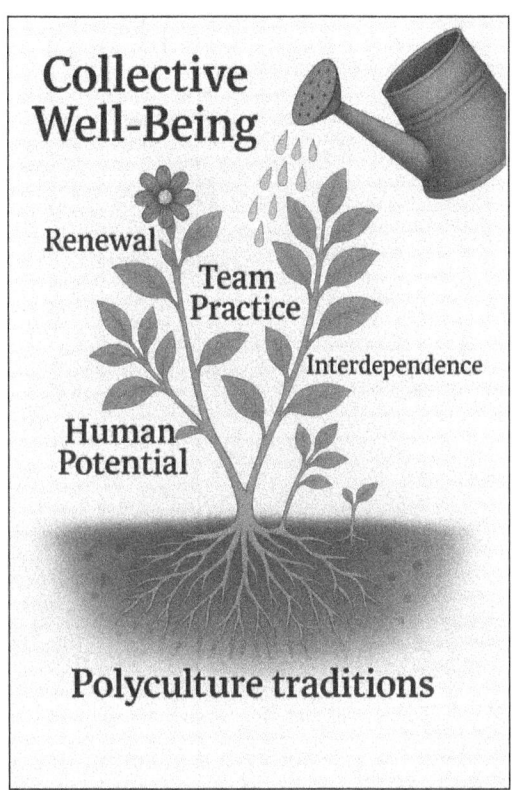

In addition to Black and Indigenous theories of knowledge, educators also continue to reference cultural wisdom from global communities to inform justice-focused, liberatory futures. How do we advance a culture of care in our daily practice?

Journaling Practice

Begin by taking a few deep breaths. For 15 minutes, write about the ideas about collective care and culture, and reflect on how they connect to your sense of belonging or role in the community. Write from a place of freedom: structurally, mentally, spiritually.

Journal Prompt

What story from a colleague, student, or caregiver continues to guide your practice? Reflect on the treasured teachings you have experienced in community.

Learning in Action

Shared Table

Prepare or share a meal with a colleague, student, or family member. As you eat, reflect on a meaningful teaching from your community or culture. Invite others to share their own. Afterward, journal about how that teaching shapes your practice.

Story Circle

With a colleague or in a small group, take turns sharing a brief story or teaching moment that shaped you. After each story, listeners respond with one question the story helped them consider. Let this exchange build shared insight through relational storytelling.

Three Sisters Reflections

Arrange three objects (ideally natural items, such as a rock or a twig) on a small surface. Assign each one a meaning: care, community, and culture. Reflect on how they interact. What does their placement teach you about balance, growth, or mutual support?

Land-Based Listening

Find a quiet outdoor space and sit without distraction. Listen to the land, its rhythms, textures, and movement. Afterward, write down one insight from your experience linked to interdependence, care, or belonging.

Students in Action

Collective Story Exchange

In small groups, students take turns leading a story circle, where each student shares an experience about a memorable moment when they felt supported and cared for in their life. Alternatively, students might share a story about a scene from a movie, TV show, graphic novel, role-playing game, or cultural story on this theme of community care in action.

- Discussion Prompt: *What lessons can we learn from this story about treating others with care and respect?*
- Students might co-create a visual class resource (such as a mural, digital slides, poster, community comic strip, etc.) that clearly displays practical ways to support care and connection in their community.

> Led by students, this activity cultivates classroom community care. Educators effectively model reciprocity and sustainability by supporting spaces for authentic student voice and leadership in connection to well-being.

Collective Care as Healing and Resistance

> "Every movement for Black liberation… has been accompanied by its singers, its dancers, its poets, its storytellers, its musicians, its artists— its theorists of the possible world, its theorists of the imagined world."
> — Christina Sharpe (2023, p. 245)

Dr. Sharpe, a leading scholar in Black Studies, invites us to consider how liberation is intrinsically linked to creativity and imagination. She reminds us that resistance is not only political; it is also creative. Liberation is carried through artistry, imagination, and theory. Collective care, too, is a creative process that has sustained spirit and community for centuries, amidst systemic strain.

In turbulent times, everyday acts of care are foundational practices of healing and resistance. Self-assessment tools support educators in recognizing self-care as essential restorative strategies to resist ongoing legacies of colonial harm. As justice-focused educators, our work aligns inner wellness with outward responsibility, and supports inclusive, accessible learning. For many of us located at multiple intersections of marginalization, collective care is far more than a teaching strategy; it is survival. Our every intentional act of care is also a radical act of protest, within education systems founded on the principles of exclusion.

We refine our practices, hold each other up, and find strength in solidarity. Every day that we return to our community, to begin again, to dare to dream, is a triumph. There is no progress without presence. We must strive to celebrate our daily wins, too. Our collective awareness is not only clarifying, it also opens space for change in our daily environment. When we care for ourselves, we offer a model to students. They see in us an example of self-respect, which in turn affirms their own.

Embracing rest, restoration, and community care re-situates our collective humanity. We must challenge social constructions of the "perpetually self-sacrificing educator" in our movement toward justice. Self-care is a fundamental form of radical resistance; educators who embrace healing strategies are exceptionally well-positioned to create transformative learning environments.

Voice from the Field

I recently experienced the power of collective care first-hand. In Spring 2025, I was invited to design and deliver a professional learning experience for Toronto Metropolitan University students. My session was part of Rooted in Identity: Finding Your Calling, a collaborative series with TMU's Black Scholarship Institute and the Tri-Mentoring Program. At the start, students made a powerful statement simply by arriving. They chose to attend my evening session despite a long day of coursework on campus. They longed to be genuinely welcomed and acknowledged in an authentic space. Our 120-minute session became an expression of collective care, with students actively co-creating the community circle; our shared cultural practice of call-and-response affirmed their experiences.

I'm on campus all day, but ours is one of few spaces where I am truly SEEN. Through culturally relevant connections, vibrant discourse, and the shared experiences of music and breaking bread, the session served as a collective act of healing.
— Student attending workshop Rooted in Identity: Finding Your Calling

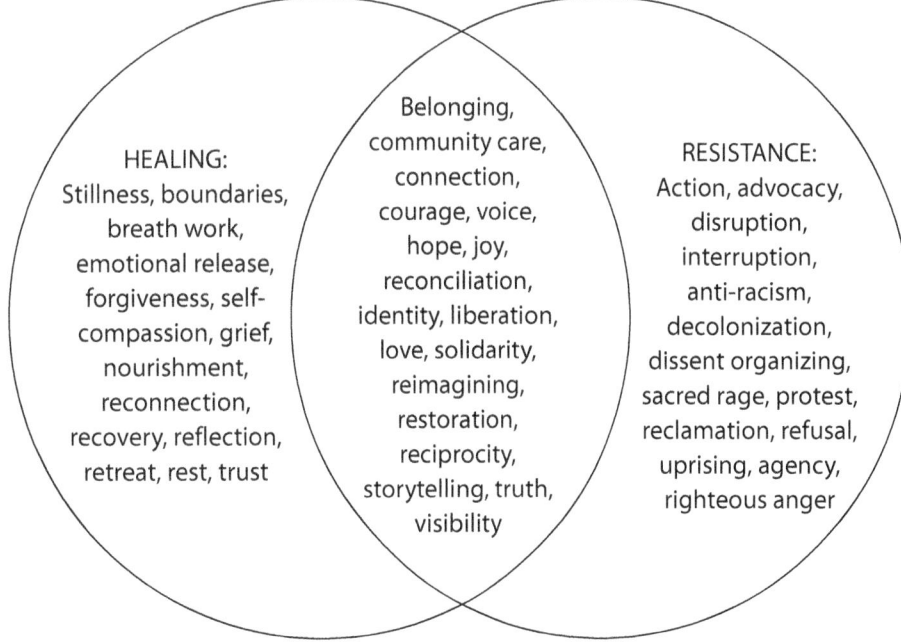

Journaling Practice

Write for 15 minutes to explore your vision for an equitable world. As always, expand your journaling process beyond the constraints of mechanics so thoughts may flow freely.

Journal Prompt

When you imagine a learning environment where everyone is seen, what does it look like, sound like, or feel like? How does this vision shape your approach to teaching and leading?

Learning in Action

Wayfinder

Sketch a simple map of a learning space you have experienced or co-created that is shaped by care, justice, and creativity. Label each part with words that reflect your values. Reflect on what this map reveals about your leadership or teaching.

Rest Reflections

Over one week, record small moments of rest or restoration. Include notes on your physical and emotional responses in these moments. This might include stillness, creative time, or boundary-setting. At week's end, reflect on how rest shaped your presence with others.

Sound Circle

Choose a song that helps you feel connected. Listen quietly, then write a short note to yourself inspired by the lyrics or rhythm. Consider sharing your reflections with trusted partners.

Liberation Visual

Use printed images or materials to create a collage that captures your vision for a justice-centred classroom. Focus on textures, color, and feeling. Reflect in writing or conversation. Consider displaying it in your space as a positive visual cue and reference point.

Students in Action

Our Future Vision

Led by students, this activity cultivates classroom community care. Educators effectively model reciprocity and sustainability by supporting spaces for authentic student voice and leadership in connection to well-being.

Students choose one medium to express their vision of a world shaped by peace, belonging, and justice. Students work individually or in small groups, and select the format that best fits their interests:

1. Create a visual (e.g., digital art, collage, poster, mural panel)
2. Record a sound piece (e.g., song excerpt, spoken word, soundscape)
3. Use movement or tableaux (e.g., short dance sequence, series of still moments)
4. Write a mini-scene script or short monologue (e.g., a short skit, speech)
5. Build a digital artifact (e.g., design a meme, video clip, digital poster)
6. Design a symbol (e.g., logo, patch, pin)

- Discussion Prompt: *What messages does your piece share about what healing, care, or resistance mean to you?*

- Create a Community Care Gallery, in the classroom or digitally, where students can display or contribute their pieces as an evolving exhibit of what community care and resistance look like in youth leadership.

Collective Care as Justice

> "Centring disability justice in our work means actively challenging ableist assumptions and creating a culture where everyone feels valued and belongs. It's a continuous process of learning and unlearning."
> — Eva Maxwell (pseudonym, personal interview, April 15, 2025).

As educators, we experience justice as a living and evolving practice in our work. Collective care is essential to our process, as we strive to co-create accessible, inclusive learning environments for a better world. Beautiful possibilities unfold as we learn and lead alongside students whose journeys call for our most intentional care.

Students in special education often navigate the most intensified intersections of ability, race, class, and gender marginalization; as educators, we respond to this reality with our deepest commitment. Our shared investment in service, particularly for those whose entire focus is special education, naturally stretches our professional and personal resources. To sustain our collective well-being, a conscious balance of energy output and input is essential. We must also include ourselves in the circle of care. Our healthy practice necessitates the discovery of joy and replenishment through self-care, connections to time-honored wisdom like radical rest, intergenerational teachings, and nature-based practices to reclaim our voice and agency.

STORY FROM THE CLASSROOM

Narrative shared by Eva Maxwell (pseudonym), Assistant Curriculum Leader of Special Education at a secondary school

Most days, I'm barely out of one conversation before the next one finds me. A hallway update turns into a classroom check-in, which rolls right into a planning call or a student support meeting. It all blurs together sometimes, but it matters. By late afternoon, I haven't had lunch yet. That's not unusual. My morning has already included urgent student needs, academic follow-ups, and real-time troubleshooting. As I return to my desk, IEP deadlines, technical issues in the new referral system, and ongoing coordination all wait for attention.

Pradeep, a Grade 11 learner with a history of learning support, had become more withdrawn in class and had interruptions in attendance. The concern wasn't flagged right away, as the details weren't captured in her ILP (Individual Learning Plan). Pradeep's mother reached out and asked for me directly. We had built a strong and trusting relationship, and she knew I would listen and respond. I met with our admin and school team to talk through what was happening and figure out the next steps. When our attendance counsellor visited the home, we got a fuller picture. Pradeep's mother was facing serious mental health challenges, and the family was living in unstable housing.

From there, I partnered with our Child and Youth Counsellor, social work team, admin, and Family Support Services to coordinate care for the family. In the weeks that followed, Pradeep's mother stayed in touch. She reached out

> often, shared updates, and let us know how much it meant to feel supported. I stayed close throughout. I checked in regularly, kept the connection strong, and honored the trust we had built. It is very challenging to manage complex care responses alongside my teaching responsibilities and full leadership role in Special Education, but I find creative solutions with our dedicated team.
> - When ILPs lack essential information, students' needs may go unrecognized or unmet. What practices could support timely, thoughtful ILP documentation while also protecting staff capacity and well-being?
> - This educator's experience shows the impact of inconsistent accommodation implementation on students and on the educators who advocate for them. How might school leaders cultivate a shared ethic of responsibility that also protects the emotional and professional wellbeing of Special Education staff?
> - This experience highlights the value of interprofessional collaboration (PSS team, Spec. Ed., Admin., Attendance, etc.) in highly sensitive situations. What strategies can schools implement to strengthen communication and coordination between different support roles and external agencies to better serve students and families?
> - This educator and her team have developed informal strategies for collective care, such as debriefings and mutual support. How might school administrators formally recognize and support these grassroots efforts to promote staff well-being, particularly in complex departments like Special Education?
> - Considering the systemic challenges described here (under-resourcing, workload, administrative burdens), what policy changes at the school or board level could create a more sustainable and healing work environment for educators, and ultimately improve outcomes for students?

Balancing Time and Capacity

The Ontario Principals' Council (2024) reported 97% of members faced "unmanageable" workloads. ETFO surveys (2023) found 77% of teachers "experienced or witnessed violence." OSSTF (2024) reports found 75% of EAs were "physically assaulted," and 31% of secondary teachers endured "physical force" from 2022 to 2023. Ministry-mandated board takeovers, abrupt policy shifts, and fiscal gaps intensify strain. It is clear that educator well-being strategies must be matched with structural transformation.

Time is always in short supply, especially in the heart of the school day. In our complex roles, the demands multiply quickly. One helpful practice is to anchor your day around two or three key priorities. Building in a few short moments of pause between tasks will help you breathe and reset. Team planning allows you to efficiently create quality materials. Connecting with colleagues at other schools can save hours of preparation. These small shifts will not erase the pressure, but they might help you stay present and well.

Assessment and evaluation is also a pressure point, especially with growing class sizes. A balanced approach helps us protect both equity and sustainability. The Ontario Ministry of Education allows triangulation, drawing on observations, conversations, and student work to support inclusive evaluation; a careful approach to type and ratio of items supports sustainability. Collaborating early on around IEPs, ILPs, and accommodations also strengthens accessibility, while working in partnership with Special Education colleagues. Professional networks offer effective solutions to foster a healthy environment for the entire school community.

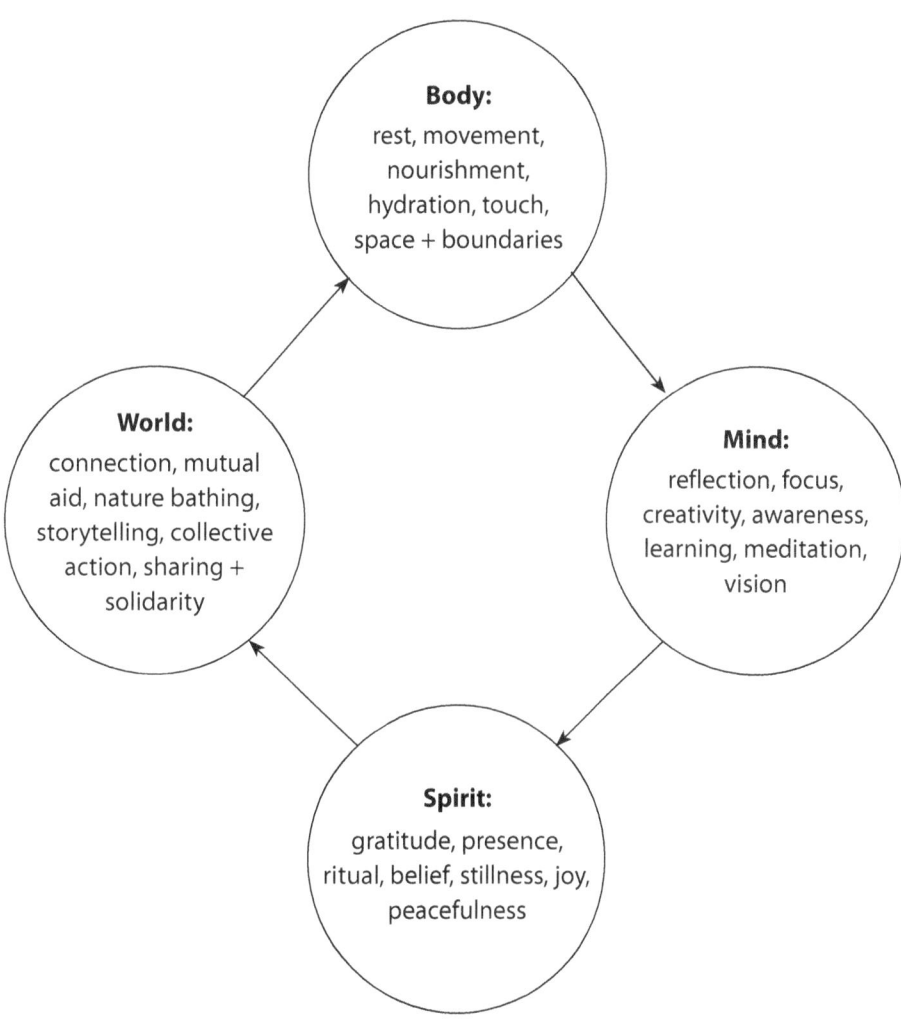

Journaling Practice

Justice work is a continuous process of learning and unlearning. Write for 15 minutes about what you've learned and what you're still questioning. You are called to engage from a place of openness, as ever, free from structural conventions.

Journal Prompt

What beliefs about disability and inclusion have you begun to question, and what has helped shift your thinking? In your current role, how do you challenge ableism in small, everyday ways?

Learning in Action

Student and Teacher

Choose one student whose connection has expanded your professional growth. Reflect privately on what they've taught you and ways you are acting on the insight. Journal your reflections.

Mirror and Window

Pair with a colleague and exchange feedback on how each of you supports access and unlearning in your roles. Name a strength and a stretch area.

Wander and Wonder

Travel through your school grounds or local neighborhood with the question *Who feels welcome here?* Pause to sketch, photograph, or map what you notice, then reflect on what your thoughts reveal about belonging.

Form and Flow

Use loose materials (e.g., clay, fabric, paper, natural objects) to create a three-dimensional representation of care, access, or transformation in your role. Reflect on what emerged as you created.

Students in Action

Mapping Care in Our Spaces

Invite students to explore a shared community space (classroom, hallway, library, schoolyard, or virtual platform) and create a care-centred map. Their map can be hand-drawn, built, created digitally, presented through movement/role play/storytelling, or created in other ways matched to their interests.

> Led by students, this activity cultivates classroom community care. Educators effectively model reciprocity and sustainability by supporting spaces for authentic student voice and leadership in connection to well-being.

1. Sketch or collage a space showing where they notice care and/or exclusion.
2. Use voice notes or video to reflect on their feelings in a specific community space.
3. Re/design the space: create a digital or hand-drawn floor plan and suggest small changes for greater inclusion.
4. Act out a short scene showing community care in action, set in a specific public space.
5. Use natural objects to symbolize what supports belonging outdoors.

- Discussion Prompt: *What makes a space feel safe, welcoming and comfortable for you? What could we add or change to help more people feel included and supported in this space?*
- Students can co-create a visual or digital class resource (e.g., poster, mural, zine, slideshow) that illustrates practical ideas to support care and inclusion in shared spaces.

Collective Care: Embodied Leadership in Action

> "One of the most important shifts for me as a leader was recognizing that vulnerability isn't a weakness; it's actually a strength that allows others to feel safe and supported in prioritizing their own needs."
> — Justin Archer (pseudonym, personal interview, April 15, 2025)

Justin Archer's insight reframes vulnerability not as something fragile or optional, but as a steady act of courage. When leaders show their humanity by acknowledging what they are carrying and where they need support, they invite a different kind of trust. They help shape a culture where well-being and growth is at the heart of collective practice.

For educators stepping into leadership, especially in fast-paced environments, the pressures are real, but so are the opportunities to lead with care. It is challenging to navigate community need, administrative demands, and our own internal expectations. And yet many new leaders are stepping into service with clarity, humility, and integrity.

Every staff member in our school communities is a leader. Whether we are in the classroom, the front office, the lunchroom, or the halls, students are always observing. They learn from how we show up, how we speak to one another, and how we respond in both calm and difficult times. Every role holds power. Every gesture of care contributes to the culture we are building together.

Voice from the Field

Barely seven weeks into my Vice Principal role, a single Friday suddenly put into sharp focus the true breadth of what leading in a very fast-paced, dynamic high school entails. Our school is a wonderfully energetic place, humming with life that pulses through every hallway! Our students come from a community that pours its heart into our school; we are blessed with active engagement. The day opened when a student bravely shared a painful experience of being threatened while out in the neighborhood after school hours. The experience shook their sense of safety. Immediately afterwards, I was also called to support a second student who was grappling with well-being and academic challenges, intensified by housing issues.

Then, just to keep things interesting, a former student, also experiencing multiple systemic barriers, caused a serious disruption that required police intervention. Of course, our school's routine administrative demands remained ever-present as these crises unfolded. Our yearbook and staff newsletter publications still required my immediate attention to meet the final and firm publication due date. Well after the official 3:45 pm dismissal, I found myself immersed in crisis response and routine tasks, a marathon stretching until 9:30 pm. This experience reveals the depth of dedication we offer in service, as educators. And in these most intense moments, the unwavering support from school staff and community partners? It truly carries us through. I've learned that leadership isn't about having every answer. It's about staying open to learning, making thoughtful decisions, and growing through the relationships that shape our school community.

— Justin Archer (pseudonym), High school vice-principal

Journaling Practice

As always, begin by focusing on your breathing and, once centred, write for 15 minutes, reflecting on vulnerability in leadership as a source of strength. Attend to the internal rhythms of your body and mind to guide your process.

Journal Prompt

Reflect on a time when someone's openness shifted the way you understood leadership.

Learning in Action

Collective Affirmation Wall

As a community, build a shared (physical or digital) space for inspiration. Each person adds one specific leadership practice they admire in someone else. Take 10 minutes for a gallery walk to read through the offerings. Afterward, consider writing a short reflection on particular teachings from the activity that resonated with you.

Body and Balance

At the start and end of one school day, pause for 90 seconds to notice your breath, posture, and physical state. Record a few words describing what you feel. Repeat for 3 to 5 days. What patterns do you notice about your stress signals?

Notes to Self

Write a short letter or record a voice note to yourself, focused on your leadership journey. Offer reassurance, name what you've learned, and reflect on ways vulnerability has shaped your growth. Plan to revisit your work in a future reflection.

Nature Noticing

Choose a small piece of the natural world (a tree, flower, or stream) and observe it for 5 minutes. Consider how it adapts, bends, or finds strength in the immediate environmental conditions around it. Write a short reflection on what that image teaches you about sustainable leadership.

Students in Action

Leadership Gallery

Led by students, this activity cultivates classroom community care. Educators effectively model reciprocity and sustainability by supporting spaces for authentic student voice and leadership in connection to well-being.

Students work individually or in small groups to create a snapshot that captures a leadership quality they value and aspire to further develop within themselves. They could express this snapshot through a variety of different formats:

1. short skit or roleplay
2. Wiki web page, drawing, digital poster
3. short video or recorded audio message
4. short dance or movement sequence
5. slide with one word and an image
6. poem, rap, or song lyric or song excerpt

Encourage students to reflect on inspiring leadership they have seen in their community at home, school, and beyond. Students might opt to share meaningful examples from fictional worlds (books, movies, role playing games, etc.).

Students can present their snapshots as part of a class gallery, digital slide deck, or quiet table display.
- Discussion Prompt: *What are some specific ways leaders help others feel seen and supported?*
- Invite students to add a short caption explaining how their snapshot creation reflects care and leadership. These captions can be anonymous and displayed collectively as a Leadership Mosaic in the physical and/or digital classroom.

Continuous Cultivation of Collective Care

> "PSS teams serving in Canada's largest school board urgently require professional growth opportunities *focused on our well-being*. Imagine the power of connection! An annual board-wide gathering is essential for our collaborative practices, team bonding, and well-being! It's time to advocate for this."
> —Shanice Donaldson (pseudonym, personal communication, April 15, 2025).

Shanice Donaldson's call to action reminds us that self-care is not optional. It is a sustaining practice that allows us to return to the work with energy, clarity, and purpose. Growth, both personal and collective, takes shape through our relationships. The ways we greet one another, offer support in moments of stress, and hold space during difficult conversations all contribute to a climate where people can thrive.

Creating a healthy environment is a shared responsibility. School culture is reflected in the everyday choices made by educators, support staff, students, caregivers, administrators, and community partners. Together, we are positioned to shape a community where everyone feels acknowledged, encouraged, and genuinely valued. Our culture of care is defined by how we show up for each other.

We must move away from the fossilized notion that leadership opportunity is assigned only to those in particular roles. Every person in a school community contributes to its strength and well-being. When we treat one another with dignity and recognize the importance of every role, we create the conditions for deeper connection and shared purpose. When care is cultivated collectively, it can grow roots. These roots strengthen our relationships, support meaningful collaboration, and build a more responsive space where all may flourish.

STORY FROM THE CLASSROOM

Narrative shared by Shanice Donaldson (pseudonym), Child and Youth Worker supporting Grades 9 and 10

I have worked closely with Mendoza, a Grade 10 student living with significant anxiety. Since elementary school, her school experience has been affected by anxiety, in terms of her capacity to be in class when stress peaks. Together with Mendoza and the broader school team, we created a proactive support plan. She could move to a calm, designated space when overwhelmed. This structure emerged from Mendoza's self-advocacy and reflected her growing confidence. The plan was already a success. She named what she needed, accepted support, and was prepared to self-advocate.

One day, Mendoza asked to leave class, but the teacher encouraged her to stay for the core of the lesson to support her learning. I understand that instinct. Balancing academic goals with wellness planning is not easy. But as the lesson progressed, Mendoza became overwhelmed and experienced a full anxiety episode and exited the building. She did not return for over a month.

It was difficult for everyone involved. Still, this moment was not about blame. It was an opportunity to pause, repair, and rebuild together. Our Professional Support Services (PSS) team returned with greater care, strengthening our communication and education strategies. I am confident we will solidify our approach while partnering with teaching staff. A plan only works when it is developed, shared, and lived by all of us. We will continue learning together.

The strong investment across all of our teams to reconvene, reflect openly, and make changes is what supported Mendoza's return. Our experience reminds me that meaningful progress is not just about getting it right. It is about responding with care, listening deeply, and remaining in relationship through moments of challenge and change.

- What specific actions might your admin team take to cultivate a stronger school-wide culture of collective care for both students and staff?
- Reflecting on your own practice, are there any beliefs you hold about student behavior or needs that could unintentionally shape how support is offered or received?
- What communication practices can strengthen collaboration and shared understanding between PSS teams and teaching staff?
- How might the insights from this case study be applied to inform professional learning that deepens collaboration between teachers and PSS staff?
- What strategies can be applied to ensure support plans are consistently implemented? Which solutions might foster greater trust and collaboration across the entire school team?

Learning In Action

There are days when even a simple reflection feels like too much. After a crisis, such as the one described in this chapter, you might feel disoriented, overwhelmed, or unsure how to begin again. In extreme conditions, it is not helpful to push ourselves to apply every strategy in our toolkit. Our hardest moments call for gentle, steady practice: one small step that helps us find our way back.

Just as we accommodate students with openness and understanding, easing cognitive and emotional demands after difficult experiences, we must extend the same care to ourselves. The space of forgiveness is the spirit of this final section. There is no journal prompt in this section. Instead, the self-compassion activity below stands alone. It is a restorative practice designed to help you return to yourself when you feel most in need of grace, space, and clarity.

Pause and Release

- Choose a quiet moment after a difficult experience or a challenging day. Sit down with a pen and paper.
- Draw a line down the centre of the page to form a T-chart: use the headings I Am Releasing… and I Am Embracing… See page 219 for a reproducible template.

In our high-intensity roles, challenges and setbacks are inevitable. It is not a professional misstep; it is a statistical reality. Establishing a practice of grace and self-forgiveness before critical moments arise allows us to respond with integrity and move forward with care.

Choose one practice.

- Under I Am Releasing…, write a sentence or phrase to clearly name and identify the experience: what didn't go as planned; what fell through; what you are carrying. Use simple words. Use neutral words; no judgment.
- Create a phrase of self-forgiveness and write it down under I Am Embracing… For example:

  I release myself from perfection.
  I show up with care.
  I grow from experience.

  Close your eyes. Repeat the phrase to yourself slowly, while breathing deeply.
- After writing both sides, fold the paper in half so the forgiveness phrases face outward. Keep your reflections in a safe, private place. From time to time, return to them as a reminder that you are always more than any one moment. Healing and growth require compassion, reflection, and time.

Rebuilding with Compassion

Choose this practice or the preceding one.

This practice is a beginning. It is a way to return to yourself with gentleness and honesty, so that when it is time to re-engage, you can do so from a place of steadiness rather than self-blame.

1. Pause and Name It: Find a quiet space and name the moment for what it is. Say to yourself, either silently or aloud, "Today was unexpected. I am feeling _____." Name the emotions without judgment. Let them surface.
2. Return to Your Humanity: Place your hand over your heart and say, "I am learning. I am growing. I will continue leading with care." Let the words land. Let them soften the space around you.
3. Ask yourself, "What is one healing action I will take today?" Choose one action; e.g., taking a walk, preparing a healthy meal, connecting with a trusted colleague, or doing nothing at all except resting.

Students in Action

Care Constellation

Give context to students:

This reflective, creative activity supports student well-being by helping them identify the quiet sources of care and calm that sustain them in times of heightened difficulty. It includes options for drawing, movement, and nature-based expression, without requiring discussion.

> A constellation is a group of stars that form a pattern in the night sky. People all over the world have named constellations and used them to tell stories, find direction, and feel connected. In this activity, you will create your own constellation: a group of stars that represent the people, places, and actions that help you feel appreciated and supported.

Choose one way to express your Care Constellation:

Educator Note: As always, we uphold our legal duty to report when we have cause to believe student safety is at risk. If a student discloses harm while in our care, they must be referred immediately for emergency support and/or intervention, as per board protocols.

1. Draw or paint your own constellation on dark paper or a digital background. Each star can represent a support: a person, a place, a memory, a routine, or something in nature that helps you feel steady.
2. Create a nature constellation by gathering small objects (leaves, stones, sticks) and arranging them into a meaningful pattern. As you place each star, decide what it represents (person, place, thing) and give it a short label or name in your mind.

3. Use movement to show what connection and care feel like for you. This can be a simple sequence of stretches, creative movement, or a breathing pattern that helps you feel centred.

- Private Reflection Prompt: *When you look at your constellation, what do you notice about the stars (people, places or actions) that help you through challenging experiences?*

Final Thoughts; A Last Offering

Our circle of care is continuous. It expands every day through the choices we make, the relationships we build, and the courage we embrace. In classrooms, hallways, offices, and schoolyards, we shape spaces where youth are seen, supported, and uplifted in possibility. Our efforts carry meaning. We are valued.

Let these final words be a quiet invitation. Just as we honor our students with patience and understanding, we are also called to extend the same ethic of care to ourselves. When we move with shared intention, care for one another, and commit to everyday practices that connect us, we make possible the kind of school community where everyone can thrive.

And let us not forget: Joy belongs here. Even in the hardest seasons. Even on the longest days. Our humanity calls us to reach for what brings light: laughter, connection, beauty.

Closing Affirmations

- I welcome joy.
- I release what is not mine to carry.
- I offer myself the care I give so freely.
- I continue with purpose.
- I believe in the future we are building.

Pause and Release

I Am Releasing…	I Am Embracing…

References and Resources

Chapter 1

Brady, J. (1995). *Schooling Young Children: A feminist pedagogy for liberatory learning.* State University of New York Press.

Biesta, G. (2017). "Don't Be Fooled by Ignorant Schoolmasters: On the role of the teacher in emancipatory education." *Policy Futures in Education*, 15(1), 52–73.

Campbell, Andrew B. (2022, June 23). HWCDSB—Becoming a Champion for Equity, Diversity and Inclusion [Video]. YouTube. https://www.youtube.com/watch?v=ksubjAV1v_c

Campbell, Andrew B.. (2023, November 22). Becoming a Champion for EDI, Social/Racial Justice and Anti-Oppressive Practices [Video]. YouTube. https://www.youtube.com/watch?v=ScOvKehEe0s&t=21s

Campbell, C. (2021). "Educational Equity in Canada: The case of Ontario's strategies and actions to advance excellence and equity for students." *School Leadership & Management*, 41(4–5), 409–428.

Freire, P. (2020). "Pedagogy of the Oppressed." In *Toward a Sociology of Education* (pp. 374–386). Routledge.

Omodan, B. I. (2022). "Analysis of Emancipatory Pedagogy as a Tool for Democratic Classrooms." *International Journal of Research in Business and Social Science*, 11(2), 348–354.

PBS NewsHour. (2024, March 15). Us vs Them: Immigration, Empathy and Psychology [Video]. YouTube. https://www.youtube.com/watch?v=x-8kxpKLqGg

University of Toronto. (n.d.). Research Services Office Equity, Diversity, and Inclusion Toolkit. https://rsi.utoronto.ca/sites/default/files/assets/files/rsi-edi-toolkit.pdf

Teach HQ. (2025). *Paulo Freire and the Emancipatory Power of Education.* https://teachhq.com/article/show/paulo-freire-and-the-emancipatory-power-of-education

Toronto District School Board. (2017). Enhancing Equity Task Force. https://www.tdsb.on.ca/Portals/0/community/docs/EETFReportPdfVersion.pdf#page=41.43

Chapter 2

Aristotle. (1998). *The Nicomachean Ethics* (D. Ross, Trans.). Oxford University Press. (Original work published c. 340 B.C.)

Arruzza, E., & Chau, M. (2021). "The Effectiveness of Cultural Competence Education in Enhancing Knowledge Acquisition, Performance, Attitudes, and Student Satisfaction among Undergraduate Health Science Students: A scoping review." *Journal of Educational Evaluation for Health Professions*, 18(3). https://doi.org/10.3352/jeehp.2021.18.3

Baires, N. A., Catrone, R., & May, B. K. (2021). "On the Importance of Listening and Intercultural Communication for Actions Against Racism." *Behavior Analysis in Practice*, 15(4), 1042–1049. https://doi.org/10.1007/s40617-021-00629-w

Boschee, F. (1990). "The Lecture: Outdated and ineffective." *NASSP Bulletin*, 74(525), 96–98. https://doi.org/10.1177/019263659007452517

Creswell, J.D. (2023, November 10). "Learning to Accept Discomfort Could Help You Thrive." *Scientific American.* https://www.scientificamerican.com/article/learning-to-accept-discomfort-could-help-you-thrive/.

DeAngelis, T. (2015). "In Search of Cultural Competence." *Monitor on Psychology*, 46(3), 64–69.

DiAngelo, R. (2018). *White Fragility: Why it's so hard for white people to talk about racism.* Beacon Press.

Eden, C.A., Chisom, O.N., and Adeniyi, I.S. (2024). "Cultural Competence in Education: Strategies for fostering inclusivity and diversity awareness." *International Journal of Applied Research in Social Science*, 6(3), 383–392. DOI: 10.51594/ijarss.v6i3.895

Hamdan, S., and Coloma, R.S. (2022). "Assessing Teachers' Cultural Competency." *The Journal of Educational Foundations*, 35(1), 108–128.

Rodriguez, V. (2012). "The Teaching Brain and the End of the Empty Vessel." *Mind, Brain, and Education*, 6(4), 177–185.

Chapter 3

Campbell, A.B. (2022, May 10). "RRDSB Speaker Series - Part # 4: The Culturally Relevant and Responsive Educator (CRRE). [YouTube]" https://www.youtube.com/watch?v=eG4G_FqsyfY&t=7

Campbell A.B., Watson, K. (2022). "Disrupting and Dismantling Deficit Thinking in Schools through Culturally Relevant and Responsive Pedagogy." *Leading for Equity and Social Justice: Systemic Transformation in Canadian Education.* University of Toronto Press.

Cepin, J., & Naimi, K. (2015). "(Non)Construction of the Teacher: An inquiry into Ontario's equity and inclusive education strategy." *Alberta Journal of Educational Research,* 61(1), 65–79. https://doi.org/10.11575/ajer.v61i1.56031

Gay, G. (2000). *Culturally Responsive Teaching: Theory, research, and practice.* Teachers College Press.

Gonsalves, A. (2024). *Becoming A Responsive Educator: Using Culturally Responsive and Relevant Pedagogy in the Classroom.* Workshop under references.

hooks, b. (1994). "Confronting Class in the Classroom." *The Critical Pedagogy Reader*, 142–150.

Gay, G. (2010). *Culturally Responsive Teaching: Theory, research, and practice* (2nd ed.). Teachers College Press.

Harrington, C. (2022, January 25). "Successful Instructors Understand their own Biases and Beliefs" (opinion). *Inside Higher Ed.* Higher Education News, Events and Jobs. https://www.insidehighered.com/advice/2022/01/26/successful-instructors-understand-their-own-biases-and-beliefs-opinion

Ladson-Billings, G. (1995). "Toward a Theory of Culturally Relevant Pedagogy." *American Educational Research Journal,* 32(3), 465–491. https://doi.org/10.3102/00028312032003465

Love, B. L. (2019). *We Want to Do More than Survive: Abolitionist teaching and the pursuit of educational freedom.* Beacon Press.

Paris, D., & Alim, H. S. (2017). *Culturally Sustaining Pedagogies: Teaching and learning for justice in a changing world.* Teachers College Press.

Chapter 4

Beaudry, S., Duff, E., & Ziegler, E. (2024). "2-spirit Indigenous Health Care and Cultural Humility." *The Journal for Nurse Practitioners,* 20(2), 1–5. https://doi.org/10.1016/j.nurpra.2023.104892

Campbell, A. B. (2023). "Allyship. [YouTube]" https://www.youtube.com/watch?v=HYyWAwOF55U

Campbell, A. B., & Swartz, L. (2023). *Stop the Hate for Goodness Sake: How can classroom teachers disrupt discrimination and promote hope, foster healing, and inspire joyful learning?* Pembroke Publishers.

Carroll, S. M. (2018). "Overing White Settler Colonial Discourse in Curricula with Anticolonial Feminism." *Journal of Curriculum Theorizing,* 33(1), 22–40.

Cole, K., & Surette, T. (2024). "'I truly think that some schools don't want to appear as if they have these issues.': Microaggressions of hegemonic influence in Canadian schools." *Canadian Journal for New Scholars in Education/Revue canadienne des jeunes chercheures et chercheurs en éducation,* 15(1), 12–25.

De Souza, L., & Schmader, T. (2025). "When People Do Allyship: A typology of allyship action." *Personality and Social Psychology Review,* 29(1), 3–31.

Konnelly, L., Bjorkman, B. M., & Airton, L. (2022). "Towards an Engaged Linguistics: Nonbinary pronouns as a site of advocacy in research and teaching." *Journal of Language and Sexuality,* 11(2), 133–140.

Lugones, M. (2007). "Heterosexualism and the Colonial/Modern Gender Aystem." *Hypatia,* 22(1), 186–219.

Moore, A. R., Coda, J., Spiegelman, J. D., & Cahnmann-Taylor, M. (2024). "Queer Breaches and Normative Devices: language learners queering gender, sexuality, and the L2 classroom." *International Journal of Bilingual Education and Bilingualism,* 27(5), 675–688.

Oxford University Press. (2024). Affirm, v. In Oxford English dictionary. https://doi.org/10.1093/OED/7303619905

Trinh, E. (2024). "Queer Allyship in TESOL: We need to ACTS now!" *TESOL Journal,* 1–17. https://doi.org/10.1002/tesj.801

Yale University. (2025). *Coming Out Guides.* https://lgbtq.yale.edu/coming-out

Chapter 5

Adichie, C.N. (2009, July). The Danger of a Single Story [Video]. TEDGlobal talk. https://youtu.be/D9lhs241zeg?si=ebrtDmLmrF_pRmgU

Braveman, P.A., Arkin, E., Proctor, D., Kauh, T., & Holm, N. (2022). "Systemic and Structural Racism: Definitions, examples, health damages, and approaches to dismantling." *Health Affairs*, 41(2), 171–178.

Diversity Council Australia (2025). Race. https://www.dca.org.au/resources/race/overview

Eizadirad, A. & Trifonas, P.P. (2025). *Handbook of Anti-Discriminatory Education*. Springer.

Global News (2020, Nov. 30). "Prince Andrew students walk out of class to protest racism within Nova Scotia school system."

Global News (2021, Oct. 19). "Over half of Canadian students see racial bullying in their schools, survey finds."

Global News (2021, Feb. 19). "School curricula haven't represented the Black perspective, says Winnipeg principal."

Gunn, F. (2021, Feb. 12). "Serious racism problem." The Canadian Press, CBC News.

Harmony Movement. (2025). Workshop materials. Harmony Movement. https://harmony.ca/

Lawrence, C. (2021). *Pathology of a Pandemic: A collection of poems*. FriesenPress.

Lawrence, C. (2025). "Reflections on the History and Intergenerational Trauma of Using the 'N' Word." In Eizadirad, A., Trifonas, P.P. (eds) *Handbook of Anti-Discriminatory Education*. Springer International Handbooks of Education. https://doi.org/10.1007/978-3-031-76485-1_54

Levins, H. (2020). "New Penn Initiative to Dismantle Racism and Advance Black Health: Health services researchers from across campus to focus on solutions." Penn Leonard Davis Institute of Health Economics. https://ldi.upenn.edu/our-work/research-updates/new-penn-initiative-to-dismantle-racism-and-advance-black-health/

Raza, A. (2022, April 13). "Being Black in School: Peel students open up about the racism they face in the classroom." CBC News.

Chapter 6

Baldwin, J. (2008). "A Talk to Teachers." *Teachers College Record (1970)*, 110(14), 17–20. https://doi.org/10.1177/016146810811001405

Burant, T., Christensen, L., Salas, K.D., Walters, S. (Eds.). (2010). *The New Teacher Book: Finding purpose, balance, and hope during your first years in the classroom, 2nd Ed.* Rethinking Schools.

Clark, J. S., Brooms, D. R., & Matias, C. E. (2021). "Unapologetic Black Inquiry: Centering Blackness in education research." In *The Handbook of Critical Theoretical Research Methods in Education* (1st ed., pp. 303–318). Routledge.

Clark, R., & Antonelli, F. (2013). *Why Teachers Leave: Results of an Ontario survey 2006–08*. Ministry of Education. https://librarysearch.library.utoronto.ca/permalink/01UTORONTO_INST/14bjeso/alma991106962046406196

Cosier, K. (2019). "On Whiteness and Becoming Warm Demanders." *Journal of Cultural Research in Art Education*, 36(1). https://doi.org/10.2458/jcrae.4941

Delpit, Lisa D. (2012). *"Multiplication Is for White People": Raising expectations for other people's children*. New Press2.

Ellerbrock, C. (2014). "Warm Demanders." In *The Sage Encyclopedia of Classroom Management* (Vol. 2, pp. 869–871). SAGE Publications Inc., https://doi.org/10.4135/9781483346243.n367

Garcia, E., & Weiss, E. (2019). "The Teacher Shortage Is Real, Large and Growing, and Worse than We Thought." The First Report in The Perfect Storm in the Teacher Labor Market Series. In *Economic Policy Institute*. Economic Policy Institute.

Gay, G. (2000). *Culturally Responsive Teaching: theory, research, and practice*. Teachers College Press.

Irvine, J. J., & Fraser, J. W. (1998). "Warm Demanders." *Education Week*, 17(35), 56–.

Jones, A. (2024). "Ontario teacher shortage to worsen in 2027, ministry document warns." The Canadian Press.

Jung, M.-K., & Vargas, J. H. C. (Eds.). (2021). *Antiblackness*. Duke University Press.

Ladson-Billings, G. (1995). "Toward a Theory of Culturally Relevant Pedagogy." *American Educational Research Journal*, 32(3), 465–491.

Ladson-Billings, G. (1998). "Just What Is Critical Race Theory and What's It Doing in a Nice Field Like Education?" *International Journal of Qualitative Studies in Education*, 11(1), 7–24. https://doi.org/10.1080/095183998236863

Mawhinney, L., Cabral, L., & Pierce, J. C. (2025). "When We Know Better, We Do Better: Educators' storied reflections on Black teacher attrition and retention." *Journal of Black Studies*, 56(1), 42–64. https://doi.org/10.1177/00219347241286262

Molyneux, T. (2021). "Preparing Teachers for Emotional Labour: The missing piece in teacher education."

Journal of Teaching and Learning (Windsor), 15(1), 39–56. https://doi.org/10.22329/jtl.v15i1.6333

Sealey-Ruiz, Y. (2021). "The Critical Literacy of Race." In K. Lomotey & R. H. Milner (Eds.), *The Handbook on Urban Education* (2nd ed.) (pp. 281-295). Routledge.

Swartz, E. (1992). "Emancipatory Narratives: Rewriting the Master Script in the School Curriculum." *The Journal of Negro Education, 61*(3), 341–355. https://doi.org/10.2307/2295252

Tenorio, R. (2010). "Brown Kids Can't Be in Our Club: Raising issues of race with young children." In *The New Teacher Book: Finding purpose, balance, and hope during your first years in the classroom*. ReThinking Schools.

Tung, R., & Villavicencio, A. (2018). "Disrupting Structural Racism: Counter-narratives of pride, growth, and transformation. *VUE (Annenberg Institute for School Reform), 48,* 3-.

Verma, R., & Apple, M. W. (Eds.). (2021). *Disrupting Hate in Education:Teacher activists, democracy, and global pedagogies of interruption* (1st ed.). Routledge.

Wun, C. (2017). "Not Only a Pipeline: Schools as carceral sites." *Occasional Paper Series (Bank Street College of Education), 2017*(38). https://doi.org/10.58295/2375-3668.1131

Chapter 7

Adjapong, E., & Porcher, K. (2025, April 28). *Self-work Before Toolkits: An interview with Dr. Yolanda Sealey-Ruiz about culturally responsive-sustaining education.* NYU Steinhardt.

Gorski, P. C. (2019). *Reaching and Teaching Students in Poverty: Strategies for erasing the opportunity gap* (2nd ed.). Teachers College Press.

hooks, b. (1994). *Teaching to Transgress: Education as the practice of freedom.* Routledge.

Lorde, A. (1984). *Sister Outsider: Essays and speeches.* Crossing Press.

Love, B. (2019). *We Want to Do More Than Survive: Abolitionist teaching and the pursuit of educational freedom.* Beacon Press.

McAuley, S. (2018, Winter). "Culturally Relevant and Responsive Pedagogy in the Early Years: It's never too early!" *ETFO Voice.*

Muhammad, G. (2020). *Cultivating Genius: An Equity Framework for Culturally and Historically Responsive Literacy.* Scholastic.

Saad, L. F. (2020). *Me and White Supremacy: Combat racism, change the world, and become a good ancestor.* Sourcebooks.

Sealy-Ruiz, Y. (2024, December 12). The Archaeology of the Self [Video]. YouTube. https://www.youtube.com/watch?v=mmST_lehb_U

Chapter 8

BakerBell, A. (2020). *Linguistic Justice: Black language, literacy, identity, and pedagogy.* Routledge.

Barbareschi, G., & Laraway, S. (2017). "Designing Culturally Inclusive Learning Space." *Journal of Educational Environments, 25*(3), 214–230.

Calkins, L. M., & Bell, A. M. (2019). "Artsinfused Literacy: Promoting joy and meaning in the classroom." *Language Arts, 96*(2), 78–88.

Campbell, Andrew B. (2023, July 23). "Cultivating Black Joy. [Video]" YouTube. https://youtu.be/scADE2FKjtI?si=IQ3pd1YOt1YfUnhp

ChandlerOlcott, K., & Crandall, B. (2012). "Exit Slips as Formative Assessment: Insights into student thinking in a digital age." In S. T. Myers (Ed.), *Professional Development for Teaching Writing in a Digital Age.* IGI Global.

Childs, K. (2024). "Black J.O.Y.: Strategies for joyful, liberatory learning." *Journal of Canadian Education Equity, 12*(1), 15–32.

Cooper, A. (2006). *The Hanging of Angélique: The untold story of Canadian slavery and the burning of Old Montréal.* HarperCollins.

Cooper, C. B. (2006). *Pockets of Hope: Communitybased Black education in antebellum America.* University of Michigan Press.

DeGruy, J. (2005). *Post Traumatic Slave Syndrome: America's legacy of enduring injury and healing.* Uptone Press.

Dery, M. (1994). "Black to the Future: Interviews with Samuel R. Delany, Greg Tate, and Tricia Rose" *South Atlantic Quarterly, 92*(4), 735–778.

Eccles, J. S., & Roeser, R. W. (2011). "Schools as Developmental Contexts during Adolescence." *Journal of Research on Adolescence, 21*(1), 225–241.

Education Elements. (2020, September 21). How Three District Leaders Are Closing the Instructionalleadership Gap [Blog post]. https://www.edelements.com/blog/how-three-district-leaders-are-closing-the-instructional-leadership-gap

EL Education. (2022, February 8). *Honoring Black Joy* [Public statement]. https://eleducation.org/blog/black-joy-emotional-safety

Emdin, C. (2016). *For White Folks Who Teach in the Hood ... and the Rest of Y'all Too: Reality pedagogy and urban education.* Beacon Press.

Eshun, K. (2003). *More Brilliant than the Sun: Adventures in sonic fiction*. Quartet Books.

Fredrickson, B. L. (2001). "The Role of Positive Emotions in Positive Psychology: The broadenandbuild theory of positive emotions" *American Psychologist, 56*(3), 218–226.

Gay, G. (2018). *Culturally Responsive Teaching: Theory, research, and practice* (3rd ed.). Teachers College Press.

Ginwright, S. (2018). "The Future of Healing: Shifting from traumainformed care to healingcentered engagement." *Medium*. https://ginwright.medium.com/the-future-of-healing-shifting-from-trauma-informed-care-to-healing-centered-engagement-634f557ce69c

Gray, D. L. (2020). "Belonging Opportunity Structures for Marginalized Youth." *Journal of Educational Equity, 15*(2), 123–145.

Heidelburg, K., Phelps, C., & Collins, T. A. (2022)."Reconceptualizing School Safety for Black Sudents. *School Psychology International, 43*(2), 1–22.

hooks, b. (1994). *Teaching to Transgress: Education as the practice of freedom*. Routledge.

Institute of Education Sciences. (2019, July 15). Including Voice in Education: Addressing equity through student and family voice [Blog post]. https://ies.ed.gov/use-work/resource-library/resource/fact-sheetinfographicfaq/including-voice-education-addressing-equity-through-student-and-family-voice-classroom-learnin

James, K. (2012). "Building Joyful School Cultures through Professional Learning Communities." *Journal of Educational Change, 13*(4), 531–549. https://doi.org/10.1007/s1083301291891

James, C. E. (2012). *Life at the Intersection: Community, class, and schooling*. Fernwood Publishing.

Jennings, P. A., & Greenberg, M. T. (2009). "The Prosocial Classroom: Teacher social and emotional competence in relation to student and classroom outcomes." *Review of Educational Research, 79*(1), 491–525.

JonesMoore, L., & Gillis, J. (2012). "Exit Slips as Rormative Assessment: Insights into student thinking in a digital age." In S. T. Myers (Ed.), *Professional Development for Teaching Writing in a Digital Age*. IGI Global.

LadsonBillings, G. (1995). "Toward a Theory of Culturally Relevant Pedagogy." *American Educational Research Journal, 32*(3), 465–491.

LewisGiggetts, T. M. (2022). *Black Joy: Stories of resistance, resilience, and restoration*. Gallery Books.

Love, B. L. (2019). *We Want to Do More than Survive: Abolitionist teaching and the pursuit of educational freedom*. Beacon Press.

Ma, A. (2023). From Birth to Death: Black Americans and a Lifetime of Disparities. Associated Press (Investigative series).

McBride, S. (2023, October 10). "The Science of Classroom Design: How data walls impact student emotions" *Edutopia*. https://www.edutopia.org/article/the-science-of-classroom-design

Morris, M. W. (2016). *Pushout: The criminalization of Black girls in schools*. New Press.

Muhammad, G. (2020). *Cultivating Genius: An equity framework for culturally and historically responsive literacy*. Scholastic.

Okonofua, J. A., Walton, G. M., & Eberhardt, J. L. (2023). "A Brief Intervention to Encourage Empathic Discipline Cuts Suspension Rates for Black Students in Half. *Proceedings of the National Academy of Sciences, 120*(11), e2301234.

Paris, D., & Alim, H. S. (2017). *Culturally Sustaining Pedagogies: Teaching and learning for justice in a changing world*. Teachers College Press.

Pianta, R. C., & Hamre, B. K. (2009). "Conceptualization, Measurement, and Improvement of Classroom Processes: Standardized observation can leverage capacity" *Educational Researcher, 38*(2), 109–119.

Pierson, R. (2013, June). Every Kid Needs a Champion [Video]. TED Conferences. https://www.ted.com/talks/rita_pierson_every_kid_needs_a_champion

Roots ConnectED. (2021). Growing in Practice: Honoring Black joy [Report]. https://www.rootsconnected.org/resources-list/growing-in-practice-honoring-black-joy

Simmons, D. (2020). "Why We Can't Afford Whitewashed Socialemotional Learning. *ASCD Express, 15*(24).

Smith, D. F. (2023). *Rooted in Joy: Humanizing pedagogy for equitable classrooms*. Equity Press.

Tatum, B. D. (1997). *"Why are all the Black kids sitting together in the cafeteria?" And other conversations about race*. Basic Books.

TeachersPayTeachers. (2024). Joy Data Wall Classroom Resource [Digital download].

Teacher Reflection Journal. (2023). Reflective Practice in Action [Blog post].

Thomas, S. E. L., & Murphey, D. (2003). *The Principal Perspective: Leading with joy and purpose*. Education Leadership.

Tichavakunda, A. A. (2022). "Black Students and Positive Racialized Emotions: Feeling Black joy at a historically white institution." *Humanity & Society, 46*(3), 419–442.

Williams, M. T. (2018). "Healing Racial Trauma: The African American experience."*Race and Social Problems, 10*(2), 95–108.

Zins, J. E., Bloodworth, M. R., Weissberg, R. P., & Walberg, H. J. (2004). "The Scientific Base Linking Social and Emotional Learning to School Success." In J. E. Zins, R. P. Weissberg, M. C. Wang, & H. J. Walberg (Eds.), *Building Academic Success on Social and Emotional Learning: What does the research say?* (pp. 3–22). Teachers College Press.

Chapter 9

Campbell, Andrew B. (2022, March 1). "Creating, Fostering & Sustaining Intentional Spaces of Belonging. [YouTube]" https://youtu.be/q7HAItav2PM?si=d4DTGhJmrvJQyaQx

Ontario Human Rights Commission. (Feb. 2022). "Executive Summary: Right to read." www.ohrc.on.ca/sites/default/files/Right%20to%20Read%20Executive%20Summary_OHRC%20English_0.pdf.

Freire, Paulo. (2000). *Pedagogy of the Oppressed.* 50th ed., New York, Bloomsbury Academic.

Gorski, Paul, and Katy Swalwell. (2023). *Fix Injustice, Not Kids and Other Principles for Transformative Equity Leadership.* ASCD, 2023.

Ighodaro, Erhabor, and Greg Wiggan. (2010). *Curriculum Violence: America's new civil rights Issue.* Nova.

James, C.E. & Turner, T. (2017). *Towards Race Equity In Education: The schooling of Black students in the Greater Toronto Area.* Toronto, ON: York University.

Ladson-Billings, Gloria. (2022). *The Dreamkeepers: Successful Teachers of African American Children.* John Wiley & Sons.

Love, Bettina. (2020). "We Want to Do More than Survive: Abolitionist teaching and the pursuit of educational freedom." BEACON.

Muhammad, Gholdy. (2023) *Unearthing Joy: A Guide to Culturally and Historically Responsive Teaching and Learning.* .

Safir, Shane, and Jamila Dugan. (2021). *Street Dat: A next-generation model for equity, pedagogy, and school transformation.* Corwin.

Chapter 10

Cole, Chelsea & Hinchcliff, Elizabeth & Carling, Rylee. (2022). "Reflection as Teachers: Our critical developments." *Frontiers in Education.* 7. 10.3389/feduc.2022.1037280.

Indigenous Services Canada.[1](2023, November 8). *Long-term Drinking Water Advisories.* Government of Canada. https://www.sac-isc.gc.ca/eng/1614387410146/1614387435325

Ladson-Billings, G. (1995). "Toward a Theory of Culturally Relevant Pedagogy." *American Educational Research Journal, 32*(3), 465–491. https://doi.org/10.3102/00028312032003465

Parekh, G., Brown, R. S., & Zheng, S. (2018). "Learning Skills, System Equity, and Implicit Bias within Ontario, Canada." *Educational Policy, 35*(3), 395–421. https://doi.org/10.1177/0895904818813303

Chapter 11

Campbell, A. B., & Swartz, L. (2023). *Stop the Hate for Goodness Sake: How can classroom teachers disrupt discrimination and promote hope, foster healing, and inspire joyful learning?* Pembroke Publishers.

Daniels, M. J. (n.d.). *Exploring the Lived Experience pf Former Special Educators in the Greater Toronto Area and their Perceptions of Work Conditions in the Special Education Classroom.* DUNE: DigitalUNE.

Elder, B. C., Rood, C. E., & Damiani, M. L. (2018). "Writing Strength-Based IEPs for Students with Disabilities in Inclusive Classrooms." *International Journal of Whole Schooling.*" *14*(1), 116-–

Hiemstra, D., & Van Yperen, N. W. (2015). "The Effects of Strength-based versus Deficit-based Self-regulated Learning Strategies on Students' Effort Intentions." *Motivation and Emotion, 39*(5), 656–668. https://doi.org/10.1007/s11031-015-9488-8

Major, A. (2012). "Job Design for Special Education Teachers." *Current Issues in Education, 15*(2). https://cie.asu.edu/ojs/index.php/cieatasu/article/view/900

Silverman, D. M., Rosario, R. J., Hernandez, I. A., & Destin, M. (2023). "The Ongoing Development of Strength-Based Approaches to People who Hold Systemically Marginalized Identities." [available from authors]

Waly, S. (2020). "Culturally Responsive Education in Today's Schools: Application and challenges." *The International Journal of Pedagogy and Curriculum, 27*(2), 39–47. https://doi.org/10.18848/2327-7963/CGP/V27I02/39-47

Chapter 12

Sealey-Ruiz, Y. (2022). "An Archaeology of Self for Our Times: Another talk to teachers." English Journal, 111(5), 21–26.

Wheeler, M. E., & Fiske, S. T. "Controlling Racial Prejudice: Social-cognitive goals affect amygdala and stereotype Astivation." *Psychological Science* 16:1 (January, 2005).

Chapter 13

Bixler, K., & Ceballos, M. (2023). "Promoting Teacher Leadership: Principal actions to promote and facilitate teacher leadership for enhanced student outcomes." *Leading and Managing*, 29(1), 21–30.

Buchanan-Rivera, E. (2022). *Identity Affirming Classrooms: Spaces that center humanity* (First edition). Routledge.

Dei, G. J. S. (1999). "Knowledge and Politics of Social Change: The implication of anti-racism." *British Journal of Sociology of Education*, 20(3), 395–409. https://doi.org/10.1080/01425699995335

Dei, G. J. S. (2000). "Removing the Margins: The challenges and possibilities of inclusive schooling." In *Removing the Margins: The challenges and possibilities of inclusive schooling*. Canadian Scholars' Press.

Gay, G. (2000). *Culturally Responsive Teaching: Theory, research, and practice*. Teachers College Press.

hooks, b. (1994). *Teaching to Transgress: Education as the practice of freedom*. Routledge. https://doi.org/10.4324/9780203700280

Jacobs, J., Beck, B., & Crowell, L. (2014). "Teacher Leaders as Equity-Centered Change Agents: Exploring the conditions that influence navigating change to promote educational equity." *Professional Development in Education*, 40(4), 576–596. https://doi.org/10.1080/19415257.2014.896272

James, C. E. (2021). "Towards Equity in Education for Black Students in the Greater Toronto Area." In *Colour Matters* (pp. 283–308). University of Toronto Press.

Khalifa, M. A., Gooden, M. A., & Davis, J. E. (2016). "Culturally Responsive School Leadership: A synthesis of the literature." *Review of Educational Research*, 86(4), 1272–1311. https://doi.org/10.3102/0034654316630383

Khalifa, M. (with Delpit, L., & Milner, H. R.). (2020). *Culturally Responsive School Leadership*. Harvard Education Press.

Kumashiro, K. K. (2000). "Toward a Theory of Anti-Oppressive Education." *Review of Educational Research*, 70(1), 25–53. https://doi.org/10.3102/00346543070001025

Ladson-Billings, G. (2014). "Culturally Relevant Pedagogy 2.0: A.k.a. the remix." *Harvard Educational Review*, 84(1), 74–84.

Muhammad, K. N. (2020). *Culturally Responsive School Leadership*. Solution Tree Press.

Poekert, P. E., Swaffield, S., Demir, E. K., & Wright, S. A. (2020). "Leadership for Professional Learning towards Educational Equity: A systematic literature review. *Professional Development in Education*, 46(4), 541–562. https://doi.org/10.1080/19415257.2020.1787209

Taylor, E., Gillborn, D., & Ladson-Billings, G. (2023). "Just What Is Critical Race Theory and What's It Doing in a Nice Field Like Education?" In *Foundations of Critical Race Theory in Education* (3rd ed., pp. 13–29). Routledge.

Wane, N. N. (2008). "Mapping the Field of Indigenous Knowledges in Anti-colonial Discourse: A transformative journey in education. *Race Ethnicity and Education,* 11(2), 183–197. https://doi.org/10.1080/13613320600807667

Wenner, J. A., & Campbell, T. (2017). "The Theoretical and Empirical Basis of Teacher Leadership. *Review of Educational Research*, 87(1), 134–171. https://doi.org/10.3102/0034654316653478

Wu, J., Eaton, P. W., Robinson-Morris, D. W., Wallace, M. F. G., & Han, S. (2018). "Perturbing Possibilities in the Post Qualitative Turn: Lessons from Taoism (道) and Ubuntu." *International Journal of Qualitative Studies in Education*, 31(6), 504–519. https://doi.org/10.1080/09518398.2017.1422289

Wise, S. (2019). *Design for Belonging: How to build inclusive school communities*. Jossey-Bass.

Chapter 14

Evans-Winters, V. E. (2005). *Teaching Black Girls: Resiliency in urban classrooms*. Peter Lang.

Gay, G. (2010). *Culturally Responsive Teaching: Theory, research, and practice* (2nd ed.). Teachers College Press.

Hammond, Z. (2015). *Culturally Responsive Teaching and the Brain: Promoting authentic engagement and rigor among culturally and linguistically diverse students*. Corwin Press.

James, C. (2010). *Seeing Ourselves: Exploring race, ethnicity, and culture*. Thompson Educational Publishing.

James, C., & Turner, T. (2017). *Towards Race Equity in Education: The schooling of Black students in the Greater Toronto Area*. York University.

Ladson-Billings, G.(1995). "Towards a theory of culturally relevant pedagogy." *American Educational Research Journal*, 32(3), 465–491.

Lareau, A. (2003). *Unequal Childhoods: Class, race, and family life*. University of California Press.

Muhammad, G. (2020). *Cultivating Genius: An equity framework for culturally and historically responsive literacy*. Scholastic.

Reay, D. (1998). *Class Work: Mothers' involvement in their children's schooling*. UCL Press.

Chapter 15

Elementary Teachers' Federation of Ontario. (2023, May 15). ETFO member survey shows violence pervasive in schools [Media release]. ETFO. Retrieved from https://www.etfo.ca/news-publications/media-releases/etfo-member-survey-shows-violence-pervasive-in-schools etfo.ca+7etfo.ca+7todaysnorthumberland.ca+7

hooks, b. (1999). *All about Love: New visions*. Harper.

Montgomery, B. L. (2021). *Lessons from Plants*. Harvard University Press.

Ontario Principals' Council. (2024). Boiling point: Principals struggle to sustain Ontario's schools [PDF]. Ontario Principals' Council. Retrieved from https://www.principals.ca/en/who-we-are/resources/Documents/LettersAndSubmissions/EN-Boiling-Point--July-4-2024-Final.pdf researchgate.net+4principals.ca+4principals.ca+4

Ontario Secondary School Teachers' Federation. (2024, June). Startling OSSTF/FEESO school violence survey results reveal need for emergency funding [PDF]. OSSTF/FEESO. Retrieved from https://www.osstf.on.ca/-/media/Provincial/Documents/News/media-releases/startling-school-violence.ashx osstf.on.ca+2osstf.on.ca+2osstf.on.ca+2

Sharpe, C. (2023). *Ordinary Notes*. Knopf Canada.

Vowel, C. (2016). *Indigenous Writes: A guide to First Nations, Métis, and Inuit issues in Canada*. HighWater Press.

Wagamese, R. (2016). *Embers: One Ojibway's meditations*. Douglas & McIntyre.

Index

2SLGBTQIA+ students
   action, 63–64
   affirmation, 55, 56–59, 64–65
   allyship, 55, 59–63, 64–65
   defined, 55
   language, 54–55
   overview, 54, 64–65
   racial slurs, 74
   reflection, 55, 64, 65
   stories from the classroom, 55–56, 57–58, 60–61
5Ws and an H activity
   described, 162–163
   template, 173

abolitionist lens, 111
accountability, 194–195
action
   2SLGBTQIA+ students, 63
   actionable activity, 63–64
   reflection, 64
adaptive strategies, 110
affinity groups, 97–98
affirmation
   affirming spaces, 59
   constructive conversations, 58–59
   defined, 55, 56
   described, 56–57, 64–65
   identity, 97–98
   queerness and other identities, 58–59
   racism, 72
   teacher expectations, 57
affirmation shares, 109
Afrocentric curriculum audits, 111
allyship
   confronting biases, 61
   defined, 55, 59
   described, 59–62, 64–65
   harmful language, 61–62
   process, 60
   reflection, 60
   stories from the classroom, 60–61
   teaching practice, 62
   true allyship, 60, 61
   types, 60
   voice from the field, 62–63
archaeology of the self, 92
assessment, 193

balancing time and capacity, 210–211
banking education, 11
barriers in society, 123–124
being present, 33–34
belonging
   creating, 117
   cultivating and sustaining, 118, 126–127, 134
   defined, 117
   elements, 117–118
   feeling, 124
   membership, 125–126
bias-interrupting interventions, 112
Black, Indigenous, and People of Color (BIPOC), 67, 68, 72
Black students
   accountability, 194–195
   assessment, 193
   classroom culture, 192
   deficit lens, 189–190
   educator's role, 188–189
   goal-setting, 197–198
   graduation coach, 187–188, 199
   liberation work, 199
   personal narratives and social justice, 197–198
   planning and curriculum, 191
   practical teaching tools, 195–198
   reflection, 195, 198
   resistance, 194–195
   setting high expectations for, 187–199

        stories from the classroom, 193–194
        teaching with high expectations, 190–194
        voices from the field, 189, 192–193, 199
body and balance, 214
brave conversations, 128
brave space, 42

care constellation, 217–218
case studies, 21–22
centre joy in teaching
        affirming identity, 97–98
        building in joy, 98
        described, 96–97, 104
        voices from the field, 97
champion / championing
        activity, 13–14
        call for action, 23
        celebrating joy, 113
        defined, 11
        EDIA, 12, 14
        educational, 12
        illustrations, 12–13
        toolbox, 22
champion logs, 113
circle of care, 112
cisheteronormativity, 55
classroom climate, 106–107, 133–135, 147–148
classroom culture, 192
classroom stories, 18–21, 29–30, 45, 55–56, 57–58, 60–61, 71, 72–73, 75–76, 82, 87, 98–103, 107, 109, 119, 121–122, 139, 148–149, 155–156, 163, 164–165, 170–171, 177, 183, 184, 193–194, 209–210, 215–216
co-creating expectations / norms, 133
collaborative enquiry, 154
collective affirmation wall, 214
collective care
        activities, 205–206, 208, 211–212, 214, 216–217
        affirmations, 218
        balancing time and capacity, 210–211
        compassion, 217
        cultivating, 215–218
        culture, 203–206
        described, 202–203, 218
        dimensions, 203
        embodied leadership, 212–215
        healing and resistance, 206–209
        journaling, 203, 205, 208, 211, 214
        justice, 209–212
        stories from the classroom, 215–216
        student-led activities, 206, 208–209, 212, 214–215, 217–218
        voices from the field, 207, 213
collective story exchange, 206
colonial legacies, 204
coming out, 58
communication, 96

community agencies, 71–72
community building / creating community
        communication, 96
        described, 94, 104
        multilingualism, 95
        student-focused morning routine, 94–95
        trust, 96
        voices from the field, 94, 96
community care, 154–156
community circles, 96
community connections, 114
community events, 31
connection, 113
courage, 33
creating sense of belonging, 42
creative exhibitions, 114
creativity, 75
critical reflection, 131–132
cultural awareness, 28, 29
cultural competence
        approaching the work, 32–34
        assessing position, 27–28
        attending community events, 31
        being present, 33–34
        building, 31–32
        commitment, 35
        cultural fluency, 28, 29
        cultural humility, 32–33
        defined, 26
        developing outside classroom, 27–31
        discomfort, 33
        engaging with an identity, 30–31
        expanding literal diet, 31
        expanding media diet, 31
        importance of, 26–27
        ongoing learning, 32
        overview, 25–26
        reflection, 35
        relationships outside identity group, 32
        stages, 28
        travel with purpose, 32
        voice from the field, 35–36
cultural curiosity, 28
cultural fluency, 28, 29
cultural heritage events, 114
cultural humility, 32–33
cultural learning opportunities, 74–75
cultural responsiveness, 28, 190–194
cultural unawareness, 28
cultural wealth, 113
culturally relevant and responsible pedagogy (CRRP), 119, 124–125, 126, 168
culturally relevant pedagogy, 83
culturally relevant, responsive, and sustaining education (CRRSE)

constituents, 38
creating a sense of belonging, 42
described, 37–38
getting to know students, 42
learning stations, 47–49
planning, 41–46
positionality, 40, 41
practice, 46–49
preparation, 39–41
questions, 50
reflection, 46, 49, 51
responsive materials, 43, 45
stories from the classroom, 45, 46–47
three Ps, 37, 50
transformation, 50
voices from the field, 38–39, 43–44
culturally relevant teaching, 37
culturally sustaining pedagogy, 37, 111
culture, 146, 192, 203–206
culture and race, 166
culture of dialogue and encouragement, 134
curriculum, 114, 191

daily routines, 108–109
decentring self, 167–168
decolonization, 168
deficit thinking
    described, 143–144
    disrupting, 145–147
    reframing, 189–190
    strength-based approach vs., 145
digital affirmation, 114
discomfort, 33
disrupt / disruption, 91
disrupting racism
    activities checklist, 82
    described, 81–82, 89–90
    Head, Heart, and Feet activity, 88–89
    overview, 80–81
    racist language, 88
    stories from the classroom, 82
    teacher tools, 83
    voices from the field, 81
    warm demander pedagogy, 83–90
diversity, 146
Diversity, Equity, and Inclusion (DEI), 14
Diversity, Equity, Inclusion, and Belonging (DEIB), 14

educators' critical reflection, 131–132
emancipatory pedagogy, 17–18
emotional labor, 83
emotional tone, 134
empowerment, 140
engagement, 113, 120, 123–124, 145–146
engaging with an identity, 30–31

equity, 17
equity, diversion, and inclusion (EDI)
    centre joy in teaching, 96–98, 104
    create community, 94–96, 104
    described, 91–92, 104
    know your why, 92–94, 104
    reflection, 92–94
    stories from the classroom, 98–103
    voices from the field, 93, 94, 96, 97
Equity, Diversion, Inclusion, and Accessibility (EDIA)
    action, 17
    championing, 12, 14, 22
    changing issues, 17
    definitions and terminology, 14–15
    described, 11–12
    emancipatory pedagogy, 17–18
    equity, 17
    learning and unlearning, 17–18
    opponents, 14
    reflection, 23–24
    stakeholders, 14
    stories from the classroom, 18–21
Equity, Diversity, Inclusion, and Belonging (EDIB), 15
Equity, Diversity, Inclusion, Decolonization, and Accessibility (EDIDA), 15
equity growth checklist, 165–166
ethics, 146
Eurocentric notions of success, 193
excellence, 196–197
expectations
    Black students, 187–199
    creating with students, 133
    setting high expectations, 137–139, 192

families, parents, and caregivers
    culturally relevant and responsive pedagogy (CRRP), 168–170
    diversifying curriculum content, 167–168
    equity growth checkpoints, 165–166
    kindness, 164–165
    privilege-based approaches, 162–164
    relationship building, 160–161
    social justice dates, 166–167
    stories from the classroom, 163, 167, 169, 170–171
    understanding equity, 161–162
    voices from the field, 166, 170
family voice notes, 110
feedback, 110, 192
form and flow, 212
future vision, 208–209

getting to know students, 42
Goal-Setting lesson
    described, 198
    template, 201

graduation coaches, 187–188, 199
Greeting Slides, 95
growth, 17, 196–197

Head, Heart, and Feet activity, 88–89
healing, 206–209
healing-centred engagement, 111
healing check-ins, 111
hidden curriculum, 125
human library, 97

identity
    affirming, 135–137
    inclusion, 119–120
    reflecting, 134
    self-esteem, 76–78
inclusion, 146
Inclusion, Diversity, Equity, Accessibility (IDEA), 15
inclusivity, 106
individual structures
    instructional innovations, 153
    positive affirmations, 150–151
    strength spotlights and strength mapping, 151–152
    students, 149
    teachers, 149
induction programming, 154
inquiry-based learning, 124–125, 153
instructional innovations / strategies, 153
intellectual curiosity
    advocating for, 140–141
    classroom climate, 133–135
    described, 130–131, 140
    educators' critical reflection, 131–132
    empowerment and recommendations, 140
    identity affirmation, 135–137
    setting high expectations, 137–139
    stories from the classroom, 139
    strategies for fostering, 131
    voices from the field, 132, 134–135, 137–138
intention, 107–108, 134
interrupt / interruption, 81
Interview Questions, 66

journaling
    described, 203
    prompts, 205, 208, 211, 214
joy anchors, 109
joy data wall, 110
joyful circles, 113
joyful classrooms / JOY framework
    advocating for, 140–141
    celebrating joy, 113–116
    championing, 113
    classroom climate, 106–107
    connection, 113
    cultivating joy, 106–107
    cultural wealth, 113
    curriculum and ritual, 114
    daily routines, 108–109
    described, 105–106, 116
    feedback and adaptive strategies, 110
    four pillars, 105
    learning and well-being, 110
    professional growth, 109
    protecting joy, 110–113
    protective strategies, 111–113
    reflection, 114
    restorative practice, 113
    stories from the classroom, 107, 109, 112
    sustaining joy, 108–110
    teaching with intention, 107–108
    voices from the field, 114–116
joyful shares, 108
Justice, Equity, Diversity, and Inclusion (JEDI), 15

kindness, 164–165
know your why (intentionality)
    described, 92, 104
    reflection, 92–94
    voices from the field, 92
knowledge sharing, 193

land-based listening, 206
leadership, 176–177, 212–215
leadership gallery, 214–215
learning
    engagement, 120, 123–124
    inquiry-based, 124–125
    ongoing, 32
    unlearning and, 17–18
learning goals, 191
learning stations
    described, 47–48
    lesson, 48–49
liberation
    described, 206
    visual, 208
linguistic justice practices, 111
literal diet, 31

mapping care, 212
meaningful tasks, 191
media diet, 31
membership, 125–126
mentor texts, 120, 123
mentoring students, 184–185
mentoring teachers, 182–184
mentorship networks, 112
metacognition, 78
mindful gratitude pauses, 109

mirror and window, 211
Mirrors, Windows, and Sliding Doors, 43
morning routines, 94–95
multilingualism, 95
My Superpower and My Growing Seed, 151–152

nationality, 163
nature noticing, 214
notes to self, 214

Pause and Release activity
    described, 216–217
    template, 219
peer mentoring, 154
Planning Lessons and Selecting Resources checklist
    described, 196
    template, 200
policy advocacy, 112
polyculture, 204–205
Positional Power Activity
    described, 41
    template, 51
positionality
    activity, 41
    described, 40
Positive Affirmations
    described, 150–151
    tools, 158–159
positive learning environment, 147–148
power challenge, 169
powerful pedagogy, 145–147
presence, 33–34
principal, 181–182
professional growth, 109

racial slurs, 73–74
racism
    active racism, 68
    addressing racist language, 88
    affirmations, 72
    anti-racism tools, 70–71
    community agencies, 71–72
    creative talents, 75
    cultural learning opportunities, 74–75
    data, 68–69
    defined, 67
    described, 67–68
    dismantling, 70–79
    disrupting racism, 80–90
    identity and self-esteem, 76–78
    passive racism, 68
    racial slurs, 73–74
    reflection, 69
    self-reflection, 78
    stories from the classroom, 71, 72–73, 75–76

    voices from the field, 77–79
rebuilding with compassion, 217
reflection, 23–24, 35, 46, 49, 51, 53, 55, 60, 64, 69, 92–94, 114, 131–132, 140, 146, 176, 179, 180, 195, 198
Reflective Checklist
    described, 138–139
    template, 142
reflective journaling, 203
reflective portfolios, 114
relationship building, 32, 113, 121–122
representation, 192–193
resistance, 194–195, 206–209
responsive materials, 43, 44, 45
rest reflections, 208
restorative covenants, 113
restorative justice circles, 111
restorative practice, 113
routines / rituals, 108–109, 114

safe space, 42, 122–124
Sample Letter to Parents / Caregivers, 172
seat at the table
    classroom, 176–179
    described, 175, 185
    formalized teacher leadership role challenges, 180
    inviting others, 182–185
    nurturing students as leaders, 177–179
    principal, 181–182
    reflection, 176, 179, 180
    school, 179–182
    stories from the classroom, 177, 183, 184
    supporting and mentoring students, 184–185
    supporting and mentoring teachers, 182–184
    teachers as leaders, 176–177
    voices from the field, 174–175, 178, 179, 181, 182–183
self-assessment, 206
self-reflection, 78
shared table, 205
Social Media Analysis Chart, 186
societal barriers, 123–124
sound circle, 208
spaces of belonging
    brave conversations, 128
    cultivating, 118, 124, 126–127
    humanizing frameworks, 127
    identity and inclusion, 119–120
    inclusive and flexible, 133
    key elements, 117–118
    love-centred, 125–127
    membership, 125–126
    relationship building, 121–122
    safety, 122–124
    stories from the classroom, 119, 121–122
    sustaining, 124–125
    traditional education models vs., 119

voices from the field, 127, 128–129
special education, 209–210
story circle, 205–206
strength, 143
strength-based approaches in education
  community care, 154–156
  deficit-based approaches vs., 145
  described, 143–145, 156–157
  enabling environment, 147–149
  engagement, 145–146
  individual structures, 149–154
  instructional innovations, 153–154
  positive affirmations, 150–151, 158–159
  powerful pedagogy, 145–147
  reflection, 146
  stories from the classroom, 148–149, 155–156
  strength consciousness, 149
  strength spotlight and strength mapping, 151–152
  voices from the field, 145, 147, 149–150, 152, 154
strength consciousness
  instructional innovations, 153
  positive affirmations, 150–151
  strength spotlights and strength mapping, 151–152
  students, 149
  teachers, 149
Strength Mapping and Growth Pathways, 152
strength spotlight, 151–152
student alliances, 97–98
student and teacher activity, 211
student-led showcases, 114
Student Profile Questionnaire activity
  described, 42
  template, 52
student pulse checks, 110
systemic barriers, 122–123

teaching for curiosity, 132
Three Sisters teachings
  described, 204
  reflections, 206
travel, 32
triangulation, 210–211
trust, 96
Two-Spirit folks, 58–59

Ubuntu, 182
Universal Design for Learning (UDL), 124–125, 153

values, 146
voices from the field, 15–16, 35–36, 38–39, 43–44, 62–63, 77–79, 81, 84–86, 93, 94, 96, 97, 114–116, 127, 128–129, 132, 134–135, 137–138, 145, 149–150, 152, 154, 166, 168, 170, 174–175, 178, 179, 181, 182–183, 189, 192–193, 199, 207, 213

wander and wonder, 212
warm demander pedagogy
  Black students, 192
  described, 83–85, 89–90
  firm black mother pedagogy, 84
  stories from the classroom, 87
  voices from the field, 84, 85–86
  warm demander for students, 86
wayfinder, 208
What Has Shifted in Me? activity
  described, 46
  template, 53
word clouds, 24
workshops, 14